CRIMELORD
THE LICENSEE

The True Story of Tam McGraw

David Leslie

MAINSTREAM
PUBLISHING
EDINBURGH AND LONDON

First published in Great Britain in 2005 by
MAINSTREAM PUBLISHING COMPANY
(EDINBURGH) LTD
7 Albany Street
Edinburgh EH1 3UG

ISBN 1 84596 049 1

A catalogue record for this book is available
from the British Library

Typeset in Stone Print and Stone Sans

Printed in Great Britain by
Clays Ltd, St Ives plc

ACKNOWLEDGEMENTS

WITHOUT THE KINDNESS, courtesy and unfailing help of the many who have travelled beside me, I could not have reached the end of this path to my first book. I treasure their friendship and sense of fun and regret only that they cannot be identified. They know who they are and I am privileged and lucky to have had their support. I would have loved to have named them, but at least I can publicly thank Terry Gray, who put the Man into Manchester; Brian Anderson of the *News of the World*; David at Alba; Kevin O'Brien, my editor at Mainstream; the lovely girls at The Tea Room, Mosspark, for supplies of tea and rolls that kept me going; and my friends in IT who persevered until I could turn on a laptop.

CONTENTS

chapter one

TREASURE TROVE

THEY WERE CHEERING JUST A FEW HOURS EARLIER AS THE goals went in.

But in the chill of dawn's first light come jeers from tired young voices, breaking with the first tones of manhood.

A replica gun appears. Then a toy knife. Insults are screamed, threats muttered. No real need to worry. Just a team of young Glasgow footballers on their way home from a match played abroad.

But ill-tempered, suspicious gendarmes have barred the way.

Leather boots and slavering dogs are on their coach, invading Scots territory, peering, poking, staring, demanding.

'Where are you from?'

'Scotland.'

'Where have you been, what have you been doing?'

'Playing football in Spain. Visiting Disneyland.'

'Is contraband hidden in your bags? Your pockets? Under seats? Have you drink, cigarettes, drugs?'

'Don't be daft; we're at school.'

'Off your coach, *mes enfants*, we want to search.'

Nothing gets past these French police, expert at rooting out the most adept smuggler, or their dogs, noses wet and trained to scent drugs at ten paces.

But then they have never before encountered the cunning of the Glasgow East Ender. The dogs are easily fooled by smoky-bacon crisps and scattered fragments of mutton pies, which the boys have innocently dropped on the floor at the sly suggestion of the driver and his co-pilot.

And as for their handlers and those who have halted the party before it can reach the sanctity of Calais' ferries, well, time to trigger their other main diversion.

And so the action moves outside to where a cop is in the process of testing the coach panels. His fist, about to check for a tell-tale dull thud – a giveaway that something has been secreted behind – is halted on the downswing by the sounds of raised voices.

The drivers have opened a debate on that most irresistible of subjects: football. Their argument is simple: France, no good; Scotland, best.

Offence is given and hopefully taken. The search is forgotten, abandoned. Tails wagging, the dogs enjoy their unexpected bounty, munching, crunching, while masters argue, debate, shout, arms waving, faces red.

And these young footballers get bored and file out of the bus. A ball is produced. A kickabout begins. Occasional passing cars hoot. The gun is examined. One of the gendarmes thinks it is identical to that worn in the holster of the cowboy at Euro Disneyland, where he and his wife took their family just a few weeks earlier. Come to think of it, isn't that same holster now hanging from the coach rack? And isn't someone wearing Western boots, spurs jangling; someone else the Stetson? He convinces himself it has to be a coincidence. Or maybe there is a simpler explanation: they were bought from one of the Disney stores.

He hears his name. A colleague is calling. The argument is unresolved but it is time to get rid of these wild, noisy young men, to send them on their way. This is the last leg of their European journey, one that began in Glasgow, took in Disneyland, then the football fields and beaches of northern Spain before returning back through France.

'Everyone on board,' shout the driver and his co-pilot. Police withdraw, the coach begins to move off, some gendarmes give good-natured salutes, receiving in return a series of gestures typical of those given by Glaswegians to acknowledge the forces of authority the world over.

The police congratulate themselves on succeeding in inconveniencing yet another busload of Brits, happy that news of this demonstration of French efficiency will be spread to would-be smugglers.

Nothing on board, for sure. Mind you, there was the cowboy gear. No, surely not. Who would steal from Disneyland? The idea is laughable.

On the coach, the kids stamp their feet on half-eaten food and empty packets, the knife is waved in play, the gun aimed in a mock fight.

Not long to the ferry and breakfast before Dover. Then home.

They watch the miles whizzing by. The views are great. Even the smallest can easily see through the windows.

Streetwise, these kids. Like to convince themselves they miss nothing. Not easily conned.

But others, older than they, are more adept.

The youngsters, and hundreds of other kids who have sat and will sit in those same seats, seeing those same French farms, don't know it, but this is no ordinary bus.

Because it carries hidden treasure. More than one and a half million pounds of it.

chapter two

THE LICENSEE

IN GLASGOW, GRATEFUL PARENTS WOULD BE AWAITING the coach and wondering how their sons had enjoyed the trip. And there were others just as eager to see it arrive safely.

Usually it was late afternoon before children were reunited with mums and dads and the secret cargo with those who had bought or brought it. The drive through England's sometimes gridlocked southern road network and then a series of motorways before the border crossing just north of Carlisle was a long haul. Then there were bags to unpack, tans to examine, stories to tell and washing machines to whirl. By the time the holidaymakers were in bed, many of their dads reckoned they had earned an hour or two propping up their local bars to banter over Celtic or Rangers or talk in lowered tones of the latest gangland scandals.

One such bar they might be found in was the Caravel in the city's East End. It was run by Thomas 'Tam' McGraw and his wife Margaret. Although Margaret's was the name that appeared above the door, it was Tam who was given the tag of 'The Licensee'. He was the gaffer, a man who could quietly get things done when help was needed, who had earned his respect rather than blown his own trumpet and had a reputation as an organiser.

Once called the El Paso, the Caravel was a drinking-hole for some of the toughest, dodgiest characters in the city. A succession of landlords had struggled to cope with the regular fights and explain to brewery bosses the mounting bills for smashed chairs, tables and glasses. Owners Tennent's tried everything to tone down the image of the place as somewhere at times akin to a Wild West saloon. New managers, new brews and even the new name were tried.

But the pub was as much a part of East End folklore as was the *Epitaph* newspaper to Tombstone, and material alterations could not transform an atmosphere that was steeped into its walls. It was easier to change the image of the Glasgow Gorbals than that of the El Paso, and many of the regulars would have gone home bemused had they not witnessed the occasional rammy. Even the new name didn't work. To those who had been drinking there for years, it was the 'Paso' and would remain so.

Inevitably, Tennent's decided enough was enough and put the place on the market. There were others said to be interested, but it was precisely the investment that Tam and Margaret McGraw were looking for, and after handing over £40,000 for the building and its contents, Margaret's spotless reputation and background guaranteed she had no difficulty persuading police and Licensing Board officers to let her open up.

In official terms, she was the boss, but Tam was never far away. His own East End background was enough for him to realise the Caravel clientele could hardly be expected to behave like kindergarten kids. There was bound to be the occasional outbreak of trouble. Even the best of friends would fall out in their cups and to try curbing arguments among men was to invite bother. If things became heated from time to time, fair enough, but there was one rule to which there were absolutely no exceptions. The Caravel had to be a drug-free zone. At a time when the stream of cannabis running into Scotland was about to become a torrent, it was no secret that Tam McGraw hated drugs, and he had made it clear that dealers who tried passing kit in the Caravel would get short shrift.

This was no polite request but was set in stone. Not only would offenders be guilty of a personal insult to the McGraws, but it only needed a policeman to walk in and see a dealer or smell a user and Margaret's hard-won licence would be in jeopardy. The Caravel prospered, and if there were flare-ups from time to time, either Tam or his friends would quickly snuff them out. One of his barmen was Joseph Hanlon. And Joe was no slouch. A promising amateur boxer, he had proved in the ring he could casily take care of himself and it would take a foolhardy customer to misbehave when Joe was about. Between them, Tam and Joe kept the Caravel on an even keel.

Fortunately, Tam was there one night when a thug took exception to what he felt was a customer's overly roaming eye. Outside, a knife appeared. Tam was quick enough to save the life of the victim, but not to prevent him being so seriously injured that a priest was called to Glasgow Royal Infirmary to give him the last rites. Tam himself was stabbed in the arm and would carry a cruel scar for the rest of his life as a reminder of that night. Thankfully, both men recovered, and some time later the man Tam had saved called at the Caravel to thank him. His name was Trevor Lawson.

It was through the pub that Tam became close, too, to Gordon Ross. Gordon had been an occasional visitor, a man who gave no trouble, who had chosen crime as a means of gaining financial security. It was a choice with which his parents might not agree, but they would never lose sight of the fact that, at the end of the day, he was their son and they loved him for that.

Tam had heard a whisper that Gordon and one of his close friends, a man we are going to call Craig, had at one stage been doing jobs in Spain for a Glasgow businessman. It was rumoured they were running drugs across the French–Spanish border in cars. It was a risky exploit, having to contend with the law, the constant threat of prison and the greed of associates. The leader of their little group had proposed pooling the profits and using the bounty to buy more drugs. His partners wondered if he could be trusted and discovered the answer to that when one of the gang asked for his cut – around £20,000 – as he wanted to move to Spain. The unfortunate was taken to the cellar of a public house near Cambuslang, hung upside down and had his head used for penalty-taking practice.

Sickened, Gordon and Craig watched helplessly, too horrified to intervene. They tried urging that he should be given his money, but, battered and bloodied, he was eventually cut down and promptly left for the Continent empty-handed, the excuse ringing in his ears that there was nothing in the kitty. The friends had a feeling that, when it came to their turn to ask for their share, the same answer would be doled out to them. And they were right. Eventually, one of their expeditions went wrong and they found themselves in prison. Out of jail, they sought out their one-time leader, who'd heard they were broke, and asked him for their money. There was nothing left, he said, all gone in expenses and in loans to others who had failed to pay up. Feeling betrayed but helpless,

Gordon and Craig visited the Caravel to drown their sorrows, pockets bulging with fresh air.

Tam McGraw saw the anger on their faces and gave them £100 each, telling them not to worry about paying him back. 'Keep it. Maybe you'll be working for me one day,' he said. 'Then you'll find I don't let my friends down.' From then on, they became close – Tam and Gordon in particular, with Tam acting as a type of surrogate father to him. He and Margaret knew from their own upbringing how tough life could be in the East End. Both had worked hard to create a home many envied, but at the same time realised that while money could bring countless benefits, it was worthless unless used in the pursuit of happiness.

One advantage of having money was that it opened the door to travel, and to many new experiences and opportunities abroad. In 1980, friends had pointed them towards a holiday location the couple would visit literally scores of times, come to love and where they would invest in a property. Admittedly it meant a five-hour flight from Glasgow, but hours of sunshine were a daily certainty. Sometimes, Tam flew with a buddy to look up old pals. Occasionally, he went alone to think. The spot was the island of Tenerife, tucked among the Canaries off north-west Africa and 300 miles from the coast of Morocco, the world's largest supplier of the recreational drug hash.

Of course, there were many in Glasgow who used hash, discreetly maybe, but frequently nonetheless. And just as in any business, where there was a demand, there were suppliers. Men like Big Ted.

chapter three

BIG TED

BIG TED RAN THE BEST RACKETS ON THE COSTA DEL SOL.
Need hash? Go see Big Ted. Transport back to the UK? Visit Big Ted. Can't get into the best nightclubs? No worries, ring Big Ted. Want a villa? Big Ted will arrange it. Problems changing money? Give Big Ted a call. A girl for the night? Ask Big Ted. Trouble with the law? Big Ted has contacts. He'll take care of that.

Everyone who mattered along the Costa knew Big Ted. In Malaga, it had become a prestige symbol to be invited to the luxury apartment he rented overlooking the Mar Mediterraneo. Anyone who wanted to do business there, in the trade that everyone knew about but talked of in hushed tones, ended up at the door of the connoisseur with a love of expensive wines and a taste for fine food. A stranger would be left with the impression that he had a finger in every pie, a sort of universal Mr Fixit.

There seemed nothing the big man could not sort. Apart, that was, from his own love life. And that was something about which you did not offer advice to Big Ted. In simple terms, he effectively and practically had two wives, both pretty, both back home, both in love with him and both wanting sole ownership. Only it wasn't so simple. Big Ted could sort everyone else but not his own worry of which to choose.

A kindly man, his bizarre double life had lasted for a decade until he decided it was time to settle down with one or the other. The difficulty was he needed time away from both to think out a solution. Finding his own space, where he could be alone, was proving impossible until, in 1989, the answer appeared in the unlikely setting of a crowded club during that period of the evening when strong drink fertilises the imagination, creating ideas and plans usually forgotten or dismissed when the effects of alcohol dissipate.

In this case, the subject of the discussion was still fresh the following morning, as Big Ted and his drinking partner from the night before – a long-time friend – mulled over the conversation. They had been joined in the club by two former school pals who operated a discreet, but successful, drugs distribution network. Nothing too naughty, they said, just hash.

Six thousand years before the birth of Jesus Christ, the Chinese had discovered in the *cannabis sativa* plant a source of food and fibre. By seven millennia later, Arabs were learning the same plant, known also as Indian hemp, had yet another remarkable property. The yellow flowers from the female *cannabis sativa* gave off a resin that, when dried, could be smoked or eaten, leaving the user with a strange but, at times, wonderful sensation of euphoria and well-being. And it had astonishing medicinal effects, dulling aches and pains, with regular users seeming to live longer and healthier lives. Smokers said that after just a few puffs from tobacco mixed with hash, they felt relaxed, even lazy, noises and sight became sharper, their hunger increased and life in general seemed to sail along on a gentle wave of humour and well-being. In the 1950s, the Moroccan government turned a blind eye as farmers, who for centuries had struggled to grow anything on the bleak slopes of the Rif mountains in the north, turned to cannabis.

Within 30 years, the country had become the world's biggest producer of hashish and not even a cosmetic crackdown in the late 1980s by the country's then ruler King Hassan II failed to stop the crops blooming. And that was hardly a surprise. Hashish was worth £3 billion a year to the frail Moroccan economy, and the standard of living for everyone involved had improved beyond their wildest dreams.

So farmers in the Rif range in the north of the country, in parts skirting the Mediterranean coast, grew the crops and in tumbledown stone sheds produced the resin that, carried from Spain in suitcases or car boots, ended up in the drawing rooms of lavish homes in the south of England or in Glasgow tenements. But demand was outstripping supply, Big Ted was told. Reliable and regular deliveries were needed. An acquaintance of his school pals ran a thriving haulage company and had contracts for carrying fruit and furniture to the UK from Spain. He was willing, for a price, of course, to have his bank balance augmented by supplementing loads with hash concealed in lorry panels and even in the furniture, in the drawers of sideboards or sealed inside the wardrobes. It needed someone in Spain to make sure the gear was always there on time to be picked up. And whoever did that would need to pay a Spanish or Moroccan supplier, take care of the lorry owner and look after his own living expenses. There would be, though, a small fortune left over.

The old school chums had fallen foul of the law and had been tipped off that their movements were being watched. It would be too dodgy for them to move to Spain, so were Big Ted and his colleague interested? The longer the pair considered the suggestion, the more they liked it. 'Only one trip,' insisted Big Ted to his friend. 'Just long enough to let me sort my head and make a few bob. But you stay on and if you need help from time to time I'll come back out.' Big Ted and his partner had shaken hands with their new business associates in the club that previous night.

Now, in the cool of daylight, they were even more convinced their decision was wise. A confirming telephone call, a whirlwind visit from Ted to his women with promises that each was the only one who mattered, and a rosy future was around the corner. It seemed no time before they were tasting beer at a bar in the Torreblanca area of Fuengirola and agreeing a deal with the Moroccan. They discovered that one of the first lessons to be learned was that, to be trusted, one had to accept that here hash was a way of life. There was so much floating around at the time it was almost impossible to miss it. Hash would be found in most of the big houses. To be invited to someone's home for dinner meant not to show shock or surprise on seeing pieces of hash of differing sizes left lying around among the cigarettes and fruit. It would be regarded as impolite not to smoke a joint because just about everyone else would be doing so. Nobody talked about it because it was no big deal.

Running hash wasn't regarded as a particularly scandalous activity. It was just what people did. While some were in business as shop-owners or bar-keepers, others did hash deals. Those like Big Ted, who came in to run the hash, became accepted as members of a family, as one of their own. They might be strangers, and unrelated, but they were another of the Costa families, they were the Hash Clan.

Hash dealers were welcomed everywhere because they were big spenders. They loved to live well and spend well – and always in cash. They made tills jingle, bar owners happy.

In some clubs, drugs would be openly available for free and it would be considered strange not to take a line of cocaine with your beer. This was a new society, something undreamed of, a time when a man willing to take a chance could become a millionaire overnight. Hash then was *the* drug; it was socially acceptable. It was the common factor between the cocktail set and families struggling to forget about the misery of run-down housing, no jobs and no hope.

It took just days for Big Ted and his partner to discover, to their astonishment, how easy it was to become wealthy, with the result that Ted's one-trip-only resolution soon vanished out of the window, floating with the prevailing winds towards North Africa. Before leaving for Spain, they had been told to look up a Moroccan named Mohammed who would arrange hash supplies. It was fortunate they had been directed to a particular bar where their man was said to hang out because they quickly learned that most of the Moroccans dealing in drugs along the Costa seemed to be named Mohammed. So finding him was not too much of a problem. And once in Spain they discovered it was incredibly easy to buy the stuff. They simply placed an order with Mohammed, paid up front for it, took delivery, packed hash into the lorries and watched them head back home to the UK. When wagons returned empty to collect another load, Big Ted and his pal would be handed a bulging parcel of banknotes from the driver, their retainer for guaranteeing all went well. In between loads, there was time to think.

Big Ted was still hard at finding a solution to his emotional problem the following year when two men literally walked into his life and changed it forever. He liked the Glaswegians the moment he first met them. Admittedly, he was at a disadvantage, having locked himself out of his car after a beer in the Las Palmeras Hotel at Fuengirola. Struggling and fuming in the heat, he turned to see the pair watching and trying hard to hide their smiles. From their own Volkswagen Golf, they somehow produced that addition to every AA patrolman's toolbox, a wire coat hanger, and had in no time used it to trip Big Ted's door handle. The keys were out of the ignition and into his hand. From there, a thank-you beer was inevitable. And, in the cool of the hotel bar, the man known as Big was introduced to his new-found Knights of the Road.

They were, he was told, Gordon Ross and the man we are calling Craig. There was an almost instant rapport, and a friendship that would last for years was born. In the events that followed, Big Ted would have most of his dealings with Craig, but at that initial meeting it was Gordon who did most of the talking. As the night went on, Ted was struck by the open fascination that women had for Gordon. He was remarkably handsome, it was true, but he also had some mystical quality, perhaps it was the movement of his green eyes or the frequent gestures of his hands, which gave notice that here was a man who expected a woman's submission. In his charm, there was a hint of both passion and cruelty. But for now, as the three men sat on bar stools in 1991 drinking cold Spanish beer from bottles, Big Ted found it difficult not to be distracted by the stares of half-naked women at his new companion. He was no slouch himself at the skill of seduction, as his own domestic situation implied, but he smiled in admiration at the Scot. Other men might have thrown the dice, desperate for a number that would give them a foothold on the bedroom ladder. Gordon, it appeared, had only to wait for shameless Eves to slide down snakes to his feet.

The Scot was only twenty-four, six years younger than his new buddy, but he was already something of a veteran in the drug-smuggling business. Admittedly, his career in crime had not made a brilliant start. Two years earlier, fascinated by risk, he and a handful of others had bought a second-hand Volkswagen Golf from a car dealer near their homes in the East End of Glasgow. He and Craig had driven to Malaga in it. Back in Scotland, they had been promised that buying hash on the Costa del Sol was as easy as picking up a tan, and much less painful. The drive, via a Dover–Calais ferry and then through France, Andorra and into Spain before the final charge down the east coast, had been long and tiresome. But once they had booked into an off-resort hostel, showered, changed and knocked back their first Bacardis, they felt better, and even more confident once they discovered that everything they'd been told was true. Buying hash by the bucket-load was simple and straightforward – provided, of course, you had the means to pay.

Within a week, their contact had pulled up outside the hostel with a van and unloaded a series of cardboard boxes. Inside were 40 kilos of resin. It had cost the pair £32,000. In Scotland, that would treble. But the profit was reward for risk, and they still faced a 1,500-mile journey north. They made it home after an uncomfortable ride and into the kitty went the profits. It seemed all too easy and the exercise was repeated. The idea had been a good one, but a consideration of the consequences had been absent from the plans. Still, in early 1989 there seemed no reason why their little plot should go wrong. After all, their first two trips had been successful, so why not their third? They were by now well accustomed to packing the hash into the car. Seat coverings were carefully removed, sections gouged out from the padding of backs and bases, the contraband carefully packed in and the covers replaced. More would fill the roof space before they set off for the uncomfortable journey home, confident they were on millionaires' row.

Sadly, that dream died on the end of the nose of a suspicious Customs officer who decided the little car appeared decidedly overloaded as it bumped off the Calais ferry into Dover docks. Luck had been with them for the first two trips, Customs officers giving them only brief visual inspections as they drove from the ferry. But those initial journeys had taken their toll on the car seating and suspension. The constant bumping had caused the packs to come loose, there were odd bulges in the seats and the suspension appeared about to collapse – hardly what was to be expected from a sturdily made and reliable German-built car carrying just two men. It needed only a cursory search. For Gordon and Craig, all that came out of the expedition was a three-year prison sentence (of which they served just over half).

In jail, Gordon thought long and hard about what had gone wrong. He knew, was certain, the idea of using a car could work. It only needed more planning, maybe the advice of a mechanic. His zest needed to be fed by money. He had tasted, albeit briefly, the thrill of fun in the sun and wanted more. So the setback of prison was to be no deterrent.

Back on the outside, as we know, when he went to the organiser of the various hash runs for his share of the pooled profits, his request fell on the stone floor of that Cambuslang basement. Shortly afterwards, with Tam's £100 in his pocket and breathing free Glasgow air, Gordon lost no time in catching up on the news that lay under the surface of the East End. In the Cottage Bar and in selected pubs in Shettleston and Baillieston his laugh was once again a familiar sound.

He caught up with old associates who liked his sense of humour and appreciated his quick eye for a pretty girl, reckoning that more often than not she would have a friend. He would sometimes call into the Caravel bar in Barlanark.

While he and The Licensee were cementing their friendship, back in Spain a relationship was in the throes of coming to an end. Big Ted and his partner had been given an ultimatum by the businessman who ran the lorry operation. The haulage-man was no fool. He had made enquiries and discovered that his lorries were helping to make the smugglers rich, very rich. Without him, he surmised, the operation could not exist.

Despite being paid well, and regularly, he felt he was worth more. But he was also a realist. Being too greedy could kill the goose that laid the golden egg. There were others in his line of business who might be willing to fill the void should he break off. And while the people he dealt with might be over in Spain, they were not to be crossed.

His request, when it was made, was, he considered, a very reasonable one. He wanted another £500 a load. Big Ted believed the price hike was fair. He was willing to pay, pointing out to his partner that they were still being left with more money than either had dreamed of making. A lot, less £500, was still an improvement on nothing. It was hardly going to bankrupt them and they could afford to carry on living in comparative luxury. True, they could refuse the increase but that might mean searching around for a new means of delivery – not an easy task, by any means, because the trust element ranked high in the cogs that ran the scheme. Finding someone else who would not ask too many questions wouldn't be easy. There was also the risk of the lorry boss feeling irked, and what was to prevent an anonymous telephone call to Customs or police giving details of any replacement?

So Big Ted was all for coughing up. To his amazement, though, his co-smuggler was not. The man was adamant, angrily protesting that they had shaken hands on a deal and a figure per load with the fleet owner. They had stuck to their end of the bargain; he should do the same. There was no budging him or the transporter, which was incredible in the light of the cash each was pocketing regularly.

Neither would give way. It was the end of the road. Big Ted was left with no alternative but to call his one-time school mates and tell them the bad news. The racket was at an end.

Under other circumstances, rancour might have prevailed, but Big Ted was liked and had built a reputation as wholly reliable. Never once had he let the side down; never had he, Oliver Twist fashion, held out his plate and called for an extra portion. His discretion was beyond challenge. He was returning home, to the renewed problem of his women, but also to an assurance that if he decided to go back into business supplying from the Spanish end, then a ready UK market would remain open to him.

Back in Britain, amidst drizzle and in the clutches of a society dominated by the demands of the Inland Revenue, Big Ted found it impossible to put from his mind the lifestyle he had been forced to leave behind. His body told him it enjoyed the rest from alcohol and liberal partaking of the product he had been supplying so successfully. But he was not a man at peace. His metabolism went to war with his brain. He missed the sun, the buzz and the money. Lots and lots of it.

Sitting over a lonely lager once 1990 had moved into 1991, looking out through rain beating against the window of his local pub while mentally reminiscing about the days of plenty, Big Ted made a decision that was to change his life. And the lives of many others.

He recalled a conversation with one of the drivers who had worked with the haulage firm that had carried so many illicit loads out of Spain. On being told the racket was coming to an end, the man had offered, out of the blue, 'If you ever decide to go into business again, count me in, give me a ring. I've been thinking of buying my own lorry and going freelance.' The possibility that the man had changed his mind during the intervening months never occurred to Big Ted as he pressed coins into the call box at the end of the bar. But it turned out there was no need to worry on that score.

Ted had the feeling as the purr gave way to a voice at the other end of the line that the driver had almost been expecting his call. And when the brief, mutual, polite enquiries about health and loved ones had been asked and answered, the response to the question that motivated the call was precisely what Big Ted had hoped. He was back in business.

chapter four

JINGLE BELLS

BACK IN HIS OLD HAUNTS AROUND MALAGA, IT WAS AS IF Big Ted had never left. All the major players welcomed him as a long-lost son. At Ronnie Knight's club, RKnights, the boss himself had a huge hug for his big-spending customer. And even Mohammed, the normally morose Moroccan with whom he had been doing business before the fall-out forced him to leave, seemed unusually voluble. 'Meesta Ted. So glad to see you,' he spluttered. 'You back just in time. Everything taking off. Lotsa money. Lotsa stuff.' And it was true.

It seemed that everywhere he went, Big Ted bumped into men and even women who, like Dick Whittington in another town centuries before, had headed to Malaga with their heads filled with visions of streets paved not with gold but with the product of a certain flowering plant that would make them all rich. Naturally, Mohammed was happy to sell them all the gear they needed. His responsibility ended with the oily brown resin handed over before his subsequent departure, his glove compartment packed with banknotes. How they got the stuff back to wherever it was they came from was neither his business nor his concern.

For the majority, a kilo or two was all they wanted or could afford. They stuffed it into suitcases, in the spare tyres of their cars, in false fuel tanks and drove away oblivious to the fact that there were dogs trained to sniff out any variety of drug or that even the sweat that broke out on their faces at the first question from a Dover Customs officer would give the game away and land them in jail.

The odds against amateurs getting away with it were poor. Professionals of the ilk of Big Ted were a different matter altogether. It took only days for him to get back into the swing of running a thriving drug-smuggling enterprise. Knowing he could be trusted not to disappear with the funds, his old buyers in the UK had been over the moon to hear he was resuming his business in Spain and more than happy to hand over payment for the first load. Even Mohammed, seeing his customer base about to resume its previously lucrative level, suggested the payment-up-front rule could be relaxed. Within a week, the first lorry had arrived and left.

Through the windows of his apartment, Big Ted stared into a sky that was blue but had a very rosy hue. He didn't know it, but in Glasgow, just over 1,300 miles to the north, things were happening that were about to have important repercussions for him.

Tam McGraw had liked Gordon Ross from the first and found the younger man and Trevor Lawson popping into the Caravel ever more frequently. It was impossible for Tam not to have learned what Gordon and some of his friends were up to. Every now and then, they would disappear for a week or so on the pretext of having a holiday in Spain and, on returning, rather than being spent up, would be briefly flush with funds.

East End gossip had it that he and Craig were back into running drugs despite the bitter lesson of Dover docks in 1989, and that a well-known figure was the brains behind what they and others were doing. Many would guess at this figure's identity, but we shall call him The Man. He insisted on a cloak-and-dagger-style operation. The fewer who knew, who were involved, the better and safer. In any society, where there is gossip there is an informer, he warned. And Glasgow was no different.

Despite The Man's warning, Craig was stopped by police and discovered with Ecstasy pills some time around late 1991 or early 1992. No one knew for sure whether an informer had grassed or if the 1989 conviction and the gossip had made him and Gordon a target for surveillance, who would be stopped and searched whenever they were seen on the streets. But the discovery meant big trouble. The tiny tablets were in demand by youngsters willing to pay £20 a time to swallow the means to last through a frenetic all-night rave, ignoring the risk of brain damage and even death. What really worried police was that some were falling into the hands of school children. Even Princess Diana, during a visit to the 36th International Congress on Alcohol and Drug Abuse, would warn: 'Imaginative children lose themselves in fantasy worlds through stories. Later they might choose to escape through Ecstasy, uppers, alcohol and addiction.'

Craig's friends warned him he was looking at a stretch, and possibly a lengthy one, behind bars. He felt he had no alternative but to go on the run and, given bail, headed for the place where so many others in whom the Scots police took an interest chose to hole up.

But it was a forlorn figure who trudged along the road near Torremolinos when Big Ted drove past one day in 1992. He was sure he recognised the face, but it took a few moments for him to realise this was one of the two Glaswegians who had done a good turn by opening up his locked car six months earlier. Big Ted did a U-turn, giving a cheery salute to the hoots and toots of Spanish drivers forced to a sudden stop, and pulled alongside. 'Hi, Craig, how are you doing?'

At first, the Scot was nonplussed, then concerned that some holidaying Glasgow cop had recognised him. A second later, the peseta dropped. 'Ted, big man, locked yourself out lately?'

As an attempt at a joke, it did not hide the fact that Craig looked lost and alone. He appeared tired and dishevelled, exactly like a man on the run, and welcomed the chance of a lift back to his lodgings in Torremolinos.

As he drove, Big Ted remembered his passenger as cheerful, smartly dressed and witty. This was a down-at-heel, different figure altogether. The bedsit to which Craig directed him was in a backstreet – it was tiny, dark, dingy, dirty and there was no way he would be allowed to continue living there. 'Get your gear, I've a room at my place. You're coming with me. There's no way you are staying in this hovel,' he was ordered. Craig made no protest.

By now, months into an expanding and profitable operation, Big Ted had swapped his apartment for a villa in the Torremolinos hinterland, among the discreet homes where the wealthy shop-owners and lawyers lived, among the plush hideouts of Brits on the run. He had more than a single spare room – a set of spares, in fact – and Craig was welcome to move in. That night, over a meal and a few beers, Craig told his story.

Despite being caught once and jailed, he and Gordon had not been put off the idea of using cars to smuggle hash. Once out of prison, they had taken a short holiday in Spain to assure their contacts they would be back in business, and it was during this break that they had met Big Ted and helped him open his car. Back in Glasgow, they had been approached by a syndicate who had been running a smuggling racket using cars since 1987 and who knew that their previous experience, while ending in disaster, would be useful. Demand for hash was insatiable, said the group. Craig and Gordon realised there might be safety in numbers and thought that carrying out a few runs for the syndicate would help them build up enough cash to resume working for themselves. The Man who ran the racket had promised them there was a fortune to be made for anyone who could get through the various checks and back over Hadrian's Wall. A few were trying the holiday-luggage route, but more were falling by the wayside than were succeeding. Cars, Craig and Gordon were convinced, were the answer. They would need enough money for a car, but the cash to buy hash would be provided. Hanging around, waiting for things to move, Craig decided to get some money together by selling Ecstasy but was caught. It was bad timing because within days Gordon told him he had managed to get them another VW Golf and they were ready to move. So Craig had taken the advice of pals and skipped bail, doing a runner and flying out via Ireland to wait for his friend, who was driving to Malaga. This time, they would go for broke and risk being hanged for a sheep as for a lamb. Instead of 40 or 60 kilos, they would buy 90 and, once near Calais, Gordon would complete the journey back to the UK on his own, while Craig would await his return to Malaga for the next run.

Big Ted found it difficult to believe what he was hearing. 'Ninety kilos,' he gasped. 'That's nearly two hundred pounds, more than fourteen stones. Where are you going to hide it? Remember you're only in a Golf and you can hardly put it in boxes on the back seats. And forgive me for asking, but that will set you back something like £63,000. Have you the money?'

'No sweat,' smiled Craig. 'It'll come with Gordon, and we've worked everything out. We've done this before. You cut out the seat padding and hide a lot in there. Where we went wrong before was in not making sure it couldn't move during the drive. Mind you, it gives your backside pelters. You might say the price of getting rich is piles. Then there's enough of a gap in the roof space to hide a lot of it. The rest will go in the door panels. It'll work. We're going over the Pyrenees into France because the frontier checks there are less stringent. You could walk an elephant through without anyone batting an eyelid.'

'But you'll make it too top heavy. The car will be all over the road and there's always the chance of ice about. The suspension will never stand it. Once you start sliding towards the edge, there's no way you'll be able to save yourselves.'

Craig smiled. 'All sorted. Wait till you see the car,' he teased.

Big Ted wondered what he meant and found out two days later when Gordon arrived from Glasgow with the Golf. Back home, a mechanic had fitted wooden blocks into the chassis and across the suspension. The result was to effectively give the car the feeling that it was sitting on top of solid rock. It bounced and shuddered like the first basic vehicles used to move across the surface of the moon. Wearily, stiffly, Gordon climbed out.

'How did it go?' asked an anxious Craig.

'Bloody hell, it feels as if I've got piles already and somebody's been shoving red hot needles into them. But if it works, it will be worth it.'

Big Ted was still dubious and tried convincing the pair to abandon the plot. 'You'll come a cropper going over the mountains,' he warned. 'Remember Michael Caine and *The Italian Job*? They had a bus full of gold and it almost went over the edge on a mountain pass because the load wasn't distributed properly. You'll have a helluva job turning because the suspension is wedged solid.'

His arguments fell on deaf ears. The Glaswegians were confident they could make it home. Handing over the money to Big Ted, they hung about the Malaga area until Mohammed could organise getting their hash to them. Craig was happy to mooch about the place with Big Ted. The two felt comfortable with one another and made the most of the freedom to trawl bars and restaurants.

Gordon too was not one to let an opportunity slip. Relaxing on the beach at Torremolinos, he noticed a damsel in distress. She was having problems working out how to adjust her lounger and as she bent to wrestle it into place he was almost mesmerised by the battle her tiny bikini top was having to contain her breasts. He could have waited for the outcome of both contests, but instead offered help. The job done, he was content to resume his own place but his Sir Galahad act and looks had clearly impressed her. She began chatting in an accent he knew was English but only later discovered was Midlands Brummie.

An hour later, they were still talking and for once Gordon was finding it hard to say a word, instead trying desperately not to laugh out loud. She had, she told him, been married to a policeman and had moved to South Yorkshire, where he reckoned his chances of promotion would be better. The marriage, she believed, was no better or worse than any other. A couple of around the same age as her and her husband had moved next door and a polite invitation for coffee had led to an occasional night out. The neighbours were outgoing and, to her astonishment, when it was proposed all four went to a rural fair she discovered the man next door was a Morris dancer. Clad in tight knickerbockers, a loose waistcoat and white shirt, he pranced about waving white scarves, bells attached to his knees ting-a-linging as his wife chanted, clapped and sang. It was, she said, the most remarkable sight – one she found hilarious and then boring while her husband was clearly hooked.

In short, he took up the pastime, increasingly accompanying his neighbours to classes and then festivals, to which she always produced an excuse not to go. She dismissed hints from friends that he was becoming unusually friendly with the dance couple, confident she would have been the first to spot if anything was amiss in the marriage.

When her husband told her he would be absent for a week attending a residential course at a police training college, she decided on a short stay with her own family. But, discovering the unexpected arrival of other relatives had created a bed shortage, she then volunteered to return home early. Opening her front door in mid-afternoon, she was at first frightened and then made curious by the sound of ringing bells, evidently coming from upstairs. The din increased as she mounted the stairs and, through an open bedroom door, she saw her husband and the wife next door in frenzied lovemaking, stark naked but for Morris-dancing bells jangling furiously about their ankles.

'What did you do?' asked Gordon.

'I left him and took his bells,' was the reply. 'Now, how about a drink? I have something I'd like you to see.' Beneath her short, black hair, brown eyes twinkled mischievously and a strap slipped ever so accidentally from a shoulder as she rose.

Later on, Craig and Big Ted came in search of their colleague, but he was nowhere to be seen. Standing beneath the balconies of the lavish Sol Don Pablo Hotel, they thought they heard a curious noise; it sounded like the ringing of bells. Craig was annoyed when Gordon finally joined them for a beer at a beach bar.

'Hell's bells, where have you been, Gordon?' he stormed. He was about to add 'the fucking stuff is here' when their friend, slightly breathless but looking as though he had freshly showered, burst into laughter.

Big Ted began singing 'Jingle bells, jingle bells . . .' and Gordon's laugh faded.

The hash was to be collected from a hotel car park in nearby Fuengirola. As soon as the bales were delivered, they were cut into strips and used to replace the roof-padding of the Golf. What could not be concealed was hidden in door panels. Then they set off.

The heat in the car was equivalent to driving in an oven. Even though they wore the minimum – sandals, shorts and T-shirts – and had the windows down, the sweat poured down their backs and into their crotches, soaking their shirts along the way.

The sight of the car swaying treacherously astounded holidaymakers but caused knowing locals to wink at one another. At each corner, the car seemed certain to topple over until it was realised the best method of changing direction was to slow to a near stop before beginning to turn the steering wheel.

As the car lurched out of sight, Big Ted was certain his new friends were driving to their doom. Later, he was to discover the pair had come close to grief as they began the ascent of the Sierra Nevada mountain range between the coastal resort of Almería and the interior city of Granada, once the seat of Moorish kings. Forced to brake sharply by an oncoming lorry as they approached a bend, the Golf rocked and slewed. Gordon stopped it inches from the flimsy barrier separating them from the oblivion of a terrifying plunge over the edge. The two had to clamber out and physically push the car back.

They tried again to make progress, this time at walking pace, and then, as the road ascended the spectacular range, they encountered ice. Along the way, as the temperature dropped, they wound up the windows, but the smell of the hidden heated resin was appalling and stifling. If it lingered, it was a certain giveaway should they be stopped, so, reluctantly, they had to suffer blasts of chilled air through open windows.

They were still dressed for the beach and the sweat froze on their bodies. In no time, they were shivering and getting odd glances. There had to be something strange about two men driving along icy roads at a crawl apparently freezing to death yet disdaining hats or sweaters and craving sharp, fresh air. Their pace was holding up the traffic in their wake and there was something decidedly peculiar about their Golf. At the slightest departure from the straight, it appeared about to topple over and on an especially sharp hairpin bend suddenly did a complete turn and began sliding backwards downhill.

It was a terrifying experience for Craig and Gordon, who clearly felt enough was enough. An hour and a half into the trip, they decided to give up and return to Torremolinos, where Big Ted was relieved to see them. 'You were mad to try it,' he said. 'Don't worry. We'll put the stuff on my next lorry and your people in Glasgow can arrange to meet up with it.'

Gordon drove the Golf back alone, meeting up with the lorry at a service halt at Toddington in Bedfordshire. There was no need to hide the hash – a solitary male driving a Golf north wouldn't arouse much suspicion – so it went into the boot and on the back seat.

In Glasgow, he told of the near disaster. 'The problem is that being top-heavy puts too much of a strain on the suspension,' he said. 'It can handle 60 kilos stashed inside it but 90 is too much. If a suspension leaf goes, we'll be stuck in the middle of nowhere with nearly a million quid's worth of hash.'

While they were grateful to Big Ted for helping them out of a spot, they could not expect him to jeopardise his own operation by regularly making the extra stop to unload the Scots' consignment. It would only need a nosy cop to investigate for disaster to destroy a very successful and lucrative enterprise. While the little syndicate had been using cars to safely bring home up to 60 kilos a run since 1987, it was hardly the way to make them millionaires.

And the risks were increasing. More and more car smugglers were being caught and Gordon had already been nicked once before. A second appearance in the dock would be certain to bring on at least six years of hearing only the turning of locks, the clanging of doors and seeing one miserable hour of sunlight a day. As they had found to their cost, hiding more in the car could be disastrous.

Giving up, though, was not an option. This was a business with huge potential encumbered with a technical problem that required only a solution. A rethink was needed.

chapter five

CLOSE SHAVES

THE MAN WAS NOT ONE TO LET MOSS GROW UNDER HIS
feet – or a good idea grow stale for lack of attention. He reasoned that, with a
little tinkering, his plan could be made to run smoothly. Bringing the gear over
by car was making money, for the guys who drove, those who distributed it in
Glasgow and himself, while the profit from each run would just about get the
next job off the ground. A corporation chairman would have told his
shareholders business was solid but not spectacular.

The plot was limited by the amount that could be carried in a car. Anything
over about 60 kilos would have compromised safety too badly. Admittedly, a
return of £138,000 on an outlay of £42,000 was nice enough, but a van . . .

The Man took a good look at the transit vans carrying workmen and their
tools around the East End of Glasgow. In the interiors of some, the wheel arches
were boxed in by a benched seat that could, with just a little adjustment by a
clever joiner, be enlarged to accommodate blocks of hash. It was worth a try. A
UK-registered workman's van would attract attention if it turned up in the
holiday resorts of the Costa del Sol, so the Golf would still handle that end of
the operation, carrying no more than a manageable 60 kilos at a time.

What was needed was a halfway point, where the van would be loaded up.
The Man's finger landed on Paris. What lay near the French capital?

Disneyland. Why, parties of kids had been going out there from Glasgow with their parents since it opened as Euro Disneyland in April 1992. (It has gone through a couple of reincarnations since then, changing its name to Disneyland Paris in October 1994 and then to the current Disneyland Park, part of the Disneyland Resort Paris.) Along with the families and kids, gangs of workmen from all over Europe had also flooded the area, putting the final touches to and maintaining the 2,000-hectare entertainment site. One extra van would hardly excite interest. The car would load up in Spain, drive to Disneyland, meet the van then head back into Spain to bring out a second cargo. Turnover would be doubled and, with it, profit.

By summer 1992, the first van had driven to Disneyland and Big Ted had waved off Craig and Gordon from Spain on their second run in the Golf shuttle car. They were carrying their loads with little attempt at concealment, because they no longer had to worry about the main danger-point, the Dover ferry terminal.

The van man, we'll call him The Driver, was another Glaswegian who had been recruited because of his reputation for not panicking in a tight spot and wisecracking his way out of an emergency. He was enthusiastic from the outset, and completed his end of the deal without complications. 'No sweat,' he told The Man when he reached Glasgow. 'A doddle. Apart from a gander through the back windows, the Customs guys hardly looked at us and the sniffer dogs were nowhere near. They're concentrating on couples in cars.'

The van runs continued, sometimes every month, or once in six weeks. Occasionally, the Golf, once unloaded, would drive all the way through to Scotland. More often than not, it would be left at Malaga, with the smugglers flying out to pick it up when a trip to Disneyland was in the offing. It meant regular wages and good earnings for the handful of men involved.

With the exception of The Man, the others in the gang enjoyed splashing their cash as fast as they earned it. The Man spent discreetly and modestly, ploughing the profits into his home and investing in businesses that would ensure a regular cash return. And, in everything, he was happy to be guided by his wife. His one weakness was for holidays in places where he knew the sun would be a constant companion. Even then, he put his sojourns to good use. Ideas and inspirations for schemes and scams, many of them illegal, constantly flitted through his mind. While he had never been a drug user, and never would be, in the hash racket he recognised the opportunities to make a fortune. And,

The Man reasoned, it could only get better. He was right, but only because fate was to join in the fun.

Around the bars and beaches of Malaga and Fuengirola, Craig and Big Ted were becoming familiar faces and spenders. Many Brits living along the Costa were assumed to be surviving on the proceeds of some crime or other, and there was no reason why they should be regarded differently. The area was a haven for dodgy characters and, for reasons that would become obvious, had been dubbed the 'Costa del Crime'.

One of the first to see the potential had been London gang leader Billy Hill. Filling the void left by so many hard men being drafted overseas to fight and die in the Second World War, Hill had allied with Jack 'Spot' Comer to rule the south-east of the capital. Inevitably, the brothers in crime fell out. Spot had the backing of the Kray twins but even they could not save him from a slashing by two up-and-coming thugs named Frankie Fraser and Alf Warren, who scared him into retirement. Hill saw the writing on the wall, packed his suitcase and in 1956 settled in southern Spain.

Billy Hill's tales of a life virtually free from over-inquisitive police and old acquaintances needing him to reach a helping hand into his wallet spread back home. Then others started following. The trickle grew to a stream in 1978, when Spain, accusing Britain of refusing to talk about handing back Gibraltar, scrapped the 100-year-old extradition treaty between the two countries. The result was a procession of Rolls-Royces and black Jaguars with darkened windows heading for the Costa towns of Malaga, Estepona, Torremolinos, Puerto Banus and Fuengirola, where the owners snapped up the most expensive properties on the market, surrounded them with high walls and fences, fitted the latest surveillance equipment and continued running their crooked businesses by telephone.

So Craig and Gordon found themselves in an area which had been and still was playing host to many of Britain's most infamous expats, including Ronnie Knight, Howard Marks, Freddie Foreman and Kenneth Noye. Drug-dealers mingled with armed robbers, contract assassins with counterfeiters. Into their midst arrived swarthy men from Colombia and the West Indies offering deals to supply vast amounts of cocaine.

Hash was one thing, but Charlie was quite another. Highly addictive, it can lead to lying, stealing, deformity, paranoia and hallucinations. The route from the main source – the mountains and jungles of Colombia – led north over the border into the USA, and the Americans were determined to quash the trade. With the collaboration of the British Foreign Office, a bogus bank was set up in Anguilla, the Caribbean paradise, and members of the most influential of the Colombian cartels were encouraged to use it for laundering drug money. The sting was called Operation Dinero.

Meanwhile, operatives from the Drug Enforcement Agency moved into southern Spain. They were looking for potential cocaine buyers, reasoning these would inevitably lead them to suppliers. In late 1992, agents looking for three Europeans targeted the Hotel Sol Principe in Torremolinos, where a barman working for the Spanish National Police had been briefed to call his handler in Malaga if they were spotted. They were, he was told, well-built, good spenders and Belgian. One was dark and good looking.

Craig, Gordon and Big Ted were in town that day. The former had arrived with £42,000 in a green hold-all and they were awaiting word that 60 kilos – clicks, they called them – of hash were arriving from Morocco for them to drive to Disneyland. Killing time, the two Scots had lunched with Craig's host and the trio took a car trip along the coast. They called by chance into the Sol Principe for a beer. As they chatted, the barman, unable to distinguish their accents from those of a man on the moon, assumed he had struck gold and called his contact. It took minutes for the Americans, with a Spanish liaison detective, to reach the hotel and arrange reinforcements to begin full-time surveillance on the suspects. By the time they arrived, though, the bar was empty. The remnants of Big Ted's cigarette still burned in the ashtray.

Seconds earlier and the fortunes of the Scots, together with their accomplices and supplier, would almost certainly have been scuppered. Why did they leave early? Through the window, Gordon had spotted a potential mate for the afternoon. Craig and Big Ted knew their friend's courtship ritual could stretch into hours, which would make them late for their date with the 60 clicks. As he made a beeline for her, his companions had followed, literally frogmarching him, despite his protests, back to the car.

For the Dinero agents, hunting three men they had never seen was the equivalent of the proverbial search for a needle in a haystack. Over the next two years, it was possible that the paths of the smugglers and the searchers crossed, but no one would ever know. In 1994, the climax of Operation Dinero would result in nine tonnes of cocaine being seized in Canada and the USA, eighty-eight members and associates of the Colombian Cali cartel being arrested worldwide, £33 million in laundered cash being confiscated and paintings by Rubens, Reynolds and Picasso impounded.

That money was small beer compared with the fortunes that would be made by the hash-smugglers. After a winter break, as spring appeared on the Scottish horizon, the future of hash smuggling into Glasgow appeared in danger of taking a nosedive. The problem began when The Man instructed The Driver to arrange the hire of another van. Arriving at the hire company late in the afternoon, he was shown a transit bus and told it was the only vehicle available. 'I must have a van,' he protested desperately. 'Now. We have to be in France tomorrow.'

They were sorry but nothing could be done. And there was no time to shop about for a replacement.

The Driver climbed in and headed for the home of The Man. If he was fazed at the appearance of a bus instead of a van, his discomfort did not show. Instead, he demonstrated the resourcefulness, coupled with an encyclopaedic memory, that had already steered him through two decades of risk.

Sharing tea with The Driver, he recalled hearing a friend talk about reading the autobiography of a well-known entrepreneur. In his younger days, the celebrity had used the cover of bus trips to Spanish holiday resorts to smuggle drugs on return journeys, unzipping seat covers and pushing his stash inside or even, on occasions, cutting slits to give access to the padding. If it worked once, reasoned The Man, it was worth another try. 'Are the seat covers zipped?'

'Zipped? What . . .?' The Driver began to protest, but he was instructed to nip into the transit and check. 'Zipped,' he said.

'Take out the padding near the back and stick paper in. Leave the padding here. When Craig and Gordon turn up, chuck out the paper and put the gear in the seat covers. If you're asked, you've taken a load of kids to Disneyland and will be going back for them in a week – that'll account for the empty bus.'

The Man's confidence was enough to convince The Driver of the sanity of this madcap scheme. At Calais, The Driver told immigration officers he was on his way to collect a party of Glasgow youngsters from Disneyland. Returning to Dover, he explained to a Customs officer boarding the coach and staring at a dozen empty seats that he was glad to have dropped off his party. A quick glance was enough to reassure the officer there was no one and nothing on board and no need to call in a sniffer dog.

CLOSE SHAVES

In Glasgow with 60 kilos of hash, The Driver gave no hint of the strain that had dogged him. He would not say it was a journey he was reluctant to repeat, but anyway that prospect would not arise. While the transit bus had been in France, The Man had been mulling over the kernel of an idea so outrageous it would be sure to work. It just needed the right team and a lot of money.

chapter six

TAKEN FOR A RIDE

THE MAN RECOGNISED THE RISK IN TRYING TO REPEAT THE
saga of the empty transit bus. It would only need one official, at either Calais or
Dover, to recall the explanation given first time around for doubts to set in.

Yet a bus would be ideal cover. There were lots of empty spaces – under the
chassis, in the engine compartment, among the luggage – for hidden booty. He
thought back to his holidays and the sight of happy youngsters craning through
bus windows. No one would ever connect them with drugs or smuggling. But
bums on seats were vital, and getting them there could be a problem.

In the poverty-wracked East End of Glasgow, there should have been no
shortage of contenders for trips to Disneyland, but few families surviving on
unemployment benefit or single mums struggling along on social security
could afford the price of a foreign holiday. The crucial question that had to be
asked was whether it was worth, in effect, paying for the security of having the
seats filled. That would mean cutting into the profits, but the alternative was an
empty vehicle with all the accompanying risks. As far as The Man was
concerned, the answer was never in doubt.

At a meeting in the Holiday Inn hotel in Glasgow, early in 1993, his co-
conspirators agreed. Better to play safe. So a sixteen-seat transit bus was hired
and for ten days, at the start of spring 1993, a party of youngsters had the treat

of their lives: a free holiday to Disneyland. The only cost, it was explained to those who heard along the East End grapevine about places on the trip being up for grabs, was £30 to help pay for fuel.

Parents who queried this incredible offer were told about a mysterious Mr Colin O'Sullivan, a wealthy Glasgow businessman with an office in Ireland who, despite making a fortune in the property market, had never forgotten his roots or what it was like to live only on hope. Word had it Mr O'Sullivan was a shy man who preferred staying in the background, but he had asked to be given a full report of the trip and it was whispered that the £7,000 bill for the party of 14 would hardly even dent his fortune. He had, their families were assured, insisted on the best for the young people and had suggested to the two adults sharing the 650-mile drive that they stay at the Davy Crockett Ranch, a series of luxury cabins set in 57 acres of forest just a quarter of an hour from the Disney parks.

The youngsters would find that being taken there from Glasgow council schemes in areas such as Arden, Tollcross, Easterhouse and Barlanark was to discover a whole new lifestyle, one they might have seen on television but which seemed completely out of their reach. The cabins boasted private bathrooms and kitchens, telephones, televisions with international channels and grounds with open-air barbecues and picnic tables. In the mornings, they would collect Continental breakfasts from the restaurant and take them back to their cabins.

When the kids returned home, they told their families they hadn't simply been to another country, but a different world. For their part, the smugglers could hardly believe the trip, and others which followed, could be so easy. On outward journeys, the bus was given only a cursory examination at the busy Dover ferry terminal. There was nothing to single it out from the hundreds of cars and other coaches heading for the Continent. Had Customs officers who exchanged a few bantering words with the two men in charge of the party decided on a more detailed examination, they might have been surprised at the amount of spending money being carried. Hidden under a seat was more than £42,000. 'To buy presents for the guys back home,' the two adults joked to one another.

From Calais car-ferry terminal, the coach headed south along the main A26 and A1 routes, stopping briefly at the popular Aire d'Assevillers-Ouest service station – roughly the halfway point of their journey through France – before carrying on to Disneyland. For most of the passengers, it was their first experience not just of being on the Continent, but of life outside Scotland. As the blue transit, hired from a Glasgow company, pulled into the huge site, said to cover an area one sixth the size of Paris, the kids were in awe. And for a week they had the adventures of their young lives, wandering through the wonders and magic of the giant Disney creation, chaperoned by the two men who had brought them to this feast of fun. Nothing seemed too much trouble for their minders.

Had the youthful holidaymakers not slept so soundly, they might have wondered why, with their trip nearing an end, the transit disappeared late one night and was missing for three hours. It had, in fact, hardly got out of first gear, being driven to the aptly named Alamo Trading Post for a vital rendezvous.

In Spain, Craig had been left with Big Ted and the Golf, while Gordon flew back to Scotland where he hung around Glasgow for three weeks, often calling at the Caravel to look up Tam McGraw, before returning to Torremolinos to meet up with them again and take delivery of 60 kilos of hash. It had already been paid for, the money coming over previously in the empty transit. Loading up the Golf with Craig and Ted's help, Gordon set off on the arduous 1,100-mile journey to Disneyland, breaking the trip by sleeping in the car. At the Alamo, the bales, stuffed into hold-alls, went into the coach, which set off back to Calais early next morning. After another rest, Gordon went back to Spain, leaving the car with Ted and Craig and then flying home to Scotland.

There were ready cash buyers for the 60 clicks when the holidaymakers returned to Glasgow. The scheme had been a rip-roaring success, leaving £87,000 to be shared out among the gang after expenses had been deducted. It was hard to believe the whole thing had run so smoothly. All around them, the smugglers were hearing and reading of others being caught for significantly smaller amounts, yet their set-up appeared flawless. The syndicate were so confident that they decided to repeat the performance at Easter in April 1993, and again, six weeks later, with the bus leaving from Pollok Shopping Centre.

This third trip, just like the first two, was booked through a Glasgow travel agency, and the format used would be repeated more than 40 times in the years that followed. One of the group, normally the man we are calling The Driver, would ask a travel representative to call an Irish telephone number, that of the man footing the bill for the holiday, Colin O'Sullivan. The Driver would explain that the millionaire liked to feel he was making the final decisions.

As soon as the telephone was answered, and the receptionist had verified she was calling the number requested by her customer, she would hand the phone to The Driver. He would then proceed to carry out a lengthy discussion with O'Sullivan, finalising numbers, arrangements and payment. The conversation would be polite and always end in mutual courtesies.

Did O'Sullivan exist? Who knows? But it has to be admitted that the numbers called were remarkably similar to some appearing in greyhound-racing magazines or catalogues offering animals for sale. And at least one advertiser, trying to flog a top-rate greyhound from his farm near Cork in the Irish Republic, was said to have been surprised to answer his telephone only to be greeted by a man with a Scottish accent asking him if the arrangements for a party of youngsters to Disneyland were satisfactory and would he be reimbursing the cost in the usual way. He was even more astonished to receive a similar call several months later. The man at the other end appeared not to be able to hear his own voice passing on details about his dogs. Much as the Irishman shouted, he could make no headway, even during pauses by the Scot. And he noticed with some bewilderment that the man from across the water appeared to be addressing his remarks to someone totally different from himself, saying things like, 'That's fine then, Colin. All systems go. I'll give the lady the other five and a half thousand and make a provisional booking for the next one, shall I?'

Sometimes The Driver would be asked to be connected to a mobile telephone and would take over when it began ringing in order to chat to 'Colin'. It would be alleged, much later, that the number called was in reality that of the man coming into the office to formalise the booking: The Driver himself, in other words. With his ring tone on silent, he would take the handset and pretend to have a conversation, in effect talking to himself. If that was the case, then the whole scenario was so realistic it fooled staff in travel offices all over Glasgow.

As for Colin O'Sullivan, he was never seen, but then one of the privileges of being wealthy was the ability to choose when or when not to show one's face in public. Maybe it was simply the case that he opted to remain in the background, never revealing himself to the hundreds of grateful families and their children. There was no doubt that O'Sullivan provided the wherewithal for a racket which, as scams go, was a steady and evidently smooth way of getting a comfortable return.

But, remarkably, there were grumblings of discontent. The natives were becoming restless. Some of the boys had by now been to Disneyland twice or even thrice. The novelty was wearing off, and when another trip was mooted there were moans of 'No' again! We're starting to tell the guides the way around.' There were even calls for 'a few dolls' to accompany the trippers. A mixed party, at that stage, was a definite no go. It would inevitably cause problems and attract too much attention.

As it was, there had already been a series of scares. But then, what else could be expected as a consequence of taking a group of streetwise kids from the toughest schemes in Glasgow and letting them loose on the unsuspecting French nation?

In theory, the Disney ideal ought to have been the balm that cooled the frustrations not just of Scots but of all peoples. Visitors were invited to allow themselves to be carried into fantasylands where beautiful maidens kissed frogs and discovered the lips were those of handsome princes, where wicked pirates were routed with minimal pain and violence, where even the most lowly could become the loftiest while never forgetting their humble roots. Old Walt had created a dreamland in which the power of imagination was intended to achieve what the United Nations could not: peace, harmony and affection between people of all races and cultures.

It was from this environment that one evening the Glasgow bus party stepped into a bar on the fringes of Disneyland for a few soft drinks while the adults tasted a mite of something stronger. Inside it was dim, busy and noisy with the sounds of many tongues. There were strapping women from . . . it sounded like Holland, Americans discussing the merits of their own Florida Disneyland compared to that of Paris, the inevitable Japanese with their flash-cameras and smiles and a party from a Dublin youth group. There was also a particularly outstanding example of the Aussie sportswoman: golden-haired, with white shorts showing off her bronzed thighs, a chest that tested the strength of her blue sleeveless blouse and a smile that would have melted Ayers Rock. In less than the time it took for the young men of Glasgow to gasp, 'Jimmy, see you that?', at least four were in love. And there the trouble began.

They had opposition. At one end of the bar stood a dozen or so Algerians, out from Paris for the day and making no secret of their intention to have a good time. Giggling and pushing in long white robes, their penchant for pale-skinned women, and the Australian in particular, was obvious. If their stares made her uncomfortable, she did not show it. No doubt her appeal was universal and by now admiration and things stronger she had come to cope with. But in the Glaswegians she discovered youthful champions. Admittedly, they were a decade too young, but age is no barrier to a proud warrior from Barlanark when he senses romance.

How it began, no one was sure. The rival armies exchanged looks and while the Scots were unable to understand a single word that spat from the lips of their adversaries, they took these to be insults. The cause of the hostilities was, of course, oblivious to it all – until, that is, a tumbler sailed through the air. It was followed by barrages in both directions of glasses, cans, cakes and even crisp packets. There were screams, shouts, infant wails and the barking of a dog. Some yelled that the police had arrived, at which point both sides beat a hasty retreat. The Celts had items to hide from the boys in blue and, on reflection, they reckoned the enemy probably had even more guilty secrets hidden within their white robes. As for the girl, she had vanished from their young lives forever, to resurface, no doubt, many times in their dreams.

That wasn't the only scare. There were times during those early holidays and even later on when the driving team must have wondered if they were in charge not of youngsters but clouds of locusts. Walt Disney has provided many magical moments to fascinate and mesmerise children throughout the years, but the antics of the Glasgow kids on the loose could leave any pantomime character looking staid in comparison.

With a wave of her magic wand, Cinderella's fairy godmother turned a pumpkin into a coach, mice into black horses and a rat became the coachman. For the young Scots' part, a simple stroll through the theme parks was all it needed for them to conjure the disappearance of a giant Pluto puppet. Souvenirs vanished from the theme parks and the Alamo Trading Post faster than the Three Bears' porridge, disappearing into pockets as wide as the mouths of the Ugly Sisters. Dumbo was bolted down, yet somehow he walked and was seen heading for the hire coach when The Driver asked his charges what they were up to. 'You'll never get that through the door,' he told them. 'And what the hell would you do with it even if you could get it back?'

The leader of the looters had thought of that. 'The woman next to my sister in Milngavie's always bragging about her garden gnomes. She's got dozens and puts them in the bath tae keep them clean. They've even got names. Just wait till me sister puts Dumbo in the middle of the lawn. The woman'll go spare.'

'Don't you think somebody will notice and tell the police?' he was asked. 'I know it's Milngavie but even there you don't see a lot of elephants in the front gardens. He's bound to be recognised.'

'No sweat. We'll paint him.'

'He's not coming. You'll have to take him back.'

So Dumbo stayed.

Aladdin was not so fortunate. The life-sized figure dressed in brightly coloured clothes and sporting a black beard duly took his seat between two miscreants. Arriving at Dover, an immigration official boarded the bus to carry out a head count, and with one of the party hiding under pals along the back seat, the man carried out his check. 'Two, four, six, eight . . .' and so on he continued, evidently under the impression that young men of school age from Glasgow matured early and that talk about the city having a sectarian problem must be rubbish, because one of the party had grown a thick beard and wore a turban.

There was no let up on the journey back to Scotland. From each service station, youngsters would emerge, pockets bulging with sweets, French chocolate, soft drinks and even, on one occasion, a can of oil.

'What are you going to do with that?' asked the incredulous driver. 'You haven't even got a car at home.'

'Nah, but it'll be handy for me da's bike.'

It was one of these exploits which was to produce the most heart-stopping moment of the entire smuggling enterprise. But that was in the future, and a few million pounds had first to be made.

chapter seven

FOOTBALL CRAZY

A LESS BENEVOLENT MAN THAN COLIN O'SULLIVAN MIGHT have regarded the discontent at the prospect of further run-ins with Dumbo, Pluto and Co. as ingratitude and worthy of punishment by calling a halt to his generosity.

But not Colin. Boys would be boys, adolescent youngsters quickly became bored and in any case, from the outset, there had been hiccups in filling the seats. Kids dropped out, changed their minds. One day they were going, next day not. At the last minute, one of the party would become ill, and a replacement would have to be found. This was a problem that taxed The Man. What was needed, he realised, was a ready, steady, reliable and credible-sounding source of bodies – a pool – gathered from a group, a team, or a club, made up from young people with a reason to travel and a motive for going abroad. Having a son of his own, he knew that something which would attract and then hold the youngsters' interest was crucial. Like a competition. Or a football tournament, for example. Football, that was it. Football was the answer, he was sure.

In 1993, Scotland was going soccer daft. A former Glasgow Rangers player, Alex Ferguson, now boss of Manchester United, had been voted Manager of the Year in England. In the city itself, Mark Hateley and Ally McCoist were banging in goals for the Ibrox club with such regularity that they seemed unstoppable. Football was not one of The Man's interests, although most of those close to him would be most likely to be seen at Parkhead – known locally as Paradise – supporting Rangers' bitter rivals, Celtic. The Man noted how, everywhere, kids were kicking footballs, seeing themselves as future stars of the Blues or Hoops.

Maybe it was true that, for most, visions of playing before huge crowds and clutching cups were pipe dreams, but then dreams cost nothing. There were plenty of adults willing to do what they could to give the young players a helping hand. And with top footballers costing millions to buy, major clubs were keen to invest in scouting networks that would hopefully root out the cream of the crop. Scotland had long been recognised as a fertile garden of footballing talent, so it was no surprise when Highbury Boys' Club was founded for lads aged 14 and 15 in the Pollok area of Glasgow. The title was a clue to the club sponsors: Arsenal, the Gunners, the legendary London side which played at Highbury stadium in the north of the capital, and the red-and-white shirts worn by the Glasgow youngsters were replicas of the strip that had graced grounds all over the world. The hope was that, if a boy demonstrated enough promise, he would be offered a trial down south.

Behind the setting up of Highbury Boys' Club in 1993 were Robert Whitelock and a one-time schoolmate, John Burgon. In the events that were to follow, not an iota of suspicion would ever fall on Robert. Never once did he doubt that what would be offered was genuine and done out of honest generosity. His sole concern was for his young charges and, in fact, at least two of the teenagers who signed for the club went on to become professionals.

The first club outing overseas was in mid-1993, when around fourteen members of Highbury Boys' Club were treated, courtesy of Colin O'Sullivan, to a ten-day stay at the French Disneyland. For more than a week, the youngsters enjoyed the wonders and magic created by the Disney empire. As much as anything, this initial trip was organised with the aim of gauging the reaction of the young players to the idea of going abroad regularly.

The Man and his friends already knew from the dissent of earlier trips that Disneyland would not be a permanent option. During the holiday, the idea of arranging matches against teams of other young people both in Britain and abroad, Spain in particular, would be mooted. Would they be interested? Would they be up for trips to other places, even long trips? Meanwhile, the kids were to enjoy themselves. And they did.

While they were off having fun, the bus made a short journey back to the Alamo Trading Post. There was business to be done. The Golf made the by now familiar journey too, and when the time came for the boys to be driven home, they hadn't a clue that 60 kilos of hash lay hidden among their luggage. Six weeks later, the hired bus was off again, this time leaving from Pollok Shopping Centre. It came back ten days later, and again there were wages for the smugglers.

Naturally, parents wanted to know how the trips had gone. How had the men in charge been? Did they drink? Were women with them? Did they stay with the boys? The young players could do nothing but give top marks. The adults drank Irn Bru or Diet Coke, were always around for help and advice and as for drugs – drugs? What drugs?

That year, there was a diversion when the club was taken to play in a tournament at Liverpool, near the world-famous Anfield ground. The Glaswegians made a good impression, reaching the final, where they narrowly lost. Their disappointment was soon assuaged, because, almost as soon as they emerged from the dressing-room, they were back into the blue minibus and heading for Dover and the Seacat to Calais en route for Disneyland. Days later, as the bus disembarked at Dover on the way back to Glasgow, it broke down and emergency repairs were needed. The crew telephoned Glasgow to report they would be delayed. Told what had happened, The Man was angry and adamant it must not be allowed to recur.

Despite this hitch at the tail end of the year, the 1993 company report would have been encouraging. 'Made lots of progress, expanded activity, created firm foundation, much room to grow, further investment recommended.' It was time to join the Premier League.

chapter eight

BUSSED AND BUST

AT THE BEGINNING OF 1994, THE MAN DECIDED TO experiment. He proposed the hire of a 36-seater bus and suggested taking a party of 32 lads from Highbury Boys' Club. Although Colin O'Sullivan would need to dig deeper than ever into his apparently unlimited resources, the idea of a much bigger squad than ever before went down well, especially when it was pointed out that the bigger vehicle would allow the cargo to be doubled. Twice as much to carry, twice as much to sell – double wages.

There was an additional motive. This venture was in the nature of a test. Driving to Disneyland wasn't a problem, but the entire racket depended on receiving, safely, hash at Davy Crockett Ranch. There was never any question of a supply shortage in Spain. Despite some domestic problems, the Moroccans boasted they could meet any requirement, but their part of the deal ended with the raw material being delivered to Big Ted and Craig in the Malaga area. The real difficulty was getting the bars of hash from there to France.

Normally, Gordon had the wheel of the Golf, but the strain of driving a top-heavy car more than 1,100 miles over mountain roads and passes was taking its toll, both on car and driver. It was a journey of almost 20 weary hours in each direction. It had been decided that the wooden blocks reinforcing the suspension would be left in place, but German car-builders had never planned for such an addition, and they were slowly loosening the chassis.

What if the Golf broke down and police became involved? Suppose they searched the car? There was no evident connection between it and a coach-load of youngsters having a ball at Disneyland. But it would mean an almost certain curtain being drawn over the dashes through the Sierra Nevada and Pyrenees. So a second-hand Ford Escort – a black RS2000 – was bought for cash at a Glasgow car auction, the purchaser giving a false name. It was to be a back-up should the Golf fail.

There was another factor to consider. The Man liked Gordon and the two discovered they had much in common, despite an age difference of almost two decades. The older of the two did not want to think of his friend brooding in a gloomy French or Spanish prison. The 36-seater was the first step in a programme that would hopefully make the entire scheme bigger, safer and extremely lucrative.

Hiring a vehicle – whether a van, transit coach or luxury bus – wasn't always straightforward. There were questions to be answered, personal particulars to be provided and details always to be avoided when the activity concerned was outside the law. Then there was a limit to the amount of hash that could be concealed without the passengers becoming aware they were part of something highly dubious. And to carry out physical alterations to any hire vehicle would invite awkward questions when it was returned to the owners. Now, if the smugglers had their own vehicle, they would be able to do with it whatever they wanted, reasoned The Man. But first things first.

Midway through January, with Christmas bills and New Year gloom covering Scotland, the parents of thirty-two boys were thrilled to wave goodbye to their offspring as they set off on a three-night stay at Disneyland. There were reasons for the shorter trip. One was obvious. Having responsibility for so many young men put an extra strain on the two adults in charge. Trying to keep thirty-two boisterous and curious teenagers in check for ten days, or even more, would have been well nigh impossible. And, for the safety of the operation, it was essential the guests got up to no major misdemeanours. Not that they would, or did, but while a spot of shoplifting or petty thieving was one thing, giving the traditional Glesga kiss to a troublesome foreigner would have invited altogether unacceptable and downright dangerous attention from the gendarmerie.

Taking such a large party for this unexpected break was helping build up and cement the cover the smugglers needed. It was so important to cultivate trust and support from parents and children alike. How well that credibility was established would be shown later. But, suffice it to say at this stage, that whatever hardships poverty threw on the East End families who became innocently and unsuspectingly drawn into the plot as it unfolded, the welfare and well-being of their children was never stinted. As is typical of Scots parents, their kids were everything, and if the mums and dads of the growing players had had even the tiniest iota of doubt that something was amiss, then Mr O'Sullivan and his friends would have been told to stick their money and largesse. The fact was that when trips were offered, seats were filled.

On 14 January 1994 it was cold, and the weathermen were predicting snow as the hired bus set off. The travel arrangements had been made through a highly respected agency, The Driver asking for his customary call to O'Sullivan just to get the final go-ahead. Within a week, the party had returned. All had gone well, the crew assuring the passengers that more trips were being planned. And in the west of Scotland, hash pipes were topped up.

In Glasgow, The Man had not been idle, encouraging his closest associates to scour auctions for a suitable bus. They examined around 200 possibilities, looking at coaches of varying sizes but rigidly sticking to the instruction not to bother checking out double-deckers. The Man said he had specific reasons for this and his associates didn't ask any questions. Eventually, they found a white 24-seater Mercedes 609D mini-coach that was coming up at an auction in Glasgow on 3 February 1994. Formerly owned by a travel company that had gone bust, it was offered at an initial £10,000 and after brief but not enthusiastic bidding was knocked down for £12,000 to a Mr G. Balmer, who paid cash for the vehicle. Balmer bore a remarkable resemblance to Graeme Mason, aged 47, from Thornliebank, Glasgow.

A close examination of the vehicle indicated it needed a makeover. Major mechanical repairs were required, it was given an extensive clean-up both inside and out and part of the flooring at the rear was raised, creating a hiding hole. When the work, costing around £8,000, was completed, the bus might not have been fit for kings, but it would be ideal for transporting the footballers from Highbury Boys' Club. It was insured for two men to drive it on behalf of a company named Barnet Travel and later in February was making its first trip to Disneyland.

Everything had been done to ensure that things went without a hitch. But who could predict human error? Problems and near disaster were in the stars. In Glasgow, happy-go-lucky Gordon was, as always, broke. He would often call on his friend Tam McGraw for a beer or Bacardi at the bar of the Caravel. Gordon had Tam rocking with laughter when he described a hair-raising journey in a VW Golf from southern Spain across the Sierra Nevada mountains. There had been 'luggage on the roof' he said, giving a knowing wink, and Tam might have guessed what he meant, but said nothing. After all, it was none of his business. He and Craig had come close to making it down the precipitous road the quick way, said Gordon, and he joked that, in their shorts and T-shorts, at least they were appropriately dressed for going straight to hell.

Tam thought the younger man looked tired and imagined this was connected to the trips he appeared to be making to Spain regularly. Now, Gordon told Tam, he was off to Malaga again after being offered a few quid for a wee job that would take only a week or so. He was to drive out there and join a handful of friends who were helping out with the assignment. It would mean leaving behind his new girlfriend. 'When I'm back, I'll bring her to meet you, Tam. She's stunning. We've moved in together and the wages will come in handy for furnishing our flat. I'm sick of always having to scratch around for money.'

Gordon, Tam thought, seemed to live in a series of highs and lows. Now he was in love and on a high, and Tam hoped it would stay that way. At home that night, Gordon's girl, too, thought he seemed exhausted and on the verge of a breakdown. She wondered what this assignment of his involved but felt, this early in their relationship, that it was not the time to push her natural curiosity. When the time was right, Gordon would explain all to her. She did sense that the job, though, if not completely illegal, was on the edge of the law and meant risks. She wanted him to stay behind but he pointed out he had already been paid expenses for the journey and it was too late to back out. They had their first row and eventually reached a compromise. She would go with Gordon. To her mind, she would be nurse-maiding him, but she knew better than to say that when he was around.

Next day, a Friday, they set off on the long drive, Gordon at the wheel. They slept on the cross-Channel ferry and, well into France, stopped at a service station to sleep in the car so they could save money. They arrived at Malaga on Sunday and headed for the beach. Other holidaymakers perceived them as a pair of happy honeymooners with not a care in the world. The girl – tall, slim, bright-eyed – attracted lustful looks from swarthy-skinned Spanish hotel staff as she emerged from a swim squeezing water from her long blonde hair. As they lay on the red-hot sands, soaking up the sun, she sensed they were being watched and turned around in the direction of the promenade wall. She noticed four men obviously gazing in their direction. Nudging Gordon, she pointed them out and he instantly smiled and beckoned the group over.

'Everything's set, Gordon,' said one, wrongly assuming the girl knew what was going on. 'The red Golf was already here and we've come over in an Escort. But there's so much stuff we're never going to make it in one journey. So it'll be there and back and there again.'

'OK,' said Gordon, conscious his girlfriend was becoming agitated and about to intervene. 'Have a meal and I'll come down and join you in a couple of hours and we can get under way.'

When the foursome left, Gordon decided to come clean. 'We're out here to drive drugs to a bus waiting at Disneyland outside Paris,' he explained.

The girl looked completely stunned. 'Gordon, I had a feeling you were up to something dodgy but not drugs. I thought it might be booze, cigarettes or even jewellery.'

Gordon realised that, if he was not completely frank now, the next few moments could see the end of their relationship. 'OK, I know this has come as a shock,' he told her, 'but it's just hash. The only problem I have with it is how bulky it is.'

'How long have you been doing this?'

'A couple of years regularly and there's never been any trouble, but this time we're taking much more than normal. That's why two trips are needed.'

'And what are you supposed to do?'

'My job is to make sure it all gets away from here safely and then to meet the guys at Disneyland and help get it loaded onto the bus. We've been using hire transits so far, but now we have a bigger bus and we'll be able to take much, much more gear.'

'But what about the border crossing? Aren't there Customs checks?'

'That's not a problem for me because my car will be clean. It's the others who have the gear and take the chances. Once I see the guys on their way, I'll motor on to Paris to wait for them. They'll drop the stuff off then come back here for another load. It'll be a doddle.'

'And you have to motor back here to meet up with them, right?'

'Yes. I'll get them loaded up, have a kip and leave in the early hours to be at Disneyland late tomorrow night. It should be a smooth run and with two people in each car they can take turns driving. We'll all get back here Tuesday evening and be back at the bus Wednesday night, because it has to leave in the middle of the night to catch the early morning Seacat from Calais.'

'So you want me to wait here for you? And once they've left on the second run, what about us?'

'We'll follow but get a later ferry just in case anybody on the bus recognises us. I'm sorry I couldn't tell you this was all about drugs, but I was sure that had I let on about this back in Glasgow, you would have walked out and I'd never have seen you again. It's been preying on my mind for days.'

The girl was astonished and wondered whether this could still be all a wind-up, but then she looked into his eyes and knew he was speaking the truth. 'Gordon, Disneyland is near Paris and that's fucking miles away,' she said.

'Yes, I know,' she was told. 'It's 1,150 in each direction. I've done the route so many times before I know it as well as the road from Shettleston to Parkhead.'

'That's 4,600 miles; it's like driving from Glasgow to New York – and then some.'

'And it's five thousand quid,' retorted Gordon. 'We're each getting five grand.'

It was clear he then considered the discussion closed, but his girlfriend was determined to have the last word. 'You look absolutely knackered,' she told him. 'If you're going to Paris, I'm coming with you. I'm not going to hang about here on my own worrying over what's happening with you.' It was settled.

Their own car clean of drugs, Gordon and the girl made it to Disneyland well ahead of the others, checked into a nearby hotel, met up with The Driver and his colleague and waited for the others to arrive. The Golf turned up in good time, but it was two hours before they spotted the Ford and the two men inside had an alarming story to tell.

Crossing into France near Perpignan, frontier police waved the car down and ordered it to pull off into a lay-by. The suspicious gendarmes searched the vehicle, checking the usual places, boot, seats, engine compartment, luggage. They found nothing because the hash was squashed into the door panels and body panels, 40 kilos of it. Reluctantly, the car was waved into France but one of the men had lost his nerve and refused to make the return trip. They'd be watched second time around, he said, and there was no way he was spending the rest of the year and God knows how much longer in jail. He took a train to Paris.

Gordon made a telephone call to Glasgow with the grim news but said he would take the place of the absconder for the second stage.

'Are you up to it?' he was asked. 'A lot of people think you need a good rest.'

Gordon was unequivocal. 'There's stuff worth more than £300,000 sitting down in Torremolinos bought and paid for and I'm not leaving it. We'll work something out.'

But it was the girl who had the final say. 'You stay here, Gordon. I'll go back in the Escort. It'll look as if we're a couple. Two guys are bound to attract interest.' Her decision was set in stone.

Gordon remained at Disneyland as the two cars headed south. In Torremolinos, with the help of Big Ted, they loaded up and it was agreed that to divert any suspicion caused by two British-registered cars travelling together they should remain a good hour apart.

The Golf left first. Inside were William Hassard, aged 30, and 33-year-old John Lyon, 33, both from Glasgow. They were carrying 113 kilos of hash, worth £260,000, in plastic bags. Behind in the Escort came the girl and one of Gordon's most trusted friends, John Templeton, aged 34, from Springboig. Forty kilos of hash lay behind the panelling.

The couple chatted pleasantly during the drive, but were unaware that, with their lighter load, they were able to move much more quickly than the Golf. Before they knew it, they caught up with the car in front. The two vehicles stopped for a break in Spain and, despite again leaving separately, arrived in virtual convoy at the frontier crossing. The occupants were about to experience a nightmare. Both cars were pulled aside and the Glaswegians realised the game was about to come to a sudden end.

The girl was later to tell friends how she and Templeton were ordered out and asked where they had come from and what was their destination. 'He's my boyfriend and we've been touring in Spain,' she said. 'We have to get back to work in Glasgow.'

The police appeared unimpressed and searched the car. They found nothing. Sniffer dogs were introduced but the vehicle had been well sprayed with everything from perfume to toilet cleanser and the dogs gave up. Two Customs officers appeared and it was clear one was convinced something was afoot. He was intent on testing his hunch to the full. Without asking permission, he produced a knife and began ripping the seats and tearing off the panelling. Inside were bags containing cannabis. Discovering the contents of the red Golf was just a formality after this. All four were arrested, the three men being carted off before a French magistrate, who jailed them for three and a half years. The French sympathy for the female cause resulted in the girl being ordered by the same court to remain at a youth hostel in Perpignan until her story that she knew nothing about the illicit load could be thoroughly checked. Her passport, documents and most of her money were confiscated.

Back at Disneyland, when the two cars failed to show, Gordon and The Driver realised something had gone seriously wrong and worked out that, had there been an accident, a message would have been telephoned to Glasgow. But when they called home, there was no news, and everyone came to the inevitable, and correct, conclusion that the smugglers had been caught. The bus was ordered back with half a load. Gordon decided there was no point in hanging about. He checked out of his hotel room and also headed for Glasgow.

Alone in Perpignan, the girl was aware her prospects were bleak – a view confirmed when, at a further court appearance, she was ordered to remain at the hostel. She was allowed a limited degree of freedom but was confined by the terms of an early evening curfew. Sensing the doors of a female jail were about to clang shut, she walked about town deep in thought for a couple of hours then, on a whim, decided to ring the flat she and Gordon shared.

To her astonishment, he answered, and, after she filled him in on what had happened, he asked how much money she had. She had secreted Scottish notes in a make up bag. It was enough to get her to Paris. 'Ring back when you get there,' she was told. Ten hours later, a combination of bus and train landed her in the city centre. Another call to Gordon instructed her to head for Charles de Gaulle airport and to pass, every hour, the British Airways information desk. While she had been travelling, Gordon had been busy. A friend whose long blonde hair gave her a very strong resemblance to that of the girl had been persuaded to loan out her passport for a couple of days, under instructions that, should anything go wrong, she was to report it had been stolen during a burglary. Another woman friend agreed to act as courier, flying to Paris via Heathrow with the spare passport hidden in her handbag. At Charles de Gaulle, she spotted the girl on her first pass of the BA desk and made the delivery. In the toilets, the girlfriend's deft use of a comb, eyeshadow and spectacles made her resemblance with the passport photo more than passing. In fact, there was little need to further the deception, the pair might have been twins: same facial shape, same colour eyes and that long blonde hair. The courier had brought money, too – given to her by Gordon's friends, who had rallied to help – for a ticket home.

The following day, the girl arrived at the flat, having first telephoned Gordon from Glasgow airport to say she was back in Scotland. As she walked through the door, she heard the sound of water and knew he was running her a welcoming bath. She had spent four terrifying days without proper food, being too upset and scared to eat anything other than chocolate bars, was tired, dirty and still frightened. His first words almost knocked her flat.

Rummaging through what was left of the belongings she had taken to Spain, he complained, 'Oh, no, you've forgotten my trainers, my blue-and-white Nikes. I left them in the hotel room near Paris. Couldn't you have picked them up?'

Elsewhere in Glasgow, the Mercedes bus had deposited its party of youngsters then headed for a depot at 151 Scotland Street, which turned out, by a freak coincidence, to be almost next door to the headquarters of the Strathclyde Police mounted section. Smartly dressed policemen and women hardly gave a glance at the bus as it turned in, or at the white transit van which came to meet it. As soon as the coast was clear, the contents of the bus were loaded into the van, which would distribute top-quality Moroccan cannabis between four main dealers in the city. The deliveryman gave the dealers the bad news: due to a technical hitch, he could serve only half their order. Not to worry, he promised, things would be back to normal in no time.

For The Man and the tiny group who knew the secret of the bus trips, it was time to move the operation on. Changes were needed, but then The Man had long intended this should be the case. It was clear that Disneyland was no longer a permanent option. True, it might be used now and again, but the long, energy-sapping and risky journeys from Spain had finally taken their toll. Three men were in jail. Big Ted had supplied 307 kilos of hash for £221,900, which should have sold in Glasgow for £706,100, leaving a profit, minus expenses, of £484,200. But half the load was now in a French Customs warehouse awaiting incineration. So the balance sheet now read: outlay £221,900, income £353,050 – still a profit of £131,150, but less expenses. The long and short of the enterprise was that £353,050 had been lost.

In May, the Mercedes was off abroad again, on another 11-day trip. This time, the party would be travelling much further, through France and into Spain, to Torremolinos. The journey would take something like 34 hours, parents of the young footballers had been warned, but once there, all would be sleeping comfortably in the 303-bedroom Las Palomas hotel. Colin O'Sullivan had felt the time had come to offer the youngsters something different from the colour of Disneyland. In the seas off the Costa del Sol, the young men could get tanned and fit, and, for the trip after this one, arrangements were being made through the Scottish Football Association for Highbury Boys' Club to take part in international tournaments.

The length of this trip made it impossible for one man to do all the driving, so this duty would be shared by one other man. In the many trips that followed it, the co-driver would not always be the same man, and sometimes there would be two of them, but at no time would the behaviour of any of the driving crews arouse suspicions that they were anything other than men wanting to ensure their charges had the time of their lives.

Once in Torremolinos, the bus was left in the hotel car park, evidently never budging from the space it occupied from the moment it arrived. In fact, a minute examination would have revealed it had mysteriously moved several inches. Under cover of darkness on the last night of the holiday, The Driver and his companion took the vehicle to one of the municipal car parks in Malaga, where it was met by a white van. Three hundred kilos of hash were transferred aboard. The cash for the deal – £210,000 – had been brought out hidden in luggage on the bus and handed to Big Ted the day after it arrived. He had returned to the Las Palomas four days later to confirm the delivery date and later again to discuss where the transfer should take place. The deal produced a profit of £480,000. It had gone so smoothly that the smugglers found it hard to take in the simplicity of the arrangement – no more arduous and life-risking drives over the mountains, no more sweats at frontier posts.

In June, the bus and the players were off again to Spain, this time to the coastal resort of Benidorm on the Costa Blanca, where they competed in a tournament against teams from the host country, Spain, as well as Portugal, England and Germany. Accreditation had been made through the Scottish Amateur Football Association, which clearly had no idea that the great game was being used to further a racket capable of financing any of the top clubs in the country.

By chance, one of the smugglers back in Glasgow happened to be passing the Scotland Street base as the bus returned. Knowing that some of the hash had been hidden in the panelling, he noticed something appearing to fall from the bus on the opposite side to him.

'Surely not,' he thought and was about to examine the object more closely when four mounted police came into sight. One of the horses gave whatever the bus had deposited a scrutiny that would have done credit to his rider but, thankfully, there was no stopping and the steeds clattered on, no doubt keen to sample their own oats. The smuggler was then horrified to discover that what lay on the road was indeed a lump of hash – only the size of a cigarette packet, but hash all the same.

In the depot, The Driver was pulling out bales of smuggled gear and, without being prompted, told his visitor, 'We've got a problem. There's a hole in the side. We've been losing stuff all the way back.'

'You should worry,' he was told. 'One of the cop nags has come within an ace of becoming the first four-legged junkie in Scotland.'

Where the thinking of The Man differed from those around him was in his vision and capability to make the most of a good idea. While the others were content to proceed with this very handsome return, he realised that, instead of a two-storey semi, the foundations were there for a tower block. The operation had been honed, fine-tuned, and shown to work and work well. Just how far could it be taken?

Even before the Las Palomas party had arrived home, he had sensed the first bus they had bought was not up to long and regular journeys overseas and had organised a meeting with most of the main conspirators. Also present was a Glasgow businessman who was about to make an investment that would mushroom the scale of his company from a corner shop to a supermarket. If there was something akin in the meeting to the movie gatherings in which Ernst Blofeld laid down the law to SPECTRE operatives in the 007 series, the atmosphere was nowhere near as formal and the setting considerably less exotic. Over the ever-present tea, in a hotel near the city centre, The Man proposed buying yet another coach and radically altering it so it would be capable of bringing home a £1 million profit each journey. Someone wondered why he was so opposed to a double-decker. The Man explained: 'You ever been on the bottom deck? It's so low you have to stoop. If the floor was any higher, your head would be wedged against the ceiling even while you were sitting down.'

The matter was never again raised. But then, it was not necessary to do so because the logic of the reply would become all too apparent. It is an indication of the trust and belief in The Man's acumen that not a voice questioned this at the time, or, indeed, ever dissented from The Man's decisions. Indeed, none of those involved in the seven-year fiddle, either directly or on the peripheries, can recall his word being doubted. This was not through fear of physical retribution, because such a prospect had not been and never would be contemplated. Rather, it was simply that he was always right. He had an uncanny instinct for knowing if, how and when a venture would come good. Of course, in this case, he had the advantage of having sounded out most of his co-conspirators beforehand.

One of The Man's first calls had been on Gordon, taking along with him a man he knew well as a regular at the Caravel pub: Trevor Lawson, a stocky demolition specialist then living in a caravan near Denny, Stirling. The three men sat huddled in Gordon's front room for two hours. As they were leaving, Trevor took their host's arm and told him, 'You know we're going to be really rich, don't you? Richer than you could ever imagine.'

The second coach, also a Mercedes, was bought from a company in the Carlisle area in June 1994 for around £52,000. But before it would be put on the road, important modifications were necessary. The Man thought back to one of his island holidays when he'd watched youngsters straining to see through the coach windows. Now the time had come for the idea he formed then to be put into practice.

The bus was driven to a coachworks in Lanarkshire, with specific instructions for the company as to what was to be done. The firm had been chosen for its expertise, and had no idea that its work had a sinister motive in this case. It was explained that the vehicle would be taking parties of children abroad and to cope with their special requirements a major reconstruction was needed. The youngsters had to be able to see out of the windows, so their seats would need to be made higher. It was a straightforward job as far as the company was concerned. The seats were taken out and two raised wooden platforms were built on either side of the central aisle along the entire length of the vehicle. When the seats were replaced, they were almost a foot higher. The coachbuilders screwed, rather than bolted, plywood panels along the sides of the platforms facing into the aisle to conceal the spaces under the seating. When the time came to load up, the smugglers simply removed the screws and then the panels. The hash, in five- or ten-kilo cakes, would be carried into the bus in suitcases, literally pushed under the seating and the panels then screwed back into place.

Mr Balmer, who paid the £20,000 bill in cash on behalf of his firm, BMH Travel, expressed satisfaction with the work. While it was being carried out, the smugglers continued using the first Mercedes, but once the new bus was ready, the 'E' registration one was sold – after it had been fully restored to its original condition. The Man had wanted it crushed, destroyed, but instead it was to end its days carrying passengers to and from towns and villages in Ireland. The big time beckoned.

chapter nine

SAUSAGE SKINS

BIG TED HAD MOVED TO SPAIN EXPECTING TO MAKE A comfortable living sending a regular delivery of hash back to the UK via his lorry-driver partner. At first, that was how it worked: no hassle, no sweat, no one else. His problem, if problem it was, was that he was good at what he did. In his Moroccan contact, Mohammed, he had more than a business acquaintance; he had a friend. Unusually for the North African, he felt he could trust his buyer Big Ted, whom he found gregarious, unlike many of the sullen and suspicious Scandinavians and Germans he did business with.

One evening, having a quiet beer in Ronnie Knight's, Big Ted was approached by two casually, but neatly, dressed men who introduced themselves as east Londoners. He had been recommended to them by Mohammed, they said. The men's story was all too familiar. They had been running a regular cannabis delivery service back to London using heavy transport when one of the drivers became greedy and wanted a bigger share of the action. He had gone to the east Londoners' Moroccan contact to place their latest order, but told them there had been a hitch in getting the money to Spain to pay for it. The Moroccan contact had dealt regularly with this outfit and had no reason not to trust them. From time to time, Customs and police did intercept cash couriers, so he agreed to let the driver have the next load, half a tonne, accepting his story that the money would be arriving within the next couple of days. The driver disappeared with the load and the money and was not seen again. It was thought he might have had a buyer waiting in Holland to pay for the cargo and the lorry, then taken a ferry to the north of England, where he had settled. When their load failed to arrive, the east Londoners contacted the Moroccan, who was still waiting for his money. Each of the parties blamed the other and the Moroccan was furious when he was told he would not be paid for a load which had not been delivered. Now, as a result, he had said he would not deal directly with them again. He and his fellow hash suppliers might have been in a form of competition with one another, but they made sure word went along the line when one was cheated and, as a result, the east Londoners were effectively black-listed. They had pleaded with their Moroccan to reconsider, and when he refused, sought help from Mohammed, who suggested they speak with Big Ted. Mohammed knew and trusted the big man, he said, and was prepared to let Big Ted act on their behalf, but he was adamant that, like his fellow suppliers, he would not deal directly with them.

'How much have you been taking?' Big Ted asked.

'It depends,' said the taller of the Cockneys. 'Sometimes half a tonne a week, sometimes two tonnes. But not every week, of course.'

Big Ted whistled. Two tonnes of hash would normally cost around £1.4 million but retail at perhaps £4.6 million. That was big bucks, but then he had heard of a London crew who had the north of the capital's cannabis scene all but sewn up and because of the amounts involved weren't in the habit of taking prisoners when anyone was crazy enough to try muscling in for a piece of the action.

'How have you been paying?' he asked.

'Always up-front, because we've had to. There's never a problem with getting the money; the difficulty is bringing it over. We have couriers, but from time to time they get greedy and lessons have to be taught. That can sometimes put others off working because they reckon they'll get the same treatment even if something goes wrong through no fault of their own. We've been approached by a team who specialise in transporting cash about the globe but they are looking for £50,000 commission for every million they shift. We think that's over the top.'

'What is it you're looking for from me?' asked Big Ted. 'Why not go to one of the others?'

'The Moroccans reckon you're the best man and the one they trust. That's saying something, because apart from the prophet Muhammad, you're probably the only guy they have any faith in. We'd appreciate it if you could look after things for us.'

Big Ted took his time before replying, so the Londoners reassured him about a potential problem that they thought might have been bothering him. 'Look, we know you've been dealing with another of the London mobs. That isn't a problem for us, and we know it isn't one for them, either. We've already sat down and talked this thing over with them. We've reached an arrangement and all we ask is that we each pay the same price.'

Big Ted knew they were speaking the truth. The group he'd been supplying had already assured him they would have no objections if this outfit sought his help, because the newcomers' interests and territory did not conflict with their own.

His visitors continued: 'There's one other thing we're prepared to do if you take us on. We've the permanent lease of a couple of warehouses on an industrial estate near Malaga airport. You can have the use of one for free, even if you want to store gear for other firms. The security will be up to you, but the estate has its own staff. Nobody ever comes snooping around and it would be handy for us because that's where we load up our lorries. If extra trailers come in, nobody will even give them a second glance.'

If Big Ted had had any doubts, this was the catalyst that waved them away. Ordering another round of beers, he shook hands with his new associates. He was glad they had brought up the issue of the rival crew. But as bottles clinked he found it difficult not to let the inward smile show. He had heard whispers about their misfortune and was told along the grapevine that they were genuinely victims. They evidently fancied themselves as knowing his business, but their intelligence service needed a shake-up. At that stage, he was handling the supply for a Midlands outfit as well as his own and the other firm's, along with the smaller but enjoyable link with Gordon and Craig. He needed a meeting with Mohammed.

'Five tonnes a month? Five thousand kilos? Not a problem,' assured the African. 'We've seen this coming and have already been increasing our crop. It's meant having to plant in some very difficult areas of the Rif but the farmers have little choice if they want to stay in their homes. It means extra work, but they have relatives in the south they can bring in to help with the harvesting and separating the resin at their sheds. After that, it's not their worry; we look after getting it from them to you.'

Big Ted knew that Mohammed was over-simplifying his description of the shipping operation. What he had not seen with his own eyes he had already learned from Mohammed himself. During darkness, lorries would take the hashish oil or resin, double-wrapped in sacking, down to the coast. The Mediterranean was closest, both to the farms and the Costa del Sol, but the mountains tended to be steeper here, whereas driving the bales south into the Sebou basin and then west to the gentler Atlantic coastline was often preferred. Once the lorries reached the beach, it was literally a case of dash or death. Light but high-speed Zodiac inflatables would be waiting inshore for the bales to be loaded, before shooting flat-out to a yacht waiting a mile or so out to sea, ready to dash into international waters if the alarm went up. The value of double-wrapping usually became apparent at this point because, as it was being thrown onto the deck of the yacht, the occasional bale would fall short and splash into the sea. Even a comparatively light 20-kilo bundle impregnated with salt water represented a loss of £14,000. Their loads on the deck, the Zodiacs would be hauled on board and used to transfer the bales to Spanish beaches.

Big Ted had once taken Gordon and Trevor Lawson to watch the Spanish end of the operation. As they stood on a deserted beach south of Torremolinos, staring into darkness, the silence of the night was shattered by the screech of the inflatables as they zoomed onto the sand. Seemingly from nowhere, two vans appeared and the cargo was bundled inside, the vehicles vanishing into the hills. When demand was high, it was an almost nightly occurrence, with the same location never being used twice in a row, although the area south of Marbella between Sotogrande and La Linea was most favoured, chiefly for the simple reason that it was about as close to the Moroccan coast as it was possible to get.

Disasters were rare, but they did happen. One night, near Fuengirola, a police helicopter appeared from nowhere and a motor launch crewed by armed troops began spraying bullets at the inflatables. It was rumoured at least one of the smugglers had been killed, but violent death was a feature of life the Spanish authorities did not wish the hordes of holidaymakers who brought with them their annual savings to be troubled with. The incident was hushed up and, after all, who was likely to kick up a fuss? During another Customs intercept, a smuggler was decapitated by the rotor blades of a police helicopter.

Anyone making inquiries the next day was greeted with a polite shrug of the shoulders. Such things were not discussed.

With so much money literally floating about, it was positively crazy that some sensible solution could not be worked out. And it was, although it was never going to be put into writing. Big Ted would later tell his Glasgow friends, 'The Moroccans have come to an agreement with some members of the Guardia Civil in Benalmadena which allows them to bring the gear in by boat during daylight. It's a lot safer and more dependable and keeps everyone happy. The arrangement is for the cops to tell us the times when there will be nobody about; they'll make sure they are patrolling somewhere else, so a boat can come in and have its cargo unloaded and away before anybody turns up to do a Customs check. It's rumoured this is costing the Moroccans between £50,000 and £100,000 a month, but they'll save more than that in what they were losing at night and in bonuses some of the crews were getting.'

Big Ted knew that Gordon and Craig had been running car-loads of hash into France and had always worried about the risks. He was happy to supply their needs, but his doubts over the wisdom of increasing the amount being taken to Disneyland turned out to be well founded. When he heard the Escort and Golf had been impounded, he waited for the inevitable next move. It came when Craig told him the plan was now to bring the bus to Mohammed, instead of vice versa. He thought that a sound idea but positively marvelled three months later when Craig sounded him out about the prospect of supplying between 600 and 700 kilos approximately every three weeks.

'That's ten times what you've been taking,' he teased. 'Where the hell are you going to stick it? Don't tell me you've produced a new breed of Jock who can swallow bales of hash. Or are you hiding it under your kilts? I've always wondered if you lot had anything valuable beneath them.'

Big Ted was well aware how touchy some Scots could be about the national dress but knew too that his friend would see he was only having his leg pulled.

'In the bus,' Craig said.

'But where? You're talking about more than two thirds of a tonne. You can hardly stick it in hold-alls or in the seats.'

'Not in the seats, under them.'

'Under the seats? That's where you put your feet.'

'No, under them. Under the floor. We've converted a bus and lifted the floor so the kids can see better through the windows. By chance, that's left a space either side running the entire length of the bus.'

Big Ted swore, not in anger but admiration. He then laughed out loud in astonishment.

'What genius came up with that?' he asked. 'It's amazing, brilliant. But how are you going to get the stuff out? Presumably the space will be too shallow for anybody to crawl in and you can hardly go fishing with a rod and line to yank it out.'

'Dead easy. The sides raised up from the aisle are just held by screws. When the bus gets back to Glasgow, we just take them out, pull the kit out then replace them. Simple.'

'And the passengers, are these still the footballers?'

'Right. They were getting bored with Disneyland so The Man decided it was time to broaden their horizons. They're really getting into this. We've even got the Scottish Amateur Football Association giving them accreditation for tournaments. The kids are brilliant and, even better, haven't a clue what's going on. They've been asking to meet Colin O'Sullivan but we keep apologising, saying he's too busy making money.'

No footballer himself, but with children of his own back home – whichever of his two families he looked on as representing home – Big Ted let his mind roam. If the bus carried 700 kilos, that would mean a profit of getting on for £1.1 million each trip: a lot of money. But what if the tournament over-ran and the footballers reached the final? Playing in it could mean losing a ferry booking and turning up at the ferry port without a ticket. Customs officers nearly always searched vehicles that didn't have a booking, and a detailed search of this vehicle would almost certainly be ruinous. How would The Man react, given the choice between breaking the hearts of the youngsters and having his entire money-making racket destroyed? Big Ted hoped it was a predicament no one would ever face. He wondered if it was a scenario the men in Glasgow had considered. Knowing Craig and Gordon so well, he sensed that, with their swashbuckling ways that would have charmed the pants off maidens two centuries earlier, they would have thrown in their lot with the youngsters and gambled all on bringing home a piece of silverware that might have cost a few pounds but made them feel like millionaires.

By August 1994, the new bus was on the road and its young passengers agreed that the raised view was a considerable improvement on anything they had previously travelled in. While they enjoyed their football, Big Ted's import and export business was now dealing with over 5,000 kilos of raw material a month. The figures were becoming astronomical. The stuff was being bought for £3,500,000 and getting sold on the streets of London, Manchester, Birmingham and Glasgow for more than £11,500,000, or, in a year, £138,000,000. Craig, who was living permanently with Big Ted, would receive a telephone call telling him when the next bus from Glasgow was due. It would sometimes stop at Benidorm or the Universal Mediterranea theme park at Salou (now called Port Aventura) but, more usually and, from the smugglers' viewpoint, more practically, the holiday party would be hosted in one of the hundreds of smart hotels along the seafront in the Malaga, Benalmadena or Torremolinos areas. Mohammed expected four days' warning to arrange supplies but such was the demand that he and Big Ted were virtually meeting every other day to organise the next consignment for whichever of the various teams had placed an order.

On the day before the party was due to head back to Glasgow, the bus would disappear for a rendezvous with a hash-packed van in a pre-selected car park and the doors opened to allow access to the area beneath the floor. Because of the lateness of the hour, the coach was invariably able to resume its original parking spot, lessening the likelihood of a curious member of the group wondering about some late-night excursion.

Most of the major smugglers simply took the consignments they'd arranged via Big Ted still wrapped in the original sacking. Good Moroccan hash had little aroma; that which did, said the experts, was to be treated with caution – something had probably been added to increase the bulk. Their preferred method of transportation was less subtle than the Scots'. They packed it into the sides of lorries or under cargoes that varied from furnishings to fruit, where there was, they fancied, little chance of discovery, although they accepted the inevitable seizure of a load from time to time by vigilant Customs officers, alerted perhaps by the demeanour of a driver, the dubiousness of his documentation or, most likely, a tip-off from a rival team of dealers.

The Glasgow team had the added problem that at Customs and immigration checks there were added chances of a fairly stringent inspection. While the football team provided the perfect excuse for taking a coach abroad, the smugglers knew that coach parties – along with couples travelling in souped-up cars – were the most likely vehicles to get searched by Customs. On coaches, the guardians of state morality had a potential galaxy of evils to root out: old ladies with suitcases packed with cigarettes, middle-aged men furtively wrapping an extra bottle of spirits in their beach towels, children clutching donkeys packed with illegal substances. Nothing should be allowed to escape the terrors of the Revenue, and parties of youngsters, boisterous Jocks at that, filled the devils in uniform at the Dover docks with positive glee at the thought of rifling through their bags and satchels in search of sin.

The Man reasoned it was crucial that every precaution be taken against the possibility of discovery. There was no way the human nose would be able to detect hash amidst the reek of diesel and oil, but highly trained sniffer dogs were another proposition altogether. So he insisted the sacking was removed and the resin wrapped in clingfilm, washed, then wrapped again. Big Ted could see his point and had to concede it was a reasonable step to take, because he too had an interest in ensuring his clients were not brought down. Such failure would mean a considerable loss to him. He discussed the problem of packaging with an old pal during a telephone conversation back home and the friend said, 'Sausages.'

'Eh?'

'Sausages. They wrap sausages in polythene. All the butchers do it nowadays. They have a machine that heats polythene then wraps it airtight around their sausages and meat. Apparently it keeps the stuff fresh and seals the smell in. Go into any butcher's shop or supermarket, pick up a joint wrapped in polythene and you can't smell a thing. It's foolproof. Get yourself an industrial wrapping machine and some sheets of polythene. You won't look back.'

Big Ted took the advice and a couple of weeks later two machines, bought second-hand from a butcher near the Scottish border for £4,500 each, were being unloaded and set up in a villa set in the hills overlooking Benalmadena.

'They can make a bit of a racket, so make sure you don't have it close to somebody who pokes their nose out to see what's going on each time a fly lands,' he had been told. 'If you can find a place with a cellar, better still.'

On the afternoon before the bus was due to turn up to be loaded, Big Ted and Craig would disappear into the hired villa where the hash had been stored once Mohammed's white-van man had made his delivery. They found that operating the machines was unpleasant work. The system functioned by blowing hot air to make the polythene pliable, and with temperatures outside often in the 80s and above, they found they had to take frequent breaks. Sweat would pour from them as the machines hissed and clunked. But when it was over and the packages had been loaded into cardboard boxes ready for the van to rendezvous with the coach, they knew there was no way even the keenest dog would get a whiff or a sniff of the secret under the seats. As word about their use spread, butchers up and down Britain would find strangers offering good money for their wrapping equipment as the machines became must-haves for all the best smuggling suppliers.

The good times had beckoned and found willing participants.

chapter ten

FUN IN THE SUN

SETTING UP THE INITIAL RUNNING OF THE NEW MERCEDES had not come cheaply. There had been the vehicle to buy, modifications to pay for and £490,000 to be found to buy 700 kilos of hash. The Man had urged those whose pockets had been steadily filling with the profits from the earlier runs not to spend too freely. Something else, something big, was coming up, he said, and those who invested in it were guaranteed to have their outlay multiplied. Some of the cash for that first load came from four principal drug-dealers in the west of Scotland who had found the market simply could not be satisfied. The rest came from the core of the smuggling gang, seven men.

They would each make fortunes. Some would use the money to increase their wealth crop to a degree where they need never worry again, others frittered it away on flash cars, clothes and fads, failing to heed the warnings of The Man that for everything in life there was a beginning and an end. And the businessman would use his share of the pot to gradually buy a distance from his co-conspirators. Once the first load had returned safely and 700 clicks were sold at £2,300 a kilo, everyone had his outlay returned with interest. From now on, the operation would be self-financing, with dealers paying before the coach set off, happy in the knowledge of a massive return.

As the autumn of 1994 approached, everyone was making money, and lots of it. Best of all, the kids, whose presence guaranteed the security of the whole operation, were having the times of their lives. They agreed that Colin O'Sullivan must have had money coming out of his ears because there would occasionally be just a three-week gap between trips. For just £30 towards the cost of fuel, they would stay in three- or four-star hotels, would eat well and enjoy the sort of lifestyle even many professional footballers with some top-flight Scottish clubs would envy.

There were matches in Benidorm, Torremolinos, Calella in the north of Spain, Barcelona and Valencia. And there was little doubt that the players were learning and improving. As the boys grew older, it was noticeable their exploits were reaching the ears of scouts from junior clubs. Some would inevitably fall by the wayside to the lure of wine, women and song, but for others the dream of turning out in the blue of their country at Hampden Park would not fade. Their trips would sometimes be split, with a week first in the south at the Costa del Sol, the explanation always being that O'Sullivan wanted to give them the chance to see as much of the country as possible. The truth was, of course, that driving a van filled with hash 300 miles from Malaga to Benidorm had been tried but discounted as too risky. It wasn't only the Spanish drivers who were lunatics; Brits were the worst, lurching along packed to the gunwales with suitcases strapped to overfilled roof racks, struggling to take hairpin bends while gazing at the scenery.

So Craig and Big Ted got on with the job of wrapping and sweating, sometimes being joined by Trevor and Gordon but regularly meeting up with The Driver and his assistant for the switch. And all the while, money rolled in until it seemed to be coming out of their ears. Everyone was enjoying a very big slice of the pie. Each time the Mercedes returned to base, the core group would expect around £160,000 each. Cash. In hand. No tax. No national insurance. The only problems were where to put it, what to do with it, what to buy with it and how to spend it. Others in the outfit were on fixed wages of from £5,000 to £10,000 – set sums for specific tasks. Everyone had his own job: there were driving duties, accommodation to work out, bookings to make, parties to organise, drug-dealers to visit, orders to take and, behind it all, The Man, constantly checking, reassuring, thinking.

In Spain, Big Ted had his end of the operation running so smoothly that he found time to relax in between deliveries. Relax might be the wrong word. He was to tell a friend: 'Me and Craig ended up running the whole place. We could go anywhere and have anything. We had the whole run of Malaga and Fuengirola. Everybody knew who we were and what our business was, but it didn't matter to them so long as the money poured through their tills.

'We'd take ten people out for the night to the best restaurants, eat the most expensive meals, have the most expensive drinks and think nothing of happily paying a bill for £2,500 in cash. We'd be out every night, seven nights a week. Once we went on an 11-day bender, coming home only once for a change of clothing.'

Big Ted was constantly hearing stories about The Man, and, at that stage, despite never having met him, he felt he knew him well. 'The operation was so smooth and successful I knew the person who had thought it all up had to be a genius. We were making millions. If any of our friends found themselves in trouble with the Spanish police, we'd offer fortunes to the cops to get the charges dropped. Anybody from back home in the UK who was on the run seemed to end up on the Costa del Sol and half of them would head for us. We were looked on almost as gods. Everywhere we went, we were fêted. Bars and restaurants would make absolutely certain there were tables available if we turned up out of the blue. They knew we were spenders and payers who never even looked at the bill.'

One of the favourite haunts of many of their guests from the UK was a notorious strip club in Fuengirola. The club boasted there were never less than 50 girls willing to dance naked for eager punters. In reality, it was, and is, little more than a glorified but exquisitely decorated brothel. It was certainly true the girls were stunning. Mainly South American, they worked two weeks on and two weeks off. Enthusiasts disappearing through the club's double wooden doors would find themselves in a dimly lit lounge where scantily clad girls would appear from nowhere to offer a dance or to share a drink. A customer interested in a more intimate tête-à-tête would first politely ask his preferred girl if she was available and, if given the nod, would be directed back through the main doors and invited to climb a flight of stairs and wait at the doors of a lift outside which, seated at a small table, was the club minder. The man made no attempt to hide the fact he was armed and his purpose was solely to ensure that the client was genuine and left in no doubt as to the consequences of trying to avoid paying the £25 fee for the girl's personal services.

The fair-skinned Europeans preferred the long black hair and gleaming white teeth of the girls from Brazil and Venezuela. Occasionally, a Scot might be dismayed to find that, when the girl started chatting to him as she undressed, she had a broad Brummie accent or a Geordie lilt. One customer complained sourly to his friends after a visit to the club that, during the sex act, the girl had bemoaned the fact he reminded her of her ex-husband. He left unsure in which respect. There is no suggestion that any of the Glasgow crew took advantage of the facilities at the club, but it is correct that some still appear familiar with the layout and arrangements.

They could certainly afford to visit not just this club but any establishment in town, their new-found wealth hanging off some like snow on a Christmas tree. And, just as the hookers were in the business of ensuring customers left happier but with lighter wallets, there were others with an eye for the main chance to enjoy the fruits of high living.

During a visit to Torremolinos by Trevor, Gordon and a couple of friends, the party decided a few hours of relaxation beneath the sun was in order. Most Continental beaches are divided into areas leased from the local town council by hotels or individuals who make a steady, but not brilliant, living hiring out sun-loungers and deckchairs on their particular stretch. The group found themselves standing before one such individual – an elderly man, whose appearance gave the impression that business had not been overly brisk. Indeed, when one of the loungers needed attention from a spanner, the man made for an ancient and rusting bicycle parked against the wooden hut from which he conducted transactions. Relaxing, the little group laughed at a succession of jokes from Trevor. Short and stocky, he looked the sort of hard man who would brook no argument, but was, in reality – at least, to his friends – a minor comedian. There seemed no situation, however gloomy, from which Trevor could not produce a wisecrack. Or was there?

After a couple of hours, the party decided they had seen sufficient bellies, breasts and sunshine and agreed it was drinks time. As they left, the little man asked if they would be back. They told him 'thank you, but no', and their final sight was of him slowly beginning to dismantle, collect and stack their loungers. Making their way into a bar a few hundred yards from where they had been lying, they tore into beers, the ice-cold drinks going down a treat. They were still there hours later as the evening was drawing to a close, merrily discussing the merits of passing women, when someone asked the time. This was the signal for Trevor to almost turn white beneath his tan and gasp, 'My watch. I've left my fucking Rolex. Hang fire, I'll be back in a few minutes.'

He was sure he remembered hanging the watch – 'a snip', as he had been promised by a Glasgow jeweller, at £12,000 – from the corner of his lounger, and rushed back to the beach, which by now was almost devoid of sunbathers and certainly of the little man, whose hut was locked. Next morning, Trevor was waiting as the old man cycled up. 'My watch. You've got my watch,' he said. The man looked blank and continued being vague when Trevor pointed to his wrist. It was time, the Scot decided, to bluff. 'A guy in the apartment over there,' he said, pointing inland, 'says he saw you put it in your pocket.'

The little man could not be moved, shaking his head and at last producing, in broken English, the promise that 'if I find anything, I keep it for you, señor.'

By now, Trevor was frantic, screaming, 'It's a £12,000 watch. It can't have fucking walked.' But his shouts were met only with shrugs as the target of his vitriol opened his tiny shed and began setting up his table. Trevor realised there was nothing for it but to give up. A month later, he was back in Torremolinos to meet up with Craig and Big Ted and happened to be drinking at a bar close to the spot where his watch had vanished. There was the same little man, pulling out from his same little hut his same loungers and, what a coincidence, one appeared to need attention. He watched, open mouthed, as a spanner was fetched – from a sparkling, brand new Renault. Trevor debated whether to make his mark on the car but did nothing. 'Fuck it,' he told himself and began smiling. 'Crafty old sod. Still, easy come, easy go,' he thought, and looked at the dial on his brand new Rolex.

Money was absolutely no hindrance to the pursuit of perfection. Craig would think nothing of laying out £900 for a designer shirt. At one stage, Big Ted was renting five villas, one to stash gear – he had decided that putting all his eggs into one basket in the Londoners' warehouse might not be the best idea – one to store and use the wrapping machines, one for himself, one in which to keep girlfriends and one in which friends would stay when they came over for a visit.

He had the absolute confidence of Mohammed. As the months and years rolled by, the Moroccan's trust bordered on the unbelievable. Whereas at the beginning he had insisted on money being paid up-front, it wasn't long before he would say, 'Give it to me in three days; I know it's there.'

Once, taking Craig to a golf course just outside Malaga, Big Ted bumped into Mohammed, who was driving a van packed with two and a half tonnes of hash.

'Ted, I was on my way to see you. This arrived last night, earlier than I expected, and I wanted you to have it.'

The day was particularly hot and they decided to adjourn for cooling drinks to Ronnie Knight's club, abandoning the van. Craig was incredulous.

'There's nearly four million quid in hash in that van and you've just left it,' he spluttered. 'And he didn't want anything from you.'

'Fuck the money; he knows he can trust me,' was the reply. And Mohammed smiled and nodded. By the time the load had left Spain, some of it under the floor of the Glasgow coach, the rest in a lorry heading for London, Mohammed had still not asked for his money and Big Ted had to telephone him to remind him it was due. 'Oh yes, don't worry, I'll call round,' was the reply, and Big Ted was convinced the Moroccan had forgotten all about it.

Despite the fun and games, the gang still took their work seriously. They were conscious that the greatest risk of discovery lay with the coach-loading part of the operation. In the crowded Costa resorts, where every inch of beach and every foot of road was used, it was impossible to find privacy. The Alamo Trading Post had been ideal. There was plenty of cover and no one would think twice about seeing baggage being loaded onto a bus. But secreting boxes, filled with polythene-wrapped packages, under a floor was an altogether more worrying matter. In the end, the gang decided they were being paranoid. The safest method was simply to park the vehicle and get on with the job regardless. It could not be helped that people were about, and on occasions those people included the police. In fact, every spot they chose seemed to be a favourite hangout for the local law. When the coach arrived outside the Fuengirola fish market for a switch, who should happen to be parked across the road but two policemen sitting in their car enjoying a cigarette. They were initially curious to see boxes being removed from a white van and evidently placed in the bus, but, after ten minutes, had lost interest and moved on. Indeed, the biggest problem facing the loaders were the swarms of wasps buzzing about the market.

There was an even more bizarre incident when the bus parked near the Fuengirola Park Hotel. Almost at the same time as the white van containing boxes drew up at the rear, a lorry pulled to a halt facing the bus. Three men emerged from the cab and one clambered onto the back of the vehicle and began stoking a smoking boiler, evidently containing white bitumen. Without a word, they proceeded to renew the road markings around the front of the bus, ignoring Big Ted and three others who were hard at work, loading it up at the back. The two operations finished almost simultaneously, the only evidence that a vehicle had been parked in the path of the workmen being two curiously unpainted sections of their work. Rather than ask the driver to reverse, they had simply skipped over the space occupied by the bus.

Loading completed, The Driver would scoop up handfuls of dirt and force it into the seams where the floor had been lifted to enhance the impression that the vehicle had not been interfered with. Once under way, there were other precautions to be taken because the risk of exposure was never far from the minds of those involved, especially the two men sharing driving duties. Despite assurances from Big Ted and Craig that the clingfilm would mask any slight aroma from the under-floor load, The Man had been very specific in his instructions as to what had to be done. In the early days of the coach arriving at Malaga, a local vet had been approached by The Driver and informed that he and his family had recently settled in the area. Until they found a home to buy, they had hired a furnished villa just outside town, but were concerned because the two family pet dogs, possibly as a result of worry caused by the heat or the change in surroundings, had begun scratching at tables, chairs and coverings. This was causing much consternation as they had no wish to bring the wrath of the Spanish landlord on themselves. Could the vet recommend a deterrent that was both unharmful to the animals but effective for keeping them at bay?

The man nodded and understood the problem – a common one – and wrote down the name of a commercial spray for them, even giving directions to the store where it could be found. Many visitors, he said, would simply have beaten the dogs, but this family – from Scotland, did you say? – well, obviously you are caring and considerate. How nice to meet such folks. Welcome to Spain.

There were two main points of worry on the return leg: the frontier post between Spain and France and, more so, the arrival terminal at Dover. Sniffer dogs, trained to pick up the scent of any drugs, were frequently used at both spots. Sometimes the passengers would be asked to leave the coach while a search was carried out; sometimes the examination would be fairly cursory. On odd occasions, they would merely be waved on once their passports and vehicle documentation had been scrutinised.

Before the youngsters boarded the bus at the start of their return journey, The Driver would carefully spray the entire floor with dog repellent. As the homeward journey progressed, he would, at each stop, re-spray the interior of the coach, telling his passengers that this was a precaution against any flea-carrying dogs being brought on board by police or Customs. The spray had no smell to humans, but animals were confused by it and tended literally to turn up their noses and scamper off in any direction. The sides and rear of the coach would get the same treatment. In addition to this, nearing the frontier The Driver would throw a half-eaten packet of crisps or a chocolate bar at one of his passengers. It was a playful gesture but with a crucial purpose. The intention was to start a food-fight so that if dogs were brought on board, they would have a further distraction from any revealing scent.

In France or Spain, should the inspection appear to be getting too thorough, The Driver would begin a conversation about the relative merits of the various national football teams, championing the merits of the Scots – a cry the young players were ever willing to reinforce. No matter how strong their desire to be diligent, the searchers were never able to resist joining in the argument and the noise would distract the Customs officers from the sounds made by their kicks and thuds against the side panels in the hope of hearing a telltale dull thud, a sure indication that something lay hidden inside. So effective were these anti-measures that, throughout the smuggling runs, Spanish or French Customs officers stopped the vehicle around 12 times and carried out searches but found nothing.

The food ploy would be repeated when the instruction was given on board the Calais to Dover ferry for drivers and passengers to return to their vehicles. Somehow, The Driver always managed to be carrying half-eaten cakes or sandwiches which ended up on the floor. Neither of the two crew-members minded the mess.

Perhaps their narrowest squeak came at Dover as a woman Customs officer strutted up the aisle making plain her suspicions that the bus was carrying contraband. To the jeers of the passengers, The Driver told her she was spot on, that there were six refugees hidden in the toilet. Angrily, she ordered them on their way, oblivious to having been within three inches of a £1-million hash bust.

Other smugglers were not so lucky, and there were lessons to be learned from their misfortunes. In 1994, four Scots women were arrested when a metal detector at Malaga airport revealed one was carrying three kilos of clingfilm-wrapped hash hidden in tinfoil. Their story was that, on the night before the end of their holiday at Benalmadena, a Spanish waiter with the imaginative name of Pepe arrived at their apartment. He said they would share £4,000 if each would hide a dozen bars of hash on their bodies. The women tried secreting the drug in their girdles and underwear but came unstuck and a judge ordered their stay extended by four and a half years. Each would spend nearly two years in the cockroach-infested Seville jail, sharing cells with drug addicts and lesbians.

Closer to home, one of the core group involved in The Man's smuggling operation, John Healy, was stopped at Gatwick Airport in November 1994 by Customs officers, who discovered he was carrying £170,000 in cash. Travelling with him was a friend, Donald Mathieson. Both were from Glasgow. Healy promised the curious investigators that there was nothing suspicious about the money. He was simply off to Alicante to buy a pub. But then, in an effort to take the heat off him, his brother-in-law came forward and said the money was his. The claimant's name was Tam McGraw.

Tam would later wonder whether he should have said nothing and allowed the money to be confiscated.

chapter eleven

KISS OF DEATH

IT WAS AN INDICATION OF THE SMUGGLERS' WEALTH THAT when, in 1994, Manchester United came to Glasgow to play at Ibrox in the International Challenge Tournament, their appearance in a city-centre hotel was overshadowed by another group. The bus team were having a rare get together with their families and friends.

Inevitably at the Reds table, the talk was of football – and, being Glasgow, that subject would doubtless have been high on the agenda of the smugglers. Certainly, they would not once be mentioning hash or buses, and if Spain came into the discussion, it would be in the context of a friendly chat over the best and worst holiday destinations.

The Man was very firm. Walls, waiters, tables, flowerpots have ears. Someone might be listening. He was pragmatic enough to accept the possibility that the police were on to what they were doing. At that stage, they were not, but it was crazy to take chances. At least one self-styled top gangster in the city had an inkling that something big and very lucrative was in operation and smarted at having the door firmly closed in his face. He was regarded as too talkative, and the scam had survived nearly four years in varying degrees of scale because those involved kept their mouths shut in public. Others involved in the business of buying and selling drugs in Glasgow had heard whispers about a major hash racket. But they failed to observe the unwritten criminal code of keeping secret a secret by asking other underworld contacts whether they knew who was behind it. The smugglers were constantly having to remind one another never to discuss their business when there was even the remotest chance of being overheard.

Throughout Europe, police forces and governments were becoming ever more aware of the growth of the drugs trade and the gathering offshore of the Colombian drug cartels in particular, waiting for a breach in the defences to flood nations with cocaine. Hash might not be taken so seriously, but in any sweep for the harder, more potent coke and smack, it was certain to be caught up. Too many were suffering prison food through their carelessness in believing they could bundle a hold-all packed with hash into the boot of a car and expect to drive through a series of Customs checks. True, there were the lucky ones who succeeded, but they were the few.

The Man constantly reminded the others that the law of averages meant that every load which made it home lessened the chances of the next consignment. Even the telephone was regarded with suspicion. Loose talk costs years, the group would be told. It was a rule one member was to break with devastating consequences.

Meanwhile, that weekend the crew lay back and enjoyed themselves. It was not surprising that one of the Manchester players kept staring over at the Glaswegian party, convinced he recognised one of the men. Gordon Ross's good looks were more likely to be imprinted on the minds of women, but the player was sure he'd seen the man before. It took a little while for things to click into place. He had taken his girlfriend of the time, a cracking looker with the figure of a Venus de Milo, but with the arms, to the Sugar Lounge in Manchester. Soon after entering, the Scot had followed and from that moment the beauty's interest in the footballer had waned. She might not have literally thrown herself at Gordon, but she had fallen in his direction perhaps, started up a conversation, asked for a light, made it obvious she was up for grabs and wondered who it was she had been with at the start of the evening. The sportsman had high hopes that she would be cooking his breakfast, but it was Gordon who would share her cornflakes via his hotel room service. Now it seemed like the player was wondering if, in this away fixture, he could sneak a crafty score with the blonde on the arm of the man who had so humiliatingly stolen his girlfriend. She was certainly very trim. He wondered. A tap on his shoulder from one of the Old Trafford Scots brought him to his senses. 'Don't even think about it,' was the advice to the player. 'Not if you want to continue to use your legs.' The young man at least had the sense to use his discretion and remain silent but he remained sullen and sulky.

Not so the opposition. The bill for the Glasgow party that weekend would top £10,000, but no one was counting, no one was producing a cheque book or credit card. Payment, together with an exceedingly generous tip, would be in cash and put down to expenses. But if that weekend showed at least one individual the value of silence, the lesson was to be lost on another.

In March 1994, Graeme Mason had been at his home in Thornliebank when the doorbell rang. He answered it to find a smartly dressed woman, whom he took to be about his own age – she turned out to be two years younger – about to break into what appeared to be a standard patter. Her name, she told him, was Hannah Martin and she was a salesperson for Kays, a well-known catalogue company: would he be interested in hearing what she had to say? She clearly made a good impression, a feeling that turned out to be mutual, because hardly was there time to reach the back of her catalogue than Hannah Martin had moved in and was sharing Graeme Mason's bed. And his secrets.

Mason's problem was he was a dreamer. He was part of the smuggling team, a cog in the wheel, but fancied himself to be the mastermind, the brains around whom the entire project revolved. And, keen to impress Hannah, he led her along the proverbial garden path, through the maze, into the woods, around the fountain and back again. He embellished, bragged and boasted with a verve and flair that would have inspired the Brothers Grimm, conjuring a story of how he led a team of international money launderers. Miss Martin, a single young woman, could not fail to be impressed and was soon to be drawn into a very real catalogue of duplicity.

Early in the relationship, Mason invited her to spend a seven-day holiday with him in Malaga. It came as a pleasant surprise and, not unnaturally, she accepted. But there was more to come. Just a few days before they were due to fly from Glasgow airport, Mason told her how she could not only have the holiday but come home with more than would be in her purse when she set off.

'Graeme, I haven't a clue what you're talking about,' she told him. 'You'll need to explain.'

And he did, describing the arrangement that had been put into place in detail, but omitting its true motive. This partial truth – and the fact that he'd said anything at all – would cost him dearly later on. Graeme told Hannah that a man would bring them a bag filled with £150,000 in cash. She and Mason were to divide the money and hide it in their cases. Some time after they arrived at their hotel in Spain, they would be contacted, the money collected from them and £2,000 less the cost of the flight and accommodation handed over. It was clean, quick and easy. No problems, no worries, no questions asked.

'But what if I'm stopped and my bags searched and they find it?' she queried.

'That's not a problem,' Graeme told her. 'All you'll be doing is taking a little more than you are supposed to have. The worst that can happen is for them to take the money from you and you then get a lawyer to fight to get it back. But nothing will be done to you.'

'You are sure of that? Why take the money overseas anyway?'

Graeme told Hannah the same lie that Gordon had once told to his loyal and unfortunate girlfriend: 'It's to be laundered, dodgy money that needs to appear it has come from a legitimate source. Anybody who wants to get anywhere in business these days is at it. It's the only way of avoiding having every penny you earn taken away by the taxman.'

The couple were due to take off early on a Sunday morning and, around midnight, two men appeared. One was John Healy, who ran a pub in Thornliebank. When he left after a few minutes, Mason produced a bag stuffed with money and the couple counted out £75,000 each, which they put into their luggage.

It was a late-booking holiday in which they only discovered their destination once they landed, and they found themselves at the Hotel Alle in Benalmadena, a short bus journey from Malaga Airport. Watching her suitcase circle the carousel after being dumped by none-too-gentle baggage-handlers had been a nightmare. Every second, she imagined it bursting open and notes flying out like feathers from a down pillow. But it arrived without a problem, the case gently gliding to her like a swan over a millpond. And no nasty Spanish Customs thug barred her way, no alarm bells sounded, no snatch-thief appeared out of the blue to grab the hidden fortune. The coach driver, delivering holidaymakers to a dozen different hotels, did not give someone else her case in error. It was there in his hand, awaiting her as she alighted at their hotel, and in their room she neatly tidied their belongings, putting the money into a hold-all and leaving it in the wardrobe.

Once checked into the hotel, Mason made a telephone call to a local number to report where he was staying and two days later, while Hannah was out, a man called and collected the hold-all. Mason and Hannah Martin made a series of six trips in all to Spain, and the arrangement would always be the same: a late booking, £140,000 to £150,000 in twenty-pound notes divided between them and earnings of £2,000 less the cost of the week-long stay.

Hannah Martin didn't know it, but she and Mason were only one of up to five families who carried money into Spain for the smugglers. It could not be taken by the bus because, despite the frequent forgetfulness of Mohammed, the deal was that payment had to be ready three to four days before the hash was delivered to Big Ted. Further, The Man was aware of the risks of the bus being stopped and searched. Hiding half a million pounds in luggage was out of the question. It could clearly not be secreted under the seating, as that would involve the floor being lifted and replaced twice. So, couriers were necessary, and what better cover than to use ordinary families from the East End of Glasgow, from places such as Barlanark, Easterhouse, Cranhill and Dennistoun? Heading out on holiday, the chances of their belongings being searched were extremely low. When had anyone heard of Customs officers at Glasgow airport opening up the cases of holidaymakers checking in for their annual summer break in the sun? None of the families were aware that there were others doing precisely the same job as themselves. All they knew about were the low personal risks and the brilliant rewards – a free seven- or eight-day holiday in Spain with spending money thrown in, and all for slipping a few bob into their cases.

Not that there weren't hairy moments. During 1996, a couple who had already been making merry at the airport bar before take-off decided to increase their alcohol intake on the flight, until a stewardess announced enough was enough. There was an argument, during which the pilot was called to issue a stiff warning and an assurance that police would be summoned to the aircraft steps the moment the plane landed at Malaga. The man was past caring about the possible repercussions – such as a demand to inspect their luggage, or, at best, being held up before they could reclaim their belongings. But the threat had a sobering effect on his wife, who had divided almost £150,000 between the family suitcases and now envisaged their bags making a never-ending lonely circuit of the carousel, at the mercy of any sticky-fingered fellow traveller. She rescued the situation only by a series of grovelling and tearful apologies, and they were allowed to leave with the rest of the passengers.

That same year, the battered and well-travelled case of one of the regular couriers was given a hard time by handlers at Malaga – so much so that it was literally bursting at the seams as it was thrown onto the rubber plates of the carousel. As other bags and cases crashed on top, it sprang partially open, revealing what appeared to be a £20 note protruding from a beach hat. It was the hat rather than the note which attracted the interest of a lively child, who raced around the circuit keeping pace with the case and attempting to rip out the contents until the horrified owner was able to come to the rescue.

Just as with Graeme Mason and Hannah Martin, all the other couriers were visited briefly the night before they left Glasgow and each was given a telephone number in Malaga to call on arrival. During that call, they would be given a time and date when they had to remain at their hotel until a collector paid a visit. The task of the collector was an important one because not only had he to be utterly trustworthy – it would have been easy for him to complete his tour of pick-ups and then vanish with the proceeds – but he had to ensure that the sum handed over by the couriers was the same as that given to them in Glasgow.

Counting money might sound like a pleasant enough task. Bank tellers, as they whisk through bundles of notes, almost have an enviable job. But try half a million pounds in varying amounts that have to be sorted into their various denominations before being counted. Initially, The Man had insisted that the dealers who bought the bulk of his hash had to pay before delivery. This is a fairly common procedure in the drugs trade, but clearly requires a high degree of trust on the buyer's part. Claims of drug busts by the police are investigated just as thoroughly by those who have paid for a load that will never arrive as by the law officers themselves. It is all too easy for a dealer to be told his consignment has been captured and confiscated when it has, in fact, been sold to a rival at a knock-down price with no questions asked.

Such was the reputation of The Man that his requirement was never disputed. However, as time went on, this stipulation was relaxed. As each full load was bringing in up to £1,600,000, counting such a huge amount was a major chore. Once sorted and checked, the money had then to be distributed, with up to half a million needed to pay Big Ted for the next consignment, wages for those outside the core group and commissions for the major players. In fact, whether the money came prior to delivery or afterwards, it still created a headache. The Man and a helper he trusted with his life regularly found themselves with stomach ailments and skin complaints after a counting session, caused by contamination from the germs that lie on every banknote as soon as it enters circulation. One note, however lightly it makes contact with a foreign body – be it a relatively harmless germ, day-to-day grime, the trace of a controlled substance on somebody's fingers – will contaminate thousands of others. It is a problem which is accepted by courts in England and has led to numerous drug charges having to be dropped, the accused being able to say that traces of, for example, cocaine discovered on their clothing or fingers may easily have come from banknotes.

He eventually decided that the solution lay in the purchase of two machines costing £1,600, commonly used in banks, into which notes are fed to be counted. Furthermore, for the monotony of carrying out the count, he would receive an additional small cut from the profits. When two of his fellow conspirators light-heartedly objected, he invited them to do the work. Once was enough. He was given his machines and his nominal overtime payment.

Not surprisingly, the money received from the four dealers would often be short, even when paying up-front, sometimes by as much as £9,000. Rather than demanding restitution, The Man would instruct Craig to ask Big Ted to negotiate with Mohammed a marginally cheaper rate per kilo.

The problem was many times worse in Spain, where Big Ted preferred his own counting machine – his hands. Five tonnes of hash a month – the amount he had built up to and the level at which the business would remain until 1997 – meant handing to Mohammed a total of £3,500,000. The thing was, Big Ted had arranged for his two pet dogs, a Red Setter and a Pomeranian, to be brought out to him in Spain. They were well trained and well behaved, or so he imagined. One hot afternoon, having spent the entire day in baking heat counting money on the floor of his living-room, he sat back to survey the sight of more than £3 million neatly stacked in bundles covering the entire floor area. Counting and checking had been a monumental task and he reckoned he had earned himself a drink. Returning to his seat, bottle in hand, Ted reckoned without the enthusiasm of the dogs for their master. During the marathon counting session, he had left them in the kitchen with access to the garden area, making sure the intervening door to the counting area was closed. Sadly, as he sat down, he realised he had only pulled the door closed, and it was resting on the latch. He could hear the dogs, anxious for a reunion, racing into the kitchen. Moving with lightning speed, he raced to click shut the door leading into the living-room. He was too late by a millisecond. Taking his protests for shouts of greeting, the dogs tore around the room, leaping high into the air in an attempt to lick his face.

When the telephone rang half an hour later, it was Craig. 'Fancy a jar?' he asked.

'Sorry,' was the doleful reply. 'I've three and a half million quid to count. Again.'

Craig sensed from his friend's tone that further questions would strain the relationship and rang off.

'One, two, three . . .' began Big Ted, while in the kitchen the dogs slept.

chapter twelve

ONE-LEGGED BALL

THROUGHOUT 1995, THE MERCEDES CONTINUED ITS TRIPS
south to the sun. In February, the boys stayed at the Hotel La Barracuda in Avda de
Esana, Torremolinos. They were hard in training for the prestigious Trofeo
Mediterraneo tournament played in Barcelona in April. Requests to take part were
carefully vetted and it was only the fact that Highbury Boys' Club were formally
entered by the Scottish Amateur Football Association that allowed it to join in.
When the time for the tournament came around, the team completed its training
by staying first at the giant 623-room Hotel Sol Principe in Torremolinos before
moving 700 miles north to take part. With the group went two-thirds of a tonne of
hash. There were further trips that year – mainly to Torremolinos but also to
Fuengirola and Malaga – and another tournament, this time in Valencia, where all
the competitors stayed in a youth hostel. The party wound down with a few days
at Hotel Alba Gardens in Benidorm, during which time the bus disappeared for a
couple of days, returning in time to collect the party and go home to Glasgow.

During one of the trips, the party almost arrived home a man short. After
stopping at a service station outside the historic French town of Lyon, the coach
set off towards the Spanish border. An hour and a half later, the passengers
were discussing the footballing abilities of one of their number when someone
remarked how unusually quiet the boy had been.

'Where is he?' someone asked.

The answer came suddenly and in a shriek. 'Fucking hell, he's not here. We've left him behind.'

The bus juddered to a halt, prompting screeches of brakes and honks of anger from the vehicles behind. There was nothing for it but to set off again and wait for an approaching junction before being able to cross through a gap in the central reservation, each mile seeming to be ten, and all the time the debate on the bus centring on whether the missing teenager had ever actually been on board. According to a headcount, he had. And his bag lay in the rack, silent and accusing as though its master were the victim of a cruel and fiendish fate. Wearily, the party arrived back at the service station to see a bored young man sitting upon a wall demanding, 'Where the fuck ya been, ya bams?'

It was worth a laugh, but by the middle of the year age had caught up with the club. The end of the football season marked the end of its existence. Most of the players were now too old for the matches the founders had envisaged and not enough new members had joined. The following year, Robert Whitelock and his friend John Burgon would start Hillwood Boys' Club for under-17s, but its members would not be offered the cut-price £30 holidays in Spain. Instead, East End families, most often mums and their kids, had taken their places. The formula, though, remained the same. When the trip was booked, The Driver would call into the offices of a travel agent and hand over £1,500, then, two weeks before the excursion, make a return visit to confirm the arrangements, have a brief discussion with Colin O'Sullivan and pay the remainder. Always in cash.

There was never anything about The Driver or the other adults who had made bus journeys to Spain looking after the young people that suggested some furtive activity was making them wealthy. They drove no flash cars, their clothes were casual, they were never heard to boast about having lots of money and indeed never appeared to have an abundance of cash with them. The same could not be said for some of the others in the syndicate.

Trevor Lawson had bought Broomhill Farm, where he had been living, at Dunipace, Stirlingshire, and was investing in other property in the Glasgow area. He had developed a worrying mania for cars. Glasgow dealer Tommy Wallace would later reckon Lawson went through twenty vehicles in just two years, many of them top-of-the-range Mercedes: 'He would buy a car and three weeks later bring it back, saying he'd seen something else and wanted that instead. Sometimes, Trevor would do a part-exchange deal; other times, he'd simply want cash.'

Trevor also developed a passion for motorcycles, racing them around the farm, occasionally crashing and leaving a £5,000 machine where it lay, preferring simply to go out and buy something new, bigger and more powerful. One day, while watching television, he saw for the first time a trotting race, horses pulling lightweight buggies carrying a whip-wielding passenger. The effect was that of cars upon Toad in *The Wind in the Willows*. That night, he was telling pals he'd discovered the ideal pursuit and developed his own track at the farm.

It was ironic that he chose to do most of his shopping for motors from Tommy Wallace. The same businessman counted among his best customers many officers from Strathclyde Police – drug-squad detectives, at that. Others from the syndicate went to Wallace for cars: 'They appeared to have so much money they didn't know what to do with it. At first, it was all Golfs – everyone wanted a VW Golf. Then they went upmarket and it was always top-of-the-range sports stuff. They'd buy a second-hand car from me and four weeks later bring it back and trade it in for an upgraded model.'

When Gordon Ross told his good friend Tam McGraw he had come into money, he was advised to invest it. 'Ice-cream vans,' Tam told him, without asking where the windfall had come from. 'Get yourself a good van and buy a reliable round, one where there'll be no hassle. You won't make a million, but it's as good a guarantee as any of a steady return.' So Gordon bought a van, paying £23,000 to take over a round at East Kilbride. He also splashed out on a BMW for himself.

Like Trevor, Gordon was suspicious of banks. Despite his flamboyance, he was also a careful man who realised that if a bank knew what he owned, then so did the bank staff, and in a moment of weakness that information could be passed to members of their family and from there, well, who knew? In older days, families from tough areas such as Glasgow and Newcastle would take no chances with handing their money over to bank managers. They hid it beneath the mattress or under floorboards, where sometimes, much to their chagrin, it provided a bonus meal for lurking mice.

Gordon and Trevor had a variation on those ancient forms of safe. They hid their money in paint tins and then buried them, keeping the secret of the locations locked away in their heads. That may have sounded strange, but money could make men do odd things.

During one of the split two-week bus holidays, divided between the Costa del Sol in the south and the Costa Blanca in the east, a couple of the Glasgow team decided to link up with the bus at Malaga and then accompany it to Benidorm, where they would spend a few days before flying home. At Malaga, they admired the trappings of wealth – the expensive yachts and flashy cars – sometimes failing to appreciate that these were within their own means thanks to their very private business. During a stroll around town – that area inland where the rich can pay for solitude away from the tourist hotels with their non-stop *viva España* and second-rate ever-grinning combos – the pair noticed, as they peered over the flower-bedecked walls surrounding an especially imposing villa, a gleaming black Dino Spyder parked in the driveway.

'That's a Ferrari, probably the fastest car on the road, even quicker than a Lamborghini,' observed one of the Scots to his friend. 'Imagine what the neighbours would say if they saw you nipping through Baillieston in one of those for a cut loaf.'

'Aye, imagine some prick leaning his bike against it as well.'

'No, honest, I've always fancied one. I know I couldn't have one back home because too many people would be asking too many questions about where the money came from. But I'd love a go.'

'Why not hire one for a couple of days? You could motor along the front in it. The birds would jump through hoops for a ride.'

'Tell you what, what if I hire one and we drive it up to Benidorm?'

Their hotel receptionist rang the local Hertz office who said, yes, they could arrange that, but there'd be a big deposit and was it a definite because the Ferrari would have to be brought down from their Granada depot? It would be extra for leaving it at Benidorm, but if sir wanted to take it on to Barcelona . . .? The answer came back, no, Benidorm it was and the deposit, well, no problem there.

It was arranged that the car would be waiting the day the bus departed for the north. Sure enough, there it stood, its cherry-red paintwork so dazzling in the morning sunlight that it almost blinded onlookers. And there was no shortage of those. Before setting off in the bus, The Driver decided to have a quick word with the two men in the Ferrari.

'Know where you're going?'

'Yes, Benidorm, the Hotel Presidente.'

'Right. You've got a map? Know the route?'

'Er, no.'

'What do you mean you haven't got a map? You're fucking kidding. It's about 500 kilometres. One wrong turn and you could be driving around Spain for days.'

'No sweat, big man, it's all sorted.'

'All sorted? You haven't got a map, don't know the road and it's all sorted?'

'Yeh, we're following you.'

The Driver was lost for words. The coach, picking up speed on good stretches to 70 or 80 kilometres an hour and carrying a full load of passengers plus 700 kilos of hash, was to act as pacemaker for a Ferrari capable of something like 280 kilometres an hour. So off they went, the Ferrari at the same sedate pace initially a few feet behind the coach until the gestures of the youngsters in the rear seat forced the gap wider. At one stage, the car surged past, horn blaring. But three or four kilometres up, it was found parked in a lay-by waiting for its guide to regain the lead. When the coach pulled into a service area, the Ferrari did the same. Approaching Alicante, one of the occupants spotted a sign for Benidorm and once more the Ferrari vanished into the distance. But on the outskirts of Benidorm, there it waited again.

'Why not go into town?' asked The Driver as the two vehicles reached the Hotel Presidente.

'Didn't know the way to the hotel.'

'You can hardly miss it. Nearly all the hotels are on the seafront and all you had to do was stop and ask, if you weren't sure.'

'Don't know the lingo.'

That night, the Ferrari was spotted buzzing past the colourful seafront bars of the resort. It was dark, the streetlights were lit, but the man at the wheel still wore the Ray-Ban sunglasses he had bought on the plane out from Glasgow. Next morning, the Hertz representative called for the car. 'Great motor, very quick,' he smiled, checking it over and satisfying himself it remained in pristine nick. 'By the way, did you find the map they left for you in the glove compartment?'

But there were occasions too when having a good time cost nothing. Billy McPhee was a hard man from Barlanark who had matured under the wing of Tam McGraw. Among his closest friends were Gordon Ross and Trevor. When the three got together, anything was liable to happen. Stocky and strong, Billy, when he worked out, cut an impressive figure and he was looking at his best when Big Ted and Gordon suggested he might enjoy a short break in Spain. If his bulk happened to impress Ted's customers and act as a little nudge that he could be called in should anyone decide to step off the rails, well, that was just fine. So Billy arrived and on his first night was taken out to a nightclub run by a well-known London heavy who had decided to give the Old Bill a rest from writing down his name on charge-sheets by investing his savings on the Costa. The man appreciated strength and saw it in Billy. Here was a guy, he decided, who could handle himself. It was time for fun.

As Billy, Big Ted and Gordon stood at the bar, listening to the cabaret – a crooner who spent the summer in Spain and winter on cruise ships – the owner approached. 'I want you to meet someone, Billy,' he said, taking the arm of a well-endowed brunette sitting alone nearby, sipping her drink and evidently bored. Introductions over, the owner asked Billy if he would spare him a moment in private. 'You want to ride her, Billy? She's well up for it. She's married to the crooner. He has a mistress, though, and she wants to show him what's good for the goose is, well, you know the rest.'

Billy could hardly believe his ears. Taking Big Ted to one side, he whispered, 'He reckons the bird wants me to give her one. I've only just said hello, can't even remember her name and she's game for it. If it's not a wind-up, it's got to be a *Guinness Book of Records* job for the fastest score ever.'

'No, it's totally kosher,' Big Ted assured him. 'Look, here's the key to one of the vans we use for shifting hash. It's a white one parked over the road with a dent in the driver's door.'

Billy sauntered back to the singer's wife and offered her another drink. 'Later,' she told him. 'You ready?' and moved off.

Outside, Billy led her to the van and in the back, naked, he in a state of shock, she of excitement, the couple gave a virtuoso if brief performance. They dressed and crossed the road back to the club, and the woman's husband was still singing as they returned. If they had hoped to creep in unnoticed, they were disappointed. The entire audience, briefed as to what had been happening, stood and applauded. The singer wondered if it was his timing or theirs which was wrong.

For some of the smugglers, wealth appeared to transport them into a world for which they were simply not prepared. Back in Scotland, a party gathered for a day's fishing on Loch Lomond. One of the group had hired an expensive motor boat, but rather than hand over cash, had promised, instead, to buy the owner a new anchor and chain. It was a beautiful afternoon as they cruised into the centre of the loch, the water so still and serene they might have been floating upon a mirror. On the deck, beers were handed round. For one of the gang, it was his first time in a small boat and he ran about like a child with a new toy.

'Guys, can I drop the anchor?' he asked.

Before leaving, they had splashed out £900 on the super-duper piece of equipment, along with 150 ft of brand new chain, at the direction of the boat owner.

The amateur sailor rushed below and emerged clutching his heavyweight toy. Leaping to the front of the boat, before his horrified colleagues could tell him to stop, he hurled it into the loch. The splash was followed by silence.

'You've chucked it overboard,' said one of the sailors.

'Yes, that's what you do with anchors.'

'But you attach the chain first.'

'Ah.'

'And you make sure the chain is long enough.'

'We had 150 ft of chain.'

'Yes. And the loch is more than 600 ft deep here.'

'Ah.'

'That's £900 literally gone down the deep.'

'Ah. Hang on, I've got an idea.'

Rushing below again, he emerged this time bearing his fishing rod and hastily cast off in the direction of the anchor.

'What are you doing?'

'Well, I might be able to hook it.'

'But the anchor is 600-odd ft down.'

'So?'

'You have 150 ft of line.'

'Ah.'

Those sorts of antics were only to be expected from young men who had been raised amid poverty and hard times. The camaraderie between the smugglers was never lost, but admittedly there were occasions when it was sorely strained. One time, two of them decided they had earned a weekend break in London. They convinced themselves that in the capital, surrounded by beautiful women and every temptation possible, they could relax and afford to buy freedom from the pressures of the bus runs and the endless, nagging possibility of discovery. They flew from Glasgow and set themselves up in the swish Royal Horseguards Hotel, mingling with minor show-business celebrities but not finding the female companionship they sought. A sympathetic cabbie, whose wife had been born in Castlemilk, took them to a West End club where, he assured the pair, all things were possible and available. He even took them to a friendly doorman who nodded them in the direction of a smartly suited Jimi Hendrix lookalike who told them, yes, he knew someone who had some Charlie: himself. So the Glaswegians settled back to enjoy themselves, ordering champagne with a panache befitting their wealth. When the mood took them, they carried out a discreet transaction with the suited man and then hunger decided it was time for them to move on. Promising the helpful doorman that their absence would be temporary, he guided them to a French restaurant within walking distance where the maître d'hôtel found them a corner table. Waiting to order, they agreed their dining experience would be considerably enhanced by a line of coke and the younger of the two headed for the gents' room. He reappeared, telling his friend that his line was waiting. 'There's a ledge runs right around the room at about knee height and it's on there.'

The restaurant was busy, though not crowded, and delay was therefore out of the question. His companion had been eagerly looking forward to getting his own hit, but opening the door to the gents' was horrified to discover it was dimly lit and covered in gleaming white tiles. The entire room – ceiling, walls and floor – was white. He saw the ledge: yes, it encircled the room, but it too was white. Somewhere on it was a line of C, his line, and he was not inclined to allow it to be wiped away by a cleaner next morning. There was only one thing for it, he decided, and, going down on his knees, began crawling around the room giving each square inch of the ledge a microscopic examination. This tactic was met with considerable astonishment, and not a little mirth, by other gentlemen wishing to use the facilities. Only one took exception at being brusquely ordered to move aside as he was about to use a urinal, but was told, 'I've lost my contact lens.' Torn between impatience and panic, the Scot was on the verge of abandoning his search when his friend, worried at his lengthy absence, appeared and, not without a couple of false starts, first pointed out the missing line then held the door closed until a straw had been whipped from the top pocket and the necessary process had been completed. Later, the pair would laugh at the escapade but their reappearance in the swanky restaurant, sweaty and their knees creased and dusty, caused comment and amusement.

As they completed their meal, they were visited at their table by one of the Hooray Henrys who had watched their efforts in the toilets with such interest. 'Excuse me, chaps,' he asked with a wink, 'you haven't got another contact lens, have you?'

In Glasgow, with so much money awash, The Man decided it was time to meet Big Ted. Ted had worked without a break for more than four years, giving a totally reliable and honest service that in most cases had made kings of paupers. The invitation to meet up with the gang in Glasgow came through Craig, who told him, 'They want to meet the man who has made them rich, the guy at the other end of the whole thing. They want me to come with you, but it's too dodgy. If I'm spotted and picked up, it's curtains for me.'

Craig was obviously depressed at seeing his friend leave, even for a short time. He had become attached to Big Ted, whose kindness had rescued him and Gordon and put their show on the road. Without him, they might still be struggling along, barely making a living in a battered Golf. Plus he missed the old faces, places and voices of Glasgow, the atmosphere, the noisy bars, the banter and even the rain. In other words, Craig was homesick.

Big Ted flew to Glasgow airport to be met in style by Trevor at the wheel of a gold Mercedes Cosworth and driven to the Hilton Hotel in the city centre, where he had been booked into a suite. After a brief rest, Trevor and Gordon collected him and the three hopped into a taxi. He was then treated to an incredible shopping spree. 'Buy whatever you want. It's all on the firm,' they told him. Two hours later, he was back at the Hilton, leaving £4,000 worth of clothing in his room. 'See you around eight,' they called.

That evening, Big Ted was picked up and taken to the Caravel, the haunt, it seemed, of the smugglers. A century earlier, he thought, these guys would have been wearing striped shirts and talking about how they'd outrun a Revenue cutter. Now the talk was of everything but drugs. As he walked through the door, the first words he heard were, 'How are you? Let's get the champagne.' It was his first meeting with so many of the group, yet he had no difficulty remembering their names. Craig had spoken of them so often he almost knew who they were without them being identified.

He was introduced to Tam McGraw, who explained that his wife Margaret ran the bar. Big Ted instantly liked the man. There was a hardness about him that required respect, yet almost a shyness with it. This was a man, he told himself, who would take charge in a crisis. In a corner, struggling to hear one another above the din of welcomes, the two chatted, Big Ted describing Spain but never mentioning the nature of the business that had indirectly brought him to the Caravel. If the other man knew of the secret, he gave no hint. For his part, Tam talked about Tenerife and Big Ted found it hard not to tell his companion the island was but a short hop from the home of one of his best friends in Spain, Mohammed the cannabis Tsar. Tam told Big Ted that he and Margaret had been visiting Tenerife for almost 20 years; they'd been over there in January for a couple of weeks. In fact, they had become so attached she had bought a villa in Playa de las Americas. If he was ever thinking of visiting, then give him a call. He wasn't, but three friends were. Were there any hotels Tam could recommend? There were, and he did. Tam asked, 'Tell me it's none of my business, but are you married?' Receiving a nod, he continued, 'Is she with you?' The reply was to the effect that he had problems he was trying to sort. 'Well, I hope you find a solution,' said Tam. 'I think we all need a woman to keep steering us in the right direction. It's fun to be single for a while but in the end we all need somebody to listen to our secrets.' Before they shook hands and drifted apart, Big Ted wondered if their paths would cross again. The Scot had confided he was contemplating a short break somewhere on the European mainland. If he visited the Costa del Sol, he assured Big Ted, then he'd certainly look him up.

A few drinks later, the party moved to another pub, the Town Tavern. The entire population of Glasgow, it seemed to Big Ted, had turned out to greet him. There were stories galore to tell and in turn he had one of his own. It might have taken several glasses of champagne to complete, but the listeners reckoned it was worth waiting to hear. The story concerned three of his friends – the same trio, he said, whom he had been discussing with Tam McGraw earlier that night in connection with a possible holiday in Tenerife.

'These three – Brian, Chris and Darren,' said Big Ted, 'have gone up to London, where they've been called to give evidence in a court case. Chris had a few quid to look after them. But Brian took over, because at home he lives with this female who's an absolute animal. And now he's off the leash.

'So there they are with a pile of dough and a big bag of weed. And Brian says, "Come on, let's go and find a hotel." Brian is a paranoid schizophrenic when it comes to cleanliness. He won't even consider drinking out of the other side of a cup that somebody else has sipped from or touched, even if he knows they are spotless. But in London it's the height of the season and the only room they can get is one in which there are three beds and they have to share. While the other two are having a smoke, Brian's gone out of the hotel to a chemist and come back with a big plastic bag for each of them. Inside is a face cloth, soap, toothbrush and toothpaste. "There's your bag," he tells Chris. "There's your bag," he says to Darren. "When you go into the bathroom, you use it and when you've finished put your own stuff back into the bag and leave it on your own bed so there won't be any mix-up. And don't go on my bed."

'Now, Darren has a reputation for being kinky, even though he's 22 stone and not a pretty guy, who doesn't get many girls. Every time he goes off, as soon as he arrives the first thing he does is to search out a prostitute. And to get warmed up, he'll buy himself a dirty book. So he's lying on his bed thumbing through the pages and clearly about to move when Brian asks, "Where are you going?" Darren tells him, "Into the bathroom", and Brian demands, "What for?" "What do you think?" says Darren and Brian begins screaming, "Not in there, not in there, not in my bathroom." Darren is desperate. "Well, get me a brass," he urges. Brian hurriedly says to Chris, who is paying for everything, "Get him a brass. I don't want him playing with himself in the bathroom."

'So they are arguing over spending on a brass and in the end Darren phones a number he's spotted in a telephone kiosk and says he's with the management of the Happy Mondays. He tells them, "I want you to send round a girl and, if she's everything I want, when the band do a concert here next month I guarantee she and yourselves will be getting a lot of work from us. I want a 5 ft 8 in. olive-skinned Asian-looking girl, young-looking, and she must be wearing a pink chemise." The other two perverts are listening to this conversation, which continues, "How long will it be before she gets here? Right, now how much is it going to be? Two hundred and fifty, OK, no problem." So, he turns to Chris and says, "You better give me another £50, because you know I'm going to have a really good time with her. I'll want the lot." Chris is persuaded to give him the money, because by this time all three are stoned on weed. About 20 minutes go by when Darren tells the other two, "You'd better fuck off, because if she turns up and there's three here she'll think there's something wrong."

'So off they go downstairs in the lift, order a drink and take a seat in the reception area near the front door, watching every car and cab that pulls up for a sight of the brass arriving. But they see nothing and an hour and a half goes by and they are thinking of ordering another drink when "ding", one of the three lift doors opens and out steps a bird, a real stunner, 5 ft 8 in., olive-skinned, long dark hair and Asian-looking. According to Chris, she just looked their way, and came walking over with one of the sexiest walks you could ever see. Brian was transfixed. She walked to him, asked, "Are you the guy? Are you Brian?" and when he says "Yes" she leans over, throws the lips on him, tongue in his mouth, giving him an extremely wet and long kiss. Then she leans back and says, "Regards from the Happy Mondays. He asked me to give you a kiss on the way out." Brian, the paragon of cleanliness, remembers where she's been and what she's probably been doing with Darren. "Arrrgh!" he screams, dashes out of the hotel, jumps in a cab and begins scouring London at two in the morning for a chemist. Eventually, he buys mouthwash and heads back to the hotel, where he scrubs his mouth so furiously his gums are bleeding. Satisfied he's got rid of any trace of the hooker, Brian gets into bed. "I hope you're satisfied," he spits at Darren, who tells him, "The best of it was, Brian, I had sex with her in your bed."

'Brian headed into the shower and spent the rest of the night sleeping in a chair.'

The end of the story was greeted with raucous laughter. It had been an effort telling it for Big Ted. Beer and champagne were mixed and, despite his years of practised boozing in Spain, he'd succumbed to the merrying joys of alcohol. He had reached that stage where men believe they can fly and are irresistible to women. Emerging from the gents' toilet, he spotted a woman with her back to him. It was all in fun but before he knew what he was doing he had picked her up and was swinging her around. She was shouting and yelling and the entire pub was in stitches of laughter. It took him some seconds to discover the reason. To his horror, he realised his unwilling dancing partner's leg had dropped off. She had been fitted with a false wooden limb, which had gone flying the moment he whirled her in his arms. Big Ted retrieved her leg and sat her in a chair while she carried out repairs. 'Don't worry,' she told him. 'It's not the first time I've been legless.' But he insisted on buying her a couple of bottles of bubbly and she had to fight back tears as she told him, 'Nobody has ever bought me champagne in my entire life.'

That night, as he slumped into bed, Big Ted told himself he envied the happiness of the friends he had known but, until that night, had never met. It was time, he told himself, to put his own house in order and suddenly he knew his long-running personal problem was finally sorted. Tomorrow, he would ring the woman he now knew he loved and ask her to move to Spain to be with him. It would mean a difficult and even traumatic call to another woman, but that had to be done, even though he knew her heartbreak and despair were certain to cut him to the bone. And he'd ring his friends and run through the list of hotels Tam had recommended in Tenerife.

When the hour came to head into the departure lounge at Glasgow airport, a party from the Caravel were there to cheer him off. One handed him a box marked 'aftershave' and told him, 'That's for looking after Craig. Don't open it until you've taken off.' As the jet bore south, Big Ted discovered he had been presented with a genuine Rolex watch. He mused it had probably cost something like £15,000 – not such a fortune in the scheme of things, when the operation of which he was a part was producing millions of pounds. There were times when he counted the takings and wondered if the makers of the board game *Monopoly* printed so much money. So vast were the piles of it washing around it was difficult to accept it was real, that there were people he knew who would have given their right arm for a fraction of what came his way. It was impossible to see it ever ending. There had to be clouds on the horizon, he thought, but until they appeared, well, he would make the most of the experience of being so wealthy that he had become bored with knowing there was nothing he needed that he could not buy. Except contentment.

He knew his lifestyle with Craig was slowly destroying him. Still in his early 30s, Big Ted had fallen into a never-ending pattern of parties, non-stop drinking, week-long benders when nights and days became blended into one gigantic bottomless glass of booze. He was living the good life and it was killing him. He knew the only way to save himself was to have his woman at his side to haul in the reins. The conversation with Tam McGraw came back and he thought about the grey-haired figure with the ready smile and wondered, not for the first or even second time, how much he knew about buses and hash and money. Just as, until that gathering at the Caravel, he had never seen or spoken with Tam, neither had he met The Man. Had their paths ever crossed? From the little he knew of Tam McGraw, there seemed to be much in common with the mysterious figure who ran the smugglers, thought out their strategy and earned such respect.

When the plane touched down at Malaga, his mind was made up. Until that trip to Glasgow, it had been impossible to think of tomorrow. Today was all that mattered. He had all the money he wanted. Berthed at Malaga was a fabulous £250,000 luxury yacht in which he had a half-share. It cost anyone seeking to hire it £750 a day plus fuel and food.

He was hardly back at his villa when Craig announced he was taking a two-week break and heading to Ireland to meet up with some old friends. He would fly to Dublin and, after a brief reunion there, travel to the north to Belfast. Big Ted was sure his own sojourn in Glasgow had partially fuelled this. Craig could not walk about the streets of Glasgow without constantly having to look over his shoulder in case he was recognised by a passing policeman or an informer. But he knew he had enough friends from Scotland living in Belfast to watch his back over there, to protect him and guarantee his continued freedom. Big Ted wondered whether he should tell his friend of his own decision, that in future someone else was to share their home. But he saw the excitement on Craig's face and decided the news could wait. In any case, he was determined that by the time he returned from Ireland she would already be installed.

Meanwhile, there was the little matter of getting richer. A phone call from one of the London crews set the wheels in motion for another delivery from Mohammed, and yet another from Scotland told him that within two weeks the bus would be back in town. This time, the passengers would not be footballers, but families who fancied a cheap break. The pattern, though, he was assured, would be the same as before and they'd be booking into the Hotel La Barracuda and moving to another hotel car park in Torremolinos to collect the load the night before their departure. The change in passengers meant adults would occasionally be travelling with their children. Almost invariably, everyone going on the trips knew one another, as friends, neighbours or relatives. Glaswegians are friendly, helpful people and mums were happy to keep a watchful eye on unaccompanied youngsters along with their own. Usually, the holidaymakers would be aged eight and upwards, but occasionally a tot would be included in the party. Having other adults there gave The Driver and his assistant more leeway and more time to look about. From time to time, though, they would feel the need to take some of the kids to one side and whisper a few words of advice. Thieving, shoplifting and general stealing, while wrong and not to be condoned, were inevitable, but there was a strict house rule that it must only be done on the outward journeys. The natural curiosity of children demanded a reason for this strange command. They were told that on the outgoing legs there would be around four stops, but homeward runs tended to be quicker in order to meet ferry times so there was less scope for larceny. A deep thinker could have pulled holes in this argument, but it was accepted by the listeners. In fact, the real reason was simply that to have police becoming involved, rushing after them to investigate alleged thefts as they headed home with a load of hash under the floor, would have been to put the operation at too great a risk.

The Driver soon found out that his instructions were being rigidly carried out. During a stop at Disneyland on the outward journey, most of the gaily decorated hats disappeared from the heads of the Seven Dwarfs and were later seen being sported along the Edinburgh Road at Dennistoun. And during the four stops on the long haul to the Costa del Sol, he would frequently see groups of his young charges emerge in blistering sunshine from service-centre shops wearing bulging mackintoshes and anoraks and asking each other, 'Does it show?'

That was not to say there weren't occasional scares on the return leg. During a trip in August 1996 to the Don Pancho Hotel in Benidorm, followed by the Sol Principe in Torremolinos, the bus was driving back towards Paris when, as dawn broke, flashing lights were switched on from behind it and the sleeping passengers awoke to the scream of sirens. Two police cars sandwiched the bus, forcing it to a stop in a service area. The Driver and the two men who had been sharing the wheel with him were convinced the game was at last up. As armed gendarmes began sauntering around the vehicle, scoffing at the UK registration, the three adults began picturing life in a French jail, where edible food is not freely dispensed but only earned by working. How would their families cope without them, they wondered. Opening the door and stepping down into the chilly morning air, they discovered the police were pointing to the vehicle headlights, which were not working. In fact, they had been driving on parking lights for most of the return journey. A furious argument ensued, not helped by the police insisting upon shouting in broken English and the Scots yelling back in their most basic Glaswegian intermingled with a handful of French, the words coming out at such a rush that it was doubtful if even a native of the city could have got the gist. During all of this, it became apparent from one of the cops' scribbles in his notebook that the crew was being issued with an on-the-spot fine of 3,000 francs and, from gestures, it was made known the bus would not be allowed to move another centimetre until the fine was paid and the electrical fault rectified. For their part, the driving team showed that, while the headlights were kaput, the windscreen wipers and indicators still worked. Further, pointing to the sky they managed to get across the message that by now it was daylight, they were only three hours from the Calais to Dover ferry – a journey that would not require the use of headlights – and that once in England, the remainder of the trip would be in the light.

The gendarmes refused to budge. The bus, they insisted, would not move. There was only one thing for it. The Driver strode off to a telephone and called an emergency number for the British embassy in Paris, asking to be put through to the nearest British consulate. He explained their predicament to the consul, that on board were 20 tired and highly distressed youngsters desperate to get home, frightened of being locked in prison. Of course, the consul and his staff sympathised and would intervene. Within minutes, a telephone crackled in one of the police cars, a brief conversation followed and the bus was grudgingly waved on its way. The service provided by British embassies and consulates overseas is first class, joked the crew as they headed for Calais. They'll even help you get 700 kilos of best-grade Moroccan hash past the cops.

It was inevitable that, with the bus doing the huge mileages expected of it and with an additional three-quarters of a tonne hidden under the floor, problems would crop up from time to time. Both the 'M' registration and its 'E' registration predecessor had been kept in immaculate condition. New tyres, including the spares, and brake pads were fitted regularly, even when garage mechanics reckoned there was enough tread remaining for another 5,000 or even 10,000 miles. It might have cost the gang up to £2,500 a time for these full-scale renewals and services, but it meant when the vehicles went for annual MOT checks, they passed with no problems and brought no attention upon themselves. And it was an added safety valve ensuring that their passengers and valuable cargo were as safe as possible. There would be other breakdowns, but never anything life- or freedom-threatening.

Leaving the ferry at Dover, The Driver had one more telephone call to make. Unlike the emergency of a few hours earlier, this was routine. The call was to a Glasgow number and when it was answered the message would be brief: 'Hi, I'm back. I've brought 720 CDs.' Or: 'Hello, I'm at Dover, got a sore back from humping 690 T-shirts.' Then he would ring off, having told the team up north another 720 or 690 clicks were on their way. The operation was running so smoothly it was almost too good to be true.

chapter thirteen

IRISH CONNECTION

THE CARAVEL BAR NO LONGER EXISTS. IT WAS DEMOLISHED by Trevor Lawson in 1996 after Margaret McGraw had become fed up with the increasingly expensive, protracted and irksome annual fight to renew her licence. Over the years, it had seen many dramas and at least one murder. It had also been the setting for the beginning of many friendships. One such was that of Tam McGraw and Emmanuel 'Manny' McDonnell.

A staunch Republican from Spamount Street in Belfast, Manny had been jailed as a teenager for illegally possessing documents that could be useful to terrorists and then in 1988 deported under the Prevention of Terrorism Act while working in Cricklewood, London. He made friends in prison and when he was released, contacted one of them who was also now on the outside. Manny suggested a meeting, not to discuss anything specific, but to mull over prison life and the doings of some of the others who'd been inside with them. They chose the Cottage Bar in Darleith Street, just off Shettleston Road in Glasgow's East End. It was 1990, and they were not to know it but the spot was to become infamous the following year when the bodies of Joe Hanlon and Bobby Glover, who had been shot dead, were discovered outside just a few hours before the funeral cortège of Arthur Thompson, Jr. was due to pass by. Young Arty had himself been murdered weeks earlier and some close to the dead man had accused Bobby in particular of being involved, along with others.

Over a pint in the Cottage Bar, Manny was introduced to a man named James, and the two got on well. James suggested that when Manny was next in Glasgow with a couple of hours to spare, he should call into the Caravel, where he was often to be found, as was his good friend Tam McGraw.

Manny had moved back to Belfast, but would frequently come over to Glasgow to visit family members or more distant relatives, usually taking the Belfast–Stranraer ferry crossing. It was during one of these trips that he decided to pop into the Caravel. Tam was there and, when Manny introduced himself, he remembered his name having been mentioned by James. The man from Belfast and the man from Glasgow quickly struck up a friendship, and when it was suggested that an Ulster folk group run by one of Manny's pals, who were planning a series of concerts in Scotland, might be a welcome attraction at the Caravel, Tam agreed.

As the months and years rolled by, the friendship became extended to their families. There would be mutual visits, Christmas cards and occasional telephone calls. There was nothing unusual about families on opposite sides of the Irish Sea becoming friendly. The west of Scotland has a ready affinity with Northern Ireland, in particular, and the McGraws already had many friends in the province. Belfast, at this time, was a city floating in a sea of troubles. Bombings, murders, shootings and terror shrouded the skies and people's minds. Children were weaned on hatred. Despite protestations from some clergy, Protestants and Catholics were taught to despise one another. Protestants were urged to join organisations such as the Ulster Defence Association or the Ulster Volunteer Force, Catholics the Provisional Irish Republican Army or the Irish National Liberation Army.

In Ayrshire and in Glasgow, sympathisers gave encouragement, money and active help to both religious factions. So it could be no surprise that the Special Branch sections of both Strathclyde Police and the Royal Ulster Constabulary would eye anyone with suspicion who appeared to have an interest in the affairs of Ulster or a friendship with a man such as Manny, who had suffered imprisonment for the Republican cause. Even though Tam's only motive for visiting Manny, or his many other acquaintances in Ulster, was the renewal of friendship, his name was put on the list of those whose visits, in future, had to be catalogued. So, for instance, when he and Margaret flew to Belfast from Glasgow airport in late July 1995 for the wedding at the Europa Hotel of family friends, the trip was recorded in official files. But by the time someone decided Tam's movements should be given the same priority as those of others of Manny's acquaintances, it was too late to record the trips that had already been made.

Manny had introduced Tam to Donegal and, in particular, to the Paradise Bar in the town. In turn, Tam mentioned the spot to friends who frequented the Caravel and suggested a group of them spending a weekend there. So Paradise was to become a haunt of many East End Glaswegians.

The local Donegal police force, mainly used to chasing after bicycles without lights and warning off poachers, was at first overwhelmed by the appearance of high-powered Mercedes or BMW cars at the Bar and wondered if some new and terrible terrorist force was in the making. They passed on their concerns to the fountain of all knowledge in Donegal and elsewhere, the local presbytery. Nothing that went on in the town or the area around it was not at some stage passed through its doors – a word here, another there, questions asked and rumours circulated. Who were these men with expensive cars who had begun arriving? Where were they from, what were they doing? They had British registration plates. Were they police looking for the drug-smugglers everyone knew used the west coast? Were they planning to rob a bank? What was going on?

The police's fears were soon allayed. The men were from Glasgow and seemed only on a mission to enjoy themselves. In fact, the local force should join them at the bar and see for themselves there was nothing sinister going on. Why, there was even talk that some television people from England would be coming over. Local gossip had it right. Instantly recognisable faces from the nightly television soaps did appear. The Paradise Bar rocketed into the list of places to be seen at and places to visit. Matthew Marsden, the mechanic Chris Collins in *Coronation Street*, was happy to be photographed, his arm around Manny. So were Sean Wilson and Michael Le Vell, Martin Platt and Kevin Webster of *Corrie*; Patrick Robinson, Ash in the medical drama *Casualty*, and Nicholas Cochrane, probably better known as Andy McDonald in *Coronation Street*. The actors took an immediate liking to Tam and when he invited them to Glasgow, they were thrilled to accept.

In Donegal, Gordon's, Trevor's and Billy's drinking sessions in the Paradise Bar became so talked about that someone suggested adding them to information sheets handed out to visitors to the area. When the local football club announced it was likely to fold because it couldn't raise £15,000 to buy its field, the Glaswegians chipped in. A jar at the bar normally filled with pennies or the occasional piece of silver became packed with banknotes. The result was the handing over to the club of the full £15,000.

Tam liked the bar and learned it could be bought. It would mean a major investment, but he set the wheels in motion in late 1995. In mid-January 1996, he and Margaret left for a two-week break in Tenerife. They returned to Glasgow the new owners of the Paradise Bar, bought for £120,000 plus £15,000 in fees and costs, the money coming from the proceeds of their ice-cream business and the Caravel. They then splashed out on a major refurbishment and brought in a Glasgow couple, John and Mary Hughes, to run it. The Dublin-based Irish government would later suggest, based on information supplied by police in Scotland, that those funds had, in reality, come from drug-dealing profits and, in particular, hash bought in Spain and transported to Glasgow under the floors of buses. It was an accusation Tam bitterly denied, and one the authorities in Scotland and Ireland have since been forced to retract, but at this point in time, the Dublin government was not to be convinced. It announced that, under legislation governing the proceeds of crime, it was confiscating the bar and would later sell it at public auction. There, the story might have ended, but it does not. Was Paradise lost? Or were eggs to become more appropriate than apples?

If drugs were talked about during the Donegal gatherings, then curious locals eager not to miss a trick failed to pick up on the discussions. Or was it merely the case that some of those closest to Tam were involved in a multi-million pound racket but had decided to leave him outside the scam because of his well-known distaste for drugs? Never once had he been known, or, to this day, would be known, to use them. Indeed, he had chastised Gordon in particular when he suspected he might have been snorting even the infrequent line of cocaine. Should something untoward be read into his being there when a number of those involved in the drug-runs partied in Donegal? Others were present and there was never to be any suggestion they were part of the racket. Or was this man with an unarguable flair for organisation the brains behind the whole scheme?

The fact was that any meeting in Northern Ireland of two or more men was, during those troubled times, sure to attract attention and suspicion. Tam was to find out for himself just how crazy a situation such uncertainty could create when he visited Belfast early in 1996 with Gordon and Trevor. It was purely a social call, a short break, during which they met up with Manny at the Europa Hotel for a quiet drink. They were unaware that the same venue had been chosen for a meeting between two paramilitaries and a contact from the Birmingham district. The Special Branch had been tipped off that something was taking place at the Europa, but their informant had been vague. All he could tell them was that a meeting had been organised. The Scots – strangers – found themselves being eyed with distrust by the paramilitary trio, while Special Branch detectives wondered if they had stumbled into not one but two groups of plotters. Their problem was in trying to work out which was the team their informant had said would be there.

The outcome was that, when the Scots left to head for another bar, so did the paramilitaries, who were determined to discover where they were going. Their doubts multiplied when the Special Branch trio began following them. Manny, no slouch at spotting surveillance techniques, was forced to tell his drinking partners they were being watched. All three teams spent an afternoon wandering through Belfast city centre wondering who was up to what, the crazy chase only being called off when the Scots checked back into their rooms at the Europa. That showed how easily the motive behind an innocent gathering could be misconstrued. Once the Special Branch had confirmed, with hotel staff, the identity of the visitors, there would be little doubt they would be filed as potential terrorist sympathisers.

Was it another coincidence that, in 1996, Tam visited Benidorm, a principal holiday destination for the buses with their parties of children and families? After all, tens of thousands of other Scots visited the same resort every year. It was during the stay with two friends, one of them English, that he was drawn into a bizarre incident. It was midsummer and the Spanish sun was four hours from its peak. But thoughtful hotel management had arranged for those of their guests who desired it to take breakfast outside, seated around the swimming pool. Under a cloudless blue sky, Tam and his two companions relaxed as they enjoyed their rolls and tea, he with his favourite six-minute boiled eggs.

A recently met acquaintance from London decided, at the invitation of the others, to join them, but appeared more interested in some of his fellow eaters – in particular, an extremely large, hairy and obese man. Even his best friends would have admitted he made Boris Karloff, in his most horrifying Frankenstein role, look elegant as he wolfed down platefuls of food and, in a series of burps and belches, shouted orders in what sounded like a Balkan tongue to an extremely well-bred young woman, whose willingness to obey left witnesses in no doubt that this was his wife. Egg yolk dribbled down his chin. He slurped coffee and spilled food on the floor.

It was an odd pairing, with the noise of the man's eating and demands for his wife to bring ever more food and drink to the table audible to everyone – not least to the most recent arrival at Tam's table, a Cockney doing business along the Costa Blanca who had enjoyed a few drinks with the Scots the previous evening. He wasn't necessarily their cup of tea, being too loud and preferring to dominate conversations, but they felt it would be rude to refuse his proposal to share the breakfast table. The Londoner became increasingly agitated at the behaviour of the Balkan. 'That's disgusting. Listen to the racket. Pigs have better manners,' he told Tam, who did his best to give the impression he was not part of the discussion. 'Some of these foreigners are a disgrace. He should be eating at a trough, not a table.'

It was at that point that the foreigner decided his breakfast needed flavouring. 'Please, pass the salt,' he asked his wife – in perfect English. She obliged, but the Cockney did not get the message. He continued his criticism, taking no notice of the fact that fellow guests could clearly hear his every word – and if they could hear, then so could the Balkan. At last, finishing his meal, the Balkan and his wife stood up and began to leave. Passing the table where Tam and the others sat, he stopped, his gigantic shadow almost blotting out the morning sun. With a graceful smile, he said 'Good morning' to Tam, again in immaculate English. He had a different greeting for his critic. Picking up the astonished agitator by the neck of his shirt, he carried him to the hotel pool, dropped him in and left without another word.

He created a splash, but elsewhere it was the name of Tam McGraw that was making waves.

chapter fourteen

TURNING ON LIGHTSWITCH

THROUGHOUT 1995 AND 1996, THE MERCEDES CONTINUED on its relentless and profitable way. Occasionally, there were problems filling the seats. On 24 March 1996, for example, there were just twelve people, made up of The Driver, three adults and eight youngsters. However, as the year progressed and school holidays arrived, demand for places would often be greater than availability. It all meant the regular sharing out of more than one million pounds by The Man amongst his associates at the end of each trip. During one spell in early summer, the bus was taking parties every three weeks. Cash was pouring in.

There was nothing to suggest that the police were on to the smugglers, although drug-squad officers in Strathclyde were constantly trying to discover the source of the hash, of which there never seemed to be a shortage. However, the concerns of their masters tended to be concentrated upon the amounts of cocaine and heroin in circulation. While the use of hash or cannabis was not condoned, it was considered harmless in comparison to the effects of other recreational drugs.

The task of tracking down drug-dealers was left to an amalgamation of several units within each force. In the case of Strathclyde, the gathering of information or intelligence was the responsibility of the Criminal Intelligence

Office, nowadays known as the force Intelligence Bureau and attached to Special Branch. This is currently one of, if not the, busiest sections of the Glasgow-based force. It generally gathers more intelligence that it can cope with, largely due to being less selective and having lighter manning levels.

The task of handling more serious crime, often involving firearms and heavy violence, was left on the desks of officers running the Scottish Crime Squad (SCS). Whilst separate from individual forces, this squad nonetheless collaborated with them and largely comprised elite seconded officers. It was the SCS which was credited with trapping heroin dealer David Santini from Glasgow. Santini was jailed for 11 years in 1997, caught with £1 million worth of heroin following the major Operation Babek ('kebab' spelt backwards). The SCS is now the Scottish Drug Enforcement Agency.

Frequently, much of the groundwork for building up a case against a specified individual or group of suspects thought to be involved with hash, heroin, cocaine, crack cocaine, Ecstasy and amphetamines was left to the individual drug squads, who would have at their disposal specialists in monitoring techniques. In the case of Strathclyde, it was the Central Surveillance Unit.

In the 1960s and '70s, men looked upon as professional criminals were included on what was known as the Supplement Z list. Because Tam McGraw had been regarded as a major player, if not the leader and organiser of a gang known as the Barlanark Team, specialising in robberies and earning him fines and spells in prison, his name appeared on the list along with dozens of others. From the 1980s and onwards, these suspects would be referred to as 'core criminals' by those compiling the police records. The media had another term for them. They were career criminals. Regularly, it would be proposed to examine closely the activities of one or more of these elite criminals. They would become officially referred to as 'target packages'.

Recommendations as to who should be classed as target packages might come from within police headquarters at Pitt Street in the city centre, or from local intelligence officers at divisional level, each force being divided up into a number of areas or divisions. From suggested names, senior officers would decide whether to go 'live' against an individual, handing over the task to the Intelligence Confidential Unit.

Going 'live' was not something to be considered lightly. It meant using every available tool to record what a target did and said during every one of his waking moments. Tracking devices would be slyly placed on his cars, vans or lorries. Photographs would be secretly taken of those he met. When the range was too great for a camera, he would simply be watched through high-powered binoculars and the details recorded. His telephones would be tapped: a delicate and frequently controversial action. To listen to telephone conversations was to intrude not merely into a man's words, but his very thoughts. It was the nearest thing possible to probing the mind. According to the rule book, permission for a tap had first to be obtained from the highest level: at that time, before the advent of devolution, the Secretary of State for Scotland. Now, such an authorisation would come from the Justice Minister in Edinburgh. There were many who wondered if, in their determination and enthusiasm, some officers always adhered to these procedures.

The police intelligence-gathering network has many tentacles. Beat officers may spot a known criminal in company and report the details. He or she might be doing no wrong – it might be a harmless chance meeting, or an encounter with an old friend from days gone by, but rightly or wrongly a report nevertheless appears. Detectives doing their regular trawls of contacts may pick up a snippet that such and such has been here or there with so and so – innocent probably; reported still. And there are informants – grasses. Men and women who have varying motives for passing to police information about others. In the underworld, they are a despised breed, the lowest of the low, shopping friends and neighbours alike for 20 pieces of silver. Money is one incentive, but only one of many. Fear is another. A man facing imprisonment may well turn traitor on his friends if it means the chance to remain free. Officially, police don't do deals, because that would mean breaking the law themselves. Unofficially, they do. Most dangerous of all is the gangster who feels ostracised, blackballed, banished to the wilderness and left out of something juicy because he is not liked or trusted. His revenge is frequently a telephone call to the police giving a detail here, a name there, a place, perhaps even a time.

On their own, these reports to or by police may appear irrelevant, worthless. But the ears of an intelligence collator will perk up when the same name begins to appear frequently, especially if there are already reports on those he is seen with. Because making a target 'live' is such an expensive business, the police felt a preliminary investigation was needed before deciding whether to proceed in earnest. Two detective sergeants were instructed to examine what Tam was up to, if anything, on the orders of a detective superintendent who is reputed to have said to them, 'Let's get him locked away and switch the lights out.' It is said that comment produced the title Operation Lightswitch. The men who were to follow Tam under its umbrella have a different theory as to how the name came about.

At the same time as the decision was made to examine Tam McGraw, Strathclyde Police were in the throes of Operation Shillelagh. The targets were Paul Ferris, who had once worked with Arthur 'Godfather' Thompson, security company chief Bobby Dempster, one of the few men who it was said Thompson feared and would step from a pavement to avoid, and Rab Carruthers. The aim of Operation Shillelagh was to track down guns and smash what police suspected was a thriving trade in weaponry between Glasgow and Northern Ireland. No charges were brought against Dempster, but both Ferris and Carruthers ended up with long prison sentences, the latter being convicted of drug offences at Manchester and being given 15 years. He was released from prison in November 2004 but died five months later. Ferris was trapped partially as a result of another operation conducted by the Metropolitan Police but with the aid of information passed on by the men who ran Operation Shillelagh.

It was some months and well into 1996 before police in Glasgow agreed to step up the targeting of Tam McGraw. They suspected, but had no evidence to back it up, that he and a team of associates might be involved in drug-dealing. His name was being mentioned ever more frequently in the context of being a major gangland leader. And so, in June 1996, it was formally agreed to proceed with Operation Lightswitch, which would be a major investigation into the smuggling of drugs, aimed at discovering whether Tam McGraw had a role in it. This was not a decision to be taken lightly, because it would involve spending a small fortune and tie up massive resources, in addition to using up a considerable degree of goodwill.

By that time, police had taken the routine precaution of arranging access to the McGraw family home-telephone records to discover whom they had been calling. A tedious, painstaking process, this involved an analyst getting confidential details of the names and addresses of all those whose telephone numbers had been rung. The expert then compiled a chart showing to whom calls were made, how many were made to which particular person and the day and time of the calls, whether mobile phones had been contacted and whose these were.

Tam McGraw on his favourite holiday destination, Tenerife, in the Canaries, with Playa de las Americas in the background.

Tam McGraw in playful mood with wife Margaret.

Playa de las Americas, the Tenerife resort where the McGraw family have holidayed for the past 25 years.

Tam McGraw with beloved family pet
Rottweiler Zoltan.

Joe Hanlon (right) dressed as a banana
for a charity function. The costume
gave him the lasting nickname
'Bananas'.

Joe Hanlon (holding camera) and
Bobby Glover in party mood.

Manny McDonnell and Tam McGraw
in Tenerife.

Manny McDonnell and
Matthew Marsden (mechanic
Chris Collins in *Coronation
Street*) at the Paradise Bar,
Donegal.

Rocky's Bar, Benidorm: one of the hotels
checked by police hunting the hash
smugglers.

Left to right: Nicholas Cochrane (Andy McDonald in *Coronation
Street*), Patrick Robinson (Ash in *Casualty*), Manny McDonnell,
Michael Le Vell (Kevin Webster in *Coronation Street*)
and Sean Wilson (Martin Platt in *Coronation Street*).

Tam McGraw and friend with, left to right, Patrick Robinson (Ash in *Casualty*), Michael Le Vell (Kevin Webster in *Coronation Street*), Sean Wilson (Martin Platt in *Coronation Street*) and Nicholas Cochrane (Andy McDonald in *Coronation Street*).

Kari Paajolahti.

Right: Document allowing Kari Paajolahti to take part in crimes.

23-DEC'98(TUE) 14:06   0171 782 4463   P.002

CONFIDENTIAL

COMMENCEMENT OF ACTIVITY

I, KARI JUHANI PAAJOLAHTI, HAVE BEEN TOLD THAT I MAY TAKE PART IN A PARTICULAR CRIME, THE IMPORTATION OF CONTROLLED DRUGS, PROVIDING THE PART I PLAY IS A MINOR ONE WHEN JUDGED AGAINST THE CRIMINAL PROPOSAL AS A WHOLE.

I MUST NOT TAKE A MAJOR ROLE IN THE PLANNING OR COMMITTING OF THE OFFENCE. I UNDERSTAND THAT ON NO ACCOUNT MUST I ACT AS AN 'AGENT PROVOCATEUR', WHETHER BY SUGGESTING TO OTHERS THAT THEY SHOULD COMMIT CRIMINAL OFFENCES THAT THEY WOULD NOT OTHERWISE HAVE COMMITTED OR ENCOURAGE THEM TO DO SO. IF I AM FOUND TO HAVE DONE SO I WILL BE LIABLE TO PROSECUTION. I UNDERSTAND THE PARTICIPATING ROLE I HAVE BEEN AUTHORISED TO UNDERTAKE AND I UNDERSTAND THAT I MUST INFORM BRIAN FERGUSON AND JOHN WILSON GORDON IMMEDIATELY OF ANY CHANGES TO THE SITUATION.

SIGNED..(PSEUDO IDENTITY)

DATE 19th December 1998

WITNESSED.....................(HANDLER)

..........................(CONTROLLER)

DATE............

The Validity of This
Document Must Be Confirmed
With John Wilson Gordon And/or
Brian Ferguson of HM Customs And Excise
0171-665-7000.

Inset: A pensive Tam McGraw.

Left to right: Tam McGraw, John 'Snads' Adams, Manny McDonnell

Tam McGraw during his
London days.

A youthful Tam McGraw at his home in Barlanark.

Arthur 'The Godfather' Thompson.

A younger Tam McGraw relaxing at home.

Tam McGraw.

Tam McGraw at his Glasgow home.

Close friend Gordon Ross, murdered in September 2002.

Barlanark Team member Eddie McCreadie with
Margaret McGraw during a break in Tenerife.

A solemn Tam McGraw
receives condolences
from close confidant
David Cassells (right)
and a friend (left) at the
funeral of Gordon Ross
in February 2003. It was
the first time in almost
five years that Tam had
been photographed.
(© Brian Anderson)

At the same time, it was noted in reports from the RUC and Special Branch that one of Tam's contacts was Manny McDonnell. What, the police wondered, could the connection be between a Glasgow publican and a convicted Irish terrorist? It was known that Tam had no known political leanings or strong views, so what was going on? Whether police felt they had found something in his telephone calls, were alarmed by evident growing interest in Ireland or had been tipped off by a jealous rival that he was up to no good, the decision was taken to go 'live', to work flat out to confirm their suspicions that Tam was up to something naughty. It was done with impressive vigour and enthusiasm.

The operation was run by the Confidential Unit from a small room in Pitt Street headquarters and the day-to-day task of running it handed to three detectives. Each day, the team would study reports of telephone taps, looking through transcripts of Tam's and Margaret's telephone conversations. They also had the use of three surveillance teams from the Central Surveillance Unit and the drug squad. As time wore on, even more resources would be brought in. But just how much light would it all throw on the smugglers?

chapter fifteen

IRISH CONNECTION II

DESPITE THE SUCCESS OF THE SMUGGLING RUNS, BY 1996 cracks were beginning to appear. Trevor had been stopped at Manchester Airport with £25,000 hidden in his trainers. He told curious Customs officers, who accused him of intending to buy drugs, that nothing was further from the truth, that he simply wanted to buy a gift for someone special and had been worried that the money exceeded the amount he should have been taking abroad. His version of what the cash was for might have been grudgingly accepted by officialdom, but back in Glasgow there were rumblings that Trevor, not satisfied with the huge amounts of money he was already getting, had embarked on a spot of freelance dealing.

Craig was becoming increasingly moody, his discontent at being exiled not helped by the two-week break in Ireland when he had met up with many old friends. Some had deliberately journeyed to Glasgow and then crossed over to Dublin to see him. Craig was still on the run, and they could not afford to risk dragging the bloodhounds in his direction by taking the more direct route from their respective homes. After the reunion, they had stayed on while he headed to the north.

The Man was also concerned at the amount of expenses being run up at the Spanish end. When each load was due to be collected, a handful of helpers

114

would be flown out to make sure all went smoothly. Their job included collecting money brought over by the families who were acting as couriers and checking that no one had become greedy and stolen any of it. They would do a spot check on it, removing one of the bundles of notes and counting it before it was all given to Big Ted. While he had never suggested his friends in Glasgow might try pulling a fly one, Big Ted took the precaution of counting it again himself. The assistants would thus be ensuring the funds were there for Mohammed to be paid. They additionally had the tasks of helping to get the hash safely from the villa, where it had been stored after wrapping, to the bus, then to oversee loading and, once that was over, to satisfy themselves that the side panels were properly secured.

The Man had noted that his assistants' costs appeared to be getting higher and higher and decided a visit to Malaga was called for. There were claims for lengthy car hires and excessive fuel bills, and the price of accommodation appeared to have suddenly risen. If nothing else, The Man's visit would be to reassure Craig that everything possible was being done to get him home and he could meet up with Big Ted to seek his view on how things were going. In the end, several visits were necessary and Big Ted found his visitor calm and focused, someone in total command of what was going on but aware he had to rely on others less perceptive than himself. Mohammed was especially impressed by the way the operation had been conducted and by the manner in which the Scots were always prepared to help out others in the same line of business. It helped build a friendly environment and lessened the chances of bickering, which frequently led to serious trouble.

There were odd occasions when the Glasgow dealers had been unable to place an order for the bus's full quota, meaning it would be returning with perhaps only three-quarters of its hidden space filled. When that happened, not that it was often, other crews dealing with Big Ted would be offered the facility to have their own gear delivered. At a price, of course. And they would never be told how it was being taken from Spain to the UK. A time, date and place was passed to them, usually a motorway service station, and a white van would be waiting with cardboard boxes, in which were the clingfilm-wrapped bundles. It might have been a gesture aimed at making the most of what the Glaswegians had lost them, but it was a good turn all the same and one which could be returned should the need arise at any time in the future.

Maybe, The Man decided as he flew home to Scotland, the problem was that the venture was running too smoothly. He wondered if the team were becoming overconfident, almost blasé about the whole affair. They were now so proficient at loading the bus that they had managed to get the turnaround down to just under an hour, but was this leading to carelessness? The Driver had told him of one loading operation that had been carried out with the coach parked over a pedestrian crossing and of another in which two of the team had chatted and shared cigarettes with a pair of patrolling policemen around the bonnet of the bus while others sweated to load up at the rear.

In fact, he knew of one loading session in which the police had turned up to see why the bus was stopped on a main street ignoring parking restrictions. Thankfully, The Driver had his wits about him. He lifted the bonnet and explained they had a mechanical fault which would be rectified as soon as the hotel arranged for a garage to sort out the problem. As the conversation continued, so did the loading.

But it only required, he knew, one slip or one over-inquisitive cop and disaster would fall. Sometimes the bus was returning with 720 clicks on board. It was lunacy to gamble with £1.6 million. What was needed was someone with a natural suspicion of all things and all people and with an inbuilt sense of self-preservation.

He recalled meeting such a man one night in the Caravel bar, an Irishman said to be involved with the Republican movement who was over to watch Celtic play at Parkhead. Would he be interested in a contract in Spain, he wondered? Well, he knew just who to ask about being put in touch . . .

In Belfast, Gordon and Trevor met The Irishman. They had been asked to ascertain from him whether he would be interested in working in Spain for a few months on a project which was neither dangerous nor arduous but which was in need of tighter security.

'What's it all about, lads?' he asked.

'Sorry, can't tell you that now. Somebody else is on their way over and will join us tomorrow. If you're interested, he'll fill in all the details.'

'This is a bit vague, isn't it? It's not a set-up? All the units here have teams in Spain, some working on drugs, some arranging arms shipments. There's no secret about that, but I'd need to know more than just "it's something in Spain".'

'Look, it's honestly a good thing and the guy will tell you himself. But if you aren't interested in the idea of going then there's no point in him even flying over.'

'OK, let's agree on this. If I like the sound of it, I'll go, but I'll only listen to what he has to say if he's prepared to be absolutely up-front. I have to be careful.'

The three shook hands and the next day The Irishman was introduced to The Man, who ignored polite questions about the standard of the flight and the journey from Belfast airport. He was anxious for an answer. Looking around to guarantee no one was within earshot, and leaning forward, The Man said, 'I'm going to put something to you and you can answer yes or no. But if you answer no then you'd better forget everything I'm going to tell you. No offence, but I hope I can trust you with what I'm about to say.

'We're running bus trips from Glasgow into Spain. The bus has a false floor and under it we're stashing hash. Nothing has gone wrong so far, but I'm concerned that things may be getting slack. I need somebody to be my eyes and ears out there. There's absolutely no need for any form of violence. If anybody is stepping out of line, then all I want is to be told and I'll have a word with whoever is causing a problem. The reason we've been able to run this so long is that it's been kept tight. If you're up for it, you can either stay around Fuengirola or Benalmadena or go out there each time there's a load. Now, what's your answer? I have to know now.'

'Yes,' said The Irishman, without taking time to consider. Had he done so, he would have been rejected. Then he added, 'What are the wages?'

'You'll be guaranteed a minimum £10,000 a time. And while you are there, if you want to do some freelancing for your own benefit then there's no problem with that, provided it doesn't interfere with what you're doing for me. It's cash in hand and will be sent over to you. One of your jobs will be to collect the money when it's brought over and act as paymaster.'

'How often?'

'It depends when the people we supply ask for a new delivery. Just now you're looking at a load every three weeks.'

The Irishman, slim, with short, dark, trim hair, gave the impression of a cat, aware and reacting to sounds and movements all around him. He missed nothing, and before The Man had arrived with Gordon and Trevor he had made sure he was seated at a corner table, facing the hotel door. He smiled. 'Every three fucking weeks. You're kidding. That's the most incredible thing I've heard of. What about the people on the bus? Are they in on it?'

'Mostly they're kids and haven't a clue. We want them kept right out of this.'

At this, The Irishman, a parent himself, laughed out loud. 'This is like something out of a movie. When do I start?'

'How about tomorrow.' It wasn't a question but a command.

The four sat together for another hour going over the workings of the racket. The Irishman was incredulous at the vast amounts being raked in and astonished to be told one or two were thought to be trying to branch out on their own. Trevor blushed when he heard this. The next evening, The Irishman took a train to Shannon and a flight to Malaga. It was a small precaution, but he'd survived in the dangerous world of guns and bombs by being careful.

In Spain, he quickly realised some changes were necessary. He insisted on making the rounds of collections from the couriers in a car hired only for that day, paying in cash and never using the same leasing company twice in a row. And he changed the routine. Instead of always calling at their hotels, those bringing over the money would sometimes be met at Malaga airport, nipping into toilets to remove the bags from their luggage before hopping onto travel-company buses to be taken to their destinations. He had been worried to learn that the same collector visited the same couriers. Patterns, he warned, were what attracted notice. A receptionist was unlikely to remember one visit by a caller to her guests, but that same face calling twice or more might ring bells.

He told The Man he wanted to recruit his own team for the work. The Man agreed but insisted on looking them over first himself. The two met in Belfast, where the new recruits were introduced. One admitted he was on the run from police in the Far East, who wanted to question him about a shooting. All had paramilitary experience. Each would receive the standard £10,000 for each trip made by the bus and the importance of keeping their mouths shut was stressed to them. 'Even my wife doesn't know what I'm doing,' said The Irishman as the group clinked glasses in the Lansdowne Hotel. 'I told her I was gun-running for the paramilitaries but she doesn't even believe that. She's convinced I'm smuggling diamonds from Holland into Glasgow.'

Ten days after that meeting, The Irishman and his tiny unit were in Torremolinos. He briefed them on precisely how things would be done, and the discipline they had been used to in the fight for control of Ulster came in useful. One of the group, tasked with a pick-up from Hannah Martin and Graeme Mason, said he had the impression the pair had been quarrelling and that there was considerable tension between them. Maybe someone, he said, ought to have a word with Graeme. It wouldn't do if there was a scene, especially if she had half the money with her at the time.

The Irishman used the skills he had picked up avoiding British soldiers and undercover operatives in Ulster to check whether there were any traces of watchers secretly monitoring the movements of the bus when it arrived. Some of the others felt he was paranoid about security, but he found it difficult to believe that such a huge operation had been running for so long without police somewhere getting a sniff of what was happening.

After a month, he flew back to Belfast, then went by ferry to Stranraer as a foot passenger, catching a bus after disembarking to Dumfries, to be collected by The Man and brought back to Glasgow. He had made minor changes, he said, but others were needed. Instead of helpers always flying direct to Spain, they should travel via Belfast, Dublin or even Amsterdam. His proposal was accepted.

'You going back over the water?' asked The Man.

'No, I've moved my family to Glasgow. We have lots of relatives over here but I'll try giving the impression I'm still heavily connected over there. The Special Branch take a look at me from time to time.'

A further month later, he was back in Glasgow for a get-together called by The Man. The smugglers got on well with one another but rarely socialised, reasoning that by being seen together regularly the police would assume they were a group and up to something. When they did meet, it was in top-class hotels such as the Glasgow Hilton or Marriott. To convene in some out-of-the-way place would have been to court suspicion. Better that they were being seen openly, as if they did not have a care or guilty thought in the world.

They had been warned to be wary of these gatherings during a conversation with associates of Manny McDonnell and Tam McGraw. The pair had checked into the Marriott with a group of friends for a weekend break. And later, Manny had a disturbing tale to tell: 'Halfway through the evening, we were warned there had been a bomb scare and that everyone would have to vacate their rooms. It was obviously a ruse. None of us had enemies who would want to blow us up. I knew exactly what would happen. While we were outside, undercover cops sneaked into our rooms and bugged them. Presumably they were wanting to know what I was doing knocking around with Tam. It was an amateurish piece of work, using all the obvious places. They even chose to unscrew the light switches and plant listening devices behind them.' For

Manny, and those who heard his description, this was how Operation Lightswitch had really got its name.

The party, Manny said, had the feeling that as they evacuated the hotel someone was filming them. Later, he would be the target for bugs yet again, during a meeting at the same hotel. On this occasion, the management were particularly apologetic but while he had been out of his room it had been necessary to move him to another. When he asked why, he was told there had been a flood in his bathroom caused by a pipe bursting. It was only minor but they could not allow a guest to be discomforted. Manny was immediately suspicious and said that, in that case, he would move his belongings, but was told this had already been done. He argued that his bathroom had been perfectly dry when he was last in the bedroom and insisted upon seeing the damage for himself. Eventually, he had his way and, just as he expected, there was no sign of flooding. He was told the problem had been cleaned up but needed to be allowed to dry out. It was clear, he said, this had been an excuse to switch him into a room which had already been bugged, and he made sure friends who were there with him were warned to be careful about what they said and to whom. In particular, he advised, they should not use the hotel telephones.

The problem for Manny was that he was of interest not only to the police but to paramilitary groups, including his own. Special Branch wanted to know why he had moved to Glasgow, what he was doing in the city and what the connection was with Tam McGraw. Back in Belfast, the UDA, UVF, PIRA and INLA, plus a host of other more minor but no less volatile outfits, were also wondering about his evident disappearance. It was, and is, a fact of life for organisations living within the murky world of terrorism that knowledge of the activities of the opposition, as well as the police, is regarded as essential. What one faction does, the others need to know, because, while terrorism thrives on high ideals and terrorists on dreams of martyrdom, the existence of both is wholly dependent upon money. Without funds, there are no weapons; without weapons, no capability to fight. Even if a group has rifles and explosives – the tools of the terror trade – without funds, the ability to use them is sorely restricted. Whichever outfit has access to the biggest pot has a head start on their rivals. And if one discovers a new source of income, that could well spell problems for the others. It was a case of dog watching dog, and Manny was up to something – but what? Even his own faction did not know, and if they were in the dark, what chance had the others? So he was playing a dangerous game, and knew it – a target for both gamekeepers and poachers, the hunters and the hunted.

Over in Glasgow, it was rumoured that police had a name at the top of their target list. But how was that name written? Tam McGraw or Manny McDonnell, The Man or The Irishman? And would there ever be an answer? One question to which there was an easy solution was this: was Tam McGraw a grass? Rivals and enemies had accused him of being a police informant. He was said to have been openly seen with police in his home, speaking in the most friendly and intimate tones.

A story had gone the rounds about one police unit actually fighting another to prevent them hauling him off to a cell. It was an accusation he publicly ignored, simply because he opted not to air his views in public. Privately, he treated it with disdain.

The proof was in the setting up of Operation Lightswitch, because it was specifically aimed at targeting him. In the course of any such operation, others will inevitably fall into the net through their contact with the main target, and Lightswitch was no different. In the end, others were taken. But it would be ludicrous to suggest police would set up a major operation with the intention of bringing down one of their own informants. No one had made such a claim when Operation Shillelagh was pointed towards Ferris, Dempster and Carruthers. And further, while it may not have been an open secret within Strathclyde Police that Tam was the subject of a task force, there were enough who knew about it to warn him had he been one of their men.

So Tam McGraw went on his way oblivious to the fact that, in the not-too-distant future, hell was about to take a bus ride to trouble. In the meantime, he went about his business and his pleasure while the hash runs continued at pace. On 23 June 1996, a party of 20 youngsters and their mothers set off for Torremolinos, returning on 7 July, reaching Dover shortly before 9 a.m. Six days later, Tam and Margaret were part of a group of eight who flew from Glasgow to Belfast en route for a party at the Paradise Bar.

There was hardly time for them to change their clothing when they arrived back in Glasgow before Tam and Margaret were off on holiday to Tenerife with two friends on 19 July. And nine days later, he was off again to Spain. His jet, carrying its 15 passengers to the sumptuous 413-bedroom Hotel Griego Mar in Torremolinos, might even have passed over the familiar white Mercedes bus as it gently made its way up the Seacat ramp in Dover. It was back 11 days later, but before the end of the month was off again, three-quarters of the seats taken, its destination being first the Hotel Sol Principe in Torremolinos and then the Hotel Don Pancho at Benidorm. The trip would last a fortnight and, at the end, thud, another million rolled into the coffers. There seemed to be money everywhere. Various van and bus trips had made, for the smugglers, around £35 million, with the ringleaders picking up almost £5 million each. But the very cash that made them so rich was about to become a problem.

chapter sixteen

FLOODED

DESPITE HIS CONCERNS, THE IRISHMAN WAS IMPRESSED BY what he saw in Spain. He knew there were many paramilitary factions in Ulster who had built up a vast knowledge and expertise of the art of secretly building illicit money-making schemes. They would have welcomed with open arms the skills of the organisational maestro who had dreamed this up.

Much of the drug operation's success was due to it being based on the inconspicuous and unobtrusive: ordinary folk taking modest holidays in an ordinary coach to the resorts that everyone else visited. During a visit to Malaga airport one day to meet a young family who had agreed to act as couriers, he watched almost in awe as their battered cases, held together with leather belts and a length of rope, were hauled out of baggage reclaim, not inviting or attracting a second glance. Who was to know of the fortunes that lay hidden inside, wrapped in elastic bands?

It was because they were ordinary that no one would ever suspect they were carrying such vast amounts. There were occasions when couples would hide the loot in their children's gaily coloured bags, the youngsters merrily, excitedly, swinging £150,000 over their shoulders as they headed towards the holiday-company buses taking them to their hotels. Sometimes he winced at the thought of a strap breaking or seam splitting and rolls of notes sailing through the air to land amidst the heaving crowds. But then he had been trained to always expect the unexpected. Once the harvest of banknotes had been gathered, it was taken to a rented villa to be counted. The same villa would never be used twice. Inside, The Irishman and two helpers would check the haul from each courier separately and then double-check to make sure the overall count equated to that of the individual totals.

It was hot work. Sweat poured down their backs and into their crotches as they bent to the task, the only sounds being that of men murmuring numbers beneath their breath. The air became increasingly rancid from smoke and the need to keep the blinds closed. They could not afford prying eyes, and The Irishman constantly feared a stranger, or a landlord, making an unexpected call and seeing the floor piled with money. He had an explanation, which would never be needed, that they were acting for a friend back home who was purchasing a yacht and the seller had insisted upon cash. That would not have been an especially unusual transaction in that part of the world and might well have been accepted without suspicion.

The final total would tell them how heavy the load would be that they'd have to heave onto the bus in the next three or four days' time. There was never less than £400,000, enough to buy around 570 clicks, while a count edging over the £500,000 mark meant a maximum 720 clicks, as much as could be packed in. Occasionally, they would forget the running total and amidst much cursing would have to start again. Sometimes, to relieve the monotony of counting hundreds of thousands of pounds, the counters would play stud poker, sharing out the money and betting £10,000 a time. From time to time, Craig would call in to check they were OK. Once satisfied the totals tallied, The Irishman or Craig would take the stash to Big Ted – who would sit down and count it all over again. And then would come the real problem.

From the outset, Mohammed had made it clear his suppliers would accept payment only in Spanish pesetas. And with each £1 worth around 192 pesetas, that meant an awful lot of pesetas, something in the region of 96,000,000 a load. There the difficulty began. It was no use trying to persuade the Moroccans to accept sterling. Trying to bank so much would lead to awkward questions, whereas it was easy to explain away pesetas. Once the changing was actually done, everything was relatively straightforward. The boxes of Spanish notes were handed over to Mohammed and, as soon as the inflatables had done their work, the telephone would burr and Big Ted's voice would simply announce, 'We have the blow.'

Once The Irishman became involved, he liked to inspect the consignment – just one of the many aspects in his make-up which irritated Big Ted, who had been used to running the Spanish end without his decisions being questioned. The hash came in bars, four to a kilo, each stamped with an eagle, wrapped in polythene and hessian sacking and packed into cardboard boxes. The security-conscious Irishman would insist upon a test smoke, lighting up a gigantic reefer that the others suspected would dry up the air for miles around. The hash would then have to be double-wrapped in the clingfilm machines and taken for loading into the bus.

Big Ted was discovering that, as the years rolled on, changing the money was becoming an ever greater headache. It was often forgotten that the Scottish element was only a part of his own operation. Five tonnes of cannabis a month meant coming up with more than 670,000,000 pesetas. For the exchanges littered all over the Costa del Sol, holidaymakers bringing in twenty or fifty pounds was one matter, but a stranger arriving with £50,000 or £100,000 was entirely another. Scores of exchanges were needed. They would frequently run out of Spanish money, begging the customers who told them they needed pesetas to buy a house or a boat to please wait, desperate not to lose their commission on such an enormous deal. And the sight of Scottish banknotes was enough to halt proceedings while the manager was called to give approval. Spanish banks might have been an option, but they tended to ask too many difficult questions where large amounts were concerned.

'Try Gibraltar,' Big Ted was told. 'The banks there are run on British lines and should be more sympathetic.'

He and a Turkish helper recommended by Mohammed began nipping over the border-crossing to The Rock. It was a nervous task, clutching bags and briefcases crammed with wads of notes and leaving Spain to be confronted by bobbies in traditional helmets. He hoped that was not an omen. Helpful as the banks there might have been, it was more than obvious what the money was being used for. One day, the Turk strolled into a Gibraltar bank asking for £800,000 to be switched to pesetas. The manager announced he would have to send to Spain for such a vast amount and could he return next day, persuading him to deposit the money in the bank overnight. To make things even more sticky, the enormous number of Scottish notes appearing in exchange safes and bank vaults was causing eyebrows to be raised. It was the sort of situation that sooner or later would draw attention and might even merit someone calling the police in Scotland.

One bank manager warned Big Ted, 'My head office says there is more Scottish money in Gibraltar than in Glasgow. They want to know why. What am I to tell them?'

'Say they're bringing their money over here because they get a better rate of exchange,' was all he could think of. He knew this was one problem which would not go away.

The bank managers and those running exchanges were still happy to face queries thrown at them from higher up the chains of command rather than lose their percentage. Indeed, the sight of Big Ted and the Turk striding through La Linea on their way to the frontier barrier prompted more than one bank manager to rush out and haul the pair into his office. He was delighted to exchange English notes, but not so eager to extend the business to those headed Bank of Scotland, Royal Bank of Scotland and Clydesdale Bank. In the end, Big Ted called The Man and begged him, 'Please stop sending so much Scottish money. Try changing it into pesetas at your end.' It was a sound idea but not so simple. Working-class families could hardly go into a bank at Arden or Thornliebank to hand over £50,000, asking for it to be changed into Spanish currency for their annual fortnight in Malaga. Dealers were asked to pay, wherever possible, in pesetas, but for each bus journey thousands of Scottish notes were still turning up.

It was a niggling sore that was now festering, but there was worse to come.

chapter seventeen

GETTING THE BULLET

AS AUTUMN LEAVES FLOATED PAST THE WINDOW OF
Hannah Martin in October 1996, her love for Graeme Mason, which had once
burned with such passion, was now down to its last embers of bitterness. Anger
and suspicion had replaced affection and hope. Where once there had been trust,
now there was anxiety, innuendo, the straining to catch a telephone conversation.
She had known from the start that their money-carrying expeditions were
outside the law, but had accepted Graeme's word that the money was only to be
laundered, cleaned up, made respectable. But then she discovered the truth.

Alone in their Thornliebank home one day, she had answered the telephone
to hear a pleasant, female voice enquiring whether 'Mr Balmer' was there. The
name meant nothing to her, and she suggested the caller had a wrong number.
It was soon clear that there was no mistake; the caller had the correct number
all right and was ringing from a garage to speak to Mr Balmer about the bus
which was being serviced. 'There must be a mistake,' Hannah replied. 'There's
no Mr Balmer here. This is Graeme Mason's home and he has a business
dealing in salvaged goods. I've never heard him mention a bus. The best I can
do is get him to ring when he comes back.'

Hannah was given the garage name and number and, when Mason returned,
she told him what had happened. He was furious. 'I've told you not to answer

the phone when I'm out,' he said. 'This is nothing to do with you.' His partner was not to be fobbed off. She persisted, and, in the arguments that followed, the truth, or at least part of it, emerged.

'Okay, we use the bus to bring gear back from Spain, and that's what the money we carry out there is for,' he said.

'Drugs? You're involved with drugs?' she demanded to know. 'Who goes in the bus? Who else is involved?'

'Kids and families from around here,' he said. 'The others help out, but don't bother about them. And it's nothing to worry about. It's just hash, only hash. Forget it.'

Hannah would not forget it, and Graeme would find, as time wore on, that there was very little that escaped her memory. Together, they made at least six cash-carrying trips. In all, the pair, just one set of couriers, took a minimum of £900,000 to Spain: enough to buy hash that would retail in Glasgow for £3 million.

Meanwhile, back in Benalmadena, Craig had not forgotten his desire to be back home in Scotland. His break in Ireland and the meeting with old friends had left him yearning to be able to walk the streets of Glasgow once more and visit his relatives at will, without the need to be furtive, ever watchful in case the city's finest should collar him.

In the past, he could at least call on Big Ted for a good night out. 'Come on,' he would insist, 'we're going out.' It would be the signal for a bender in which days would replace hours, the boozing and pleasure-seeking halting only when sleep or hunger made a break an alternative to collapse. Their expeditions had become legendary and it was almost a matter of pride to Craig that their status as champions of the Costa junketing set was retained. But Big Ted, too, was remembering. He had gone out to Spain a tall, lithe, fit, eleven and a half stones. Now, eight years on, the unceasing diet of drink and rich food had swollen him to over seventeen stones. His only exercise was in the regular hash-wrapping sessions when, true, the sausage machines did make him pour with sweat, but that was hardly an alternative to dieting or living sensibly.

Craig seemed to resent that Big Ted now preferred to stay at home, having moved in his woman while the Scot was in Ireland. With her had come their three kids, who were now happily ensconced in a private school specialising in educating the children of expats. Big Ted and his woman each had their own spanking new jeeps and, in addition to the half-share in the yacht, he owned two other boats. There were those who felt he wanted for nothing. But he had a niggling feeling that all was not as it should be. He had run the operation safely for years, taking pains to be on good terms with anyone and everyone with whom he had dealings, aware of the value of goodwill. Now, increasingly, clouds were crossing the skyline.

Billy McPhee came over to meet up with Craig, who was showing signs of restlessness. What Craig probably needed was a long discussion about his problems with a good listener who would suggest solutions. Billy's method of soothing his friend, though, was not to be found in any agony-aunt column. He came from an environment in the East End of Glasgow in which a pub rammy was an accepted part of the evening's entertainment. But in Spain, and especially along the Costa, things were different and more complex. Big Ted had accepted ribald comments or gibes with a laugh, knowing they were not meant to be malicious and could be returned with interest with no fear of causing offence. There was a happy camaraderie among the Brits, especially the men concerned with the drug trade. They knew they could literally afford to laugh off ridicule and taunts, aware that they had no malicious intent. But Billy did not see it that way. His reputation in Glasgow as a man not to be mocked was one he saw as essential to be extended to Spain. 'Sticks and stones may break my bones but names will never hurt me' was an old adage which, he ought to have seen, was generally accepted. But it was not for him, and the outcome was trouble.

Calling into the 27 Club one night, his lady on his arm, Big Ted was seized by a worried manager. 'Please, you have to do something. Your friends Billy and Craig are starting fights. We cannot have this because if it gets to the police, there will be big trouble. They have made it plain they will not let anyone get a reputation for causing bother and upsetting holidaymakers.'

It was a situation Big Ted discussed with The Man in person during further visits to Glasgow. They agreed something had to be done about Craig, whose plight was well known in Glasgow, where he was a well-liked figure. Tam McGraw talked over the situation with Gordon Ross, and they wondered whether a drive currently in place by Strathclyde Police could turn out to be a help. Worried by the ever-increasing number of bullets flying about, police had embarked on a campaign to take guns off the streets. Police in general tend to hunger after promotion. Higher rank means higher pay. Higher pay means higher pension. Senior rankers can carry on working and drawing top money considerably longer than those lower down the line. There is often a slavish adherence to decrees from the very top, even if the men who have to carry out those instructions may disagree with them. It is one thing to have an idea that sounds good, but quite another to be at the frontline having to carry it out. The gaffers knew that they needed to find guns. Men coming up with the goods would do themselves no harm at all. So guns would be produced. Here and there, a hint would be dropped that if a firearm was to turn up, a charge might be forgotten, an indiscretion ignored.

Gordon had an informal chat with a Glasgow detective, a man with a reputation for being trustworthy, not afraid of using his own discretion instead of always toeing the party line. Craig, he told the policeman, knew the whereabouts of at least one gun; it was buried in a cemetery. Would specifying the exact location open the door to a deal being arranged allowing the exile to return? The officer took the proposal to colleagues but could get no assurances. Craig would have to come back and lay the weapon on the table of the interview room. Only then would a prospective deal join it there. It was disappointing for Gordon, so Tam took a hand. There were rumours of drugs, guns and even a rocket launcher being offered. Again, nothing was reciprocated.

It was disappointing for Craig and his friends and the frustration he showed in Big Ted's company was not being eased by the arrival of The Irishman. In the background from which The Irishman came, the freedom fighters to which he belonged genuinely looked on themselves as undercover patriots fighting a desperate guerrilla war against the British Army. Many had served with that same Army and brought to their new comrades-in-arms the disciplines instilled in the professionals. Nothing was to be taken for granted; caution was essential for survival; organisation was the byword. So The Irishman found himself at odds with Big Ted's casual, laid-back technique, even though it was one which had shown outstanding success for eight years. This led to friction. Big Ted would later tell The Man, 'Craig had asked me to put The Irishman up and I agreed but found him difficult to understand. I knew he had been used to taking nothing for granted, but there were limits. When he first arrived, he'd be up at six in the morning, knocking on my bedroom door with a boiled egg and tea. I wasn't used to being around that early but did my best to go along with it and tried to help him settle in. After a few days, he asked, "Why are you being so nice to me?" I found him intimidating and felt he needed to learn how to relax. So one night I took him to a club near Fuengirola owned by an Edinburgh guy. All the criminals used it. As we had a drink, some girls came and sat next to our table. They kept looking in our direction, a fact we couldn't help but notice. Eventually, one of the girls leans across and asks, "Who the hell are you?" It was meant in fun but The Irishman looks at her and says, "What the fuck are you asking for?"

'It was bad enough to have Craig obviously jealous of my having a woman around and him wanting to order everybody about. But then The Irishman brings over some of his people and guns begin appearing. He and Craig were in our villa one day and he was demonstrating how this handgun worked to one of the drivers who collected the hash, and it went off by accident, right next to the driver's ear. The bullet whistled past his head. An inch to the right and it would have killed him.'

Big Ted knew he had to begin distancing himself both from the newcomers and the new-style Craig. He could almost feel the heat heading towards them.

There was also heat in Glasgow, especially in the immediate vicinity of Tam McGraw. Operation Lightswitch had begun for real. Initial surveillance and, more profitably, telephone taps had shown his links to Manny McDonnell, Gordon Ross – a convicted drug-runner – and Trevor Lawson. In particular, Gordon and Trevor had been showing signs for some time of having come into money – lots of it. But where was it coming from? It had to be drugs. But how?

An astounding array of resources was made available to the drug squad who were tracking Tam, including 17 unmarked vehicles, each manned by a driver and back-up, a black hackney cab, a motorcycle and even a helicopter. And if more was needed, it would be forthcoming. Tam would be watched 24 hours a day. Every telephone call was to be checked, everyone he met thoroughly checked out and, if possible, the reason for the meeting ascertained. As an added precaution, very few – only a handful, in fact – of the officers involved would have the whole picture. Most were tasked to follow an individual or watch a location without knowing why.

On occasions, they would go through the 'Butterfly Syndrome', being ordered to stop following one target and switch to another without a reason being given. Surveillance would always be directed from Pitt Street and, to the dismay of the unit members, they were never allowed to 'think outside the box'. They could only do exactly what they had been told. They came to realise that the men they were targeting were professionals who, despite being unaware of the interest in them, ran their activities like a military operation. Often, they would carry out what police termed 'multiple reciprocals', taking precautions such as moving up and down the same street several times to learn if they were being followed.

Officers experienced in surveillance methods tried communicating their concerns about the way the operation was being handled to their control centre at Pitt Street, but to no avail. They argued that sometimes the simple way was the best and quoted one classic example. Orders had been given for them to place an intensive watch on Tam's home in Mount Vernon, Glasgow. It meant teams continually driving past, walking around, hanging about and even making use of a spy camera fitted into a nearby street light and directed at his home. Soon after this was under way, one of the team radioed his superiors. 'He's out. There's no sign of life, nobody about. We might as well call this off.'

The reply was terse: 'Stick at it.'

A day later, someone had the bright idea of knocking on the door of a neighbour with the excuse of having a package that had to be delivered in person. 'Tam and Margaret? Oh, they've been away. Don't know when they'll be back.'

Cost to taxpayer? £20,000.

In fairness, when things went wrong, it wasn't necessarily the fault of the Strathclyde team. A secondary target was followed from Bellshill and seen to take a train to London. A number of officers hopped on with him, believing he was taking £60,000 to buy amphetamines. Out of courtesy and protocol, the Metropolitan Police were made aware of what was going on and the London force asked to take over when the target arrived in their city. He was lost before he had left King's Cross station. Weeks later, he was caught in Scotland carrying six kilos of amphetamine paste.

In yet another incident, the police were tipped off that a suspect was on his way to Scotland from England with ten kilos of heroin. They were given a detailed description of his car and a full surveillance team was ordered to literally hit the vehicle as soon as it was spotted in Glasgow. In the north side of the city, police pounced when the car stopped at traffic lights, the strike team smashing both driver- and passenger-side windows. It showed how effective they could be, only they wreaked havoc on the wrong car. It was identical to the one they had been told about, but was the wrong one nevertheless. Inside, as batons smashed at the glass, an innocent mother and her two children, stricken with terror, huddled on the back seat.

GETTING THE BULLET

The watch on Tam McGraw was, according to the police reports, producing results. On 1 November 1996, he was spotted checking into the Marriott Hotel in Argyle Street, Glasgow, with Gordon, Trevor and Manny. Late in the evening, the four were seen emerging and climbing into a car. It was followed to the village of Croy in the Highlands, where it cruised around for some time and then returned to Glasgow, arriving at the pub of John Healy in Thornliebank in the early hours. A story would later be leaked to a local newspaper suggesting the group had been a hit team in search of a gangster suspected of passing information to police. As the month was ending, Tam was noted at Glasgow airport flying to Belfast. He returned the next day and if police wondered where he had been and what he had been up to, most of the regulars in the Paradise Bar in Donegal could have let them in on the secret.

While the watchers were secretly observing him, the bus was still ploughing its prosperous way back and forth to Spain, though not without the occasional mishap. An axle snapped as it journeyed through Catalonia, and for four days the two drivers and eighteen passengers had to kick their heels around a village until mechanics at the local garage could organise a replacement part from Barcelona. Then, during one of the return runs, an oil filter became clogged with dirt, slowing progress to a maximum 28 miles per hour and resulting in the trip home taking a nightmare three-and-a-half days. Back in the East End of Glasgow, they were telling stories about a missing coach party, although no one thought to tell the police.

This was highly unfortunate for the police, because at this stage, despite their surveillance, monitoring, phone taps, intelligence-gathering and all-round reliance on snouts, the police still had no inkling that the white Mercedes bus with the BMH lettering on its side, such a familiar sight in Scotland Street, should have been their target.

chapter eighteen

CHINESE WHISPERS

AT THE BEGINNING OF 1997, AN INTERNAL MEMO WAS circulated around police stations in Strathclyde announcing the appointment of 46-year-old Detective Superintendent Bob Lauder as the new head of the drug squad. An intense, dedicated workaholic, he had spent most of his police career as a detective, including a spell as a sergeant in the tough Gorbals area of Glasgow. He was familiar with major criminals, having worked as a detective inspector with the Scottish Crime Squad, and had seen service as a detective chief inspector at Kilmarnock, in Ayrshire, where he led the search for the killer of attractive young mum Shona Stevens, bludgeoned by a hammer-wielding maniac in November 1994 – an unsolved murder that remains constantly in his thoughts.

One of his first tasks was to be briefed on major operations involving his new team, and he was told of Operation Lightswitch, launched in June 1996 to look into drugs smuggling. As chief hunter, he would not be expected to join in every chase, rather to keep an eye on what was happening, give advice where he felt it was needed and make sure resources were being used wisely. He would be given a daily report from his surveillance team.

The police at this stage were becoming convinced that, if there was big-time smuggling into Scotland, then the mastermind was Manny McDonnell, whose regular trips to Spain were attracting growing interest. It was noticed that he appeared close to Tam McGraw and John Healy in particular. Manny, the police decided, was a man to watch. Meantime, the checks on Tam suggested he was in regular contact with Gordon and Trevor.

On 24 January 1997, Gordon and Trevor flew from Glasgow to Malaga. When they arrived, they would meet up with Big Ted, who had a bizarre story to tell. Next to the villa his family shared in Benalmadena was the home of a Cockney couple and their two children. The two women had become firm friends, forever chatting over the garden fence, watching their children splash in their respective pools. The menfolk had never met, and such was the etiquette of the growing congregation of Brits that asking another man about his business was considered out of order. Big Ted hadn't a clue what his neighbour did to be able to afford to live in such style. But, in the middle of one night, he was awoken to discover the answer. 'You'll never guess it,' he told Gordon and Trevor. 'The bugger had a sausage wrapper going full blast. It was three in the morning and he must have woken half the bloody neighbourhood. My missus woke and asked me what was making the noise. I just said "sausages" and told her to go back to sleep. She gave me a funny look but did as she was told.'

A couple of weeks later, he was invited next door to a drinks party and introduced to his neighbour for the first time. 'You know when you're wrapping those sausages?' said Big Ted, enjoying the astonished expression on the face of the other. 'Try doing it somewhere else or the police will be round to barbecue you.'

'The silly bugger will bring the cops down on everybody,' he now told his visitors from Scotland. 'There are too many people becoming involved and too much carelessness.'

The Scots stayed for just a day before moving on, to where he did not know. It was around this time that Craig also disappeared. Big Ted assumed he had decided to take his chances, having reached a deal with the police. He was sorry to see a man who had been such a good friend for so long quit. He remembered the sorry, forlorn figure he had spotted by the roadside so long ago and how the two had raised hell along the Costa. But of late the relationship had become strained and Big Ted could not help but wonder why Billy had been brought into the set-up.

On 26 January 1997, Gordon and Trevor were arrested by immigration officials at Vancouver airport along with a fellow Scot, Charles 'Chick' Glackin, aged 34. All three had flown on a KLM jet from Amsterdam and walked into a trap. The Royal Canadian Mounted Police had been tipped off by police in Scotland that three men would be arriving carrying suitcases packed with money to fund a drug deal. As they walked to passport control, all three were arrested. Gordon was searched and £10,000 in used notes discovered in his shoes. After checks of the others and their luggage, the Mounties triumphantly announced that each had between £30,000 and £40,000 in used readies.

A forensic examination of one of Gordon's credit cards revealed that it showed traces of cocaine. That was enough for the Canadian authorities to refuse him entry, but checks with Strathclyde police turned up the fact that he and Trevor both had criminal records. That night, they were put on a flight back to the UK, Gordon insisting on paying extra to travel first class, where he sat handcuffed and shackled as the other passengers boarded, the Mounties only relenting once the plane had taken off, unlocking the chains to allow Gordon and Trevor to eat.

Chick was not so lucky. Police in Glasgow had been hunting him for four years, although, in fairness, he and Tam McGraw had tried coming to an agreement with law forces to get him home earlier. Desperate to extradite him back to Scotland, the Canadians jailed him for 30 days for trying to get in with a fake passport – enough time, they reckoned, to sort out the necessary paperwork. 'He did not give us any trouble. Indeed, he was quite a gentleman,' the Mounties announced. In February, Chick was back in Glasgow, starting a three-year sentence for being in possession of Ecstasy pills.

It was a grim ending to what had, in fact, not been a drug-buying expedition but a skiing holiday at the plush Whistler resort in British Columbia. The Mounties might have got their men, but they did not understand them. The Scots could afford the best and had set out determined to enjoy themselves, no matter what it cost. In the end, they saved their money, but what happened was an indication of things to come.

While Chick was waiting to be flown back to Barlinnie prison, known to many as the Big House, to the east of Glasgow, Tam and Margaret were off in another direction, to their favourite destination, Tenerife, spotted by police leaving Glasgow airport on 7 February and flying back two weeks later.

Just under a month after that, an incident was to occur which would have a profound effect on the outcome of Operation Lightswitch. And it would all hinge on a table napkin. Deep in the bowels of Pitt Street was the equipment used to monitor the telephone conversations of Tam McGraw and others. The ears of the secret listeners tingled when they heard a meeting being set up at a restaurant in Glasgow between Tam, John Healy and Manny. The police were convinced something of importance was on the menu and two women detectives from the Central Surveillance Unit were told to hurry to the Chinatown restaurant in New City Road, Glasgow, and watch for the trio arriving. It was just after five on the afternoon of 17 March 1997.

At 5.20, one of the detectives watched as John Healy went inside. Both of the women followed him in and, to his astonishment, they decided to sit at the very next table to his, even though he was the only diner in the restaurant. One woman had her back to him, while each time he looked up he discovered himself looking into the face of the other. He was immediately suspicious, but decided that, as the meeting was purely social, with no sinister or illegal purpose, he would go along with the strange game. Twenty minutes later, he used his mobile phone to ascertain the whereabouts of his friends, to be told they were almost at the door. They joined him four minutes later. Manny in particular wondered why, with the restaurant empty, the only two groups of customers had sat next to one another. 'What's going on here?' he asked Healy and, jerking his head in the direction of the women, continued, 'You know them?'

'Don't think so,' was the reply. 'I sat here and they came in and plonked themselves down next door.'

'Cops,' said the man from Belfast. 'It's the sort of thing cops would do. They must be waiting for somebody.'

As waiters scurried to the two tables, delighted their considerate customers had made things easy by sitting together, the two women ate in virtual silence, straining to hear what the men were discussing. It would have been an awkward task at the best of times, especially with one officer having her back to the conversation. To add to the inconvenience, one of the three, Tam, spoke in broad Glaswegian at such a rate of knots that a Hansard shorthand writer would have thrown up his or her hands in despair. Even worse, Manny's Irish had even his companions craning forward to understand. During the meal, he told his friends about an incident involving his niece, who had been stopped by Customs officers at Glasgow airport and told to empty her baggage, the resulting search unearthing the fact that she had exceeded her cigarette import allowance. There were aeroplane passengers using airports all over Europe to smuggle in vast quantities of cigarettes and tobacco; she could probably have walked through any other Customs check without a word being said, but had chosen Glasgow and was stopped, he moaned.

'Customs seem to have drives every now and again to catch people out,' said Tam. 'One of the families living near me came back last year from Benidorm after they'd had to sit around for four hours in the blazing heat waiting for their flight. When they got to Glasgow, Customs people were stopping just about everybody. They'd have been quicker coming back by bus.'

'How was Tenerife?' he was asked by Healy, wondering if the tan he saw on the face of his relative was the result of the recent holiday on the island.

'Brilliant,' he was told. 'And we're off again next week.'

The meal – a typically excellent one – over, John Healy paid the bill and the men left, still laughing over the plight of Manny's unlucky niece. But the report the two police officers compiled of their understanding of her misfortune would leave a very bitter taste.

chapter nineteen

BENIDORM BOB

IF THERE WAS A SWEET-AND-SOUR FLAVOUR ABOUT THE Chinatown meal, elsewhere in Scotland smiles were also being wiped away. The grin on the face of Mr Happy, which had fronted the 'Glasgow's Miles Better' campaign, disappeared when the city council announced it could no longer afford the annual copyright fee of £28,000 – the equivalent of just over six kilos of hash. Former Scotland, Celtic and West Ham football legend Frank McAvennie said he would be selling his Milngavie home to pay a £750 fine after being caught with cocaine at Glasgow airport. And, in the far north, the picturesque Sutherland village of Bettyhill was recovering from a raid by armed drug-squad police, who pounced on a makeshift laboratory where four Londoners were set to manufacture speed worth £130,000. It was probably just as well for their would-be customers that the gang was caught. Instead of turning out the drug, their bungling chemist mucked up the recipe and produced two gallons of a solvent used to make gloss paint. On the A74 road, near Carlisle, Operation Moss ended with a high-speed chase in which police stopped a car and inside discovered £150,000 worth of drugs that had been driven from Spain.

The same evening as that little drama, on Saturday 29 March, Tam and Margaret McGraw were lapping up the Tenerife sunshine. Their leaving had not gone unnoticed. A tiny spy camera, hidden in the street light opposite their Mount Vernon home, had watched them leave for Glasgow airport four days earlier. Its installation was watched, with some hilarity, by interested neighbours, whose curiosity had been aroused by the sight of a team of workmen evidently replacing a perfectly good bulb and ignoring an adjoining lamp which remained in the dark.

The McGraws were not the only travellers. The Chinatown meeting had encouraged Strathclyde detectives to step up their monitoring of Tam and the other two diners, and to place a virtually full-time watch on their movements. As the result of a report by the listeners checking on calls made by John Healy, the police began wondering whether there could be any connection with a trip to Torremolinos around this time made by two Glasgow men, Donald Mathieson and Robert Gillon. They had driven to the Continent in a Land-Rover via the Dover to Calais ferry on 29 March and headed south. It would have been impossible to follow them every step of the way but there was, in any case, no need. Earwigging the telephone calls had told them the destination was the Scirocco Hotel in Torremolinos. Drug-squad officers in Glasgow, still without any clue as to the use of buses or that a smuggling operation of immense proportions was happening under their noses, decided to pass on their suspicions to their Spanish counterparts. During a call to regional police headquarters in Malaga, the Scots politely suggested that Mathieson and Gillon were worth watching.

That task was enthusiastically taken on by Chief Inspector Ignacio 'El Latigo' Bulanyos. His nickname meant 'The Scourge', and it had been well earned. Scores of smugglers were pining away in Spanish jails as a result of his determination to clear the drug menace from his beloved beaches. He immediately ordered a watch on the pair and reported back to Glasgow that they had indeed turned up at the Scirocco, where they had been noticed chatting to a dark-haired woman. Further enquiries with the hotel receptionist revealed her to be none other than Hannah Martin. It is an indication of just how far police in Scotland were from the real story at this stage. They had nothing to link Hannah to Graeme Mason and their regular deliveries of money. Even more significantly, they did not realise that Robert Gillon was one of the co-drivers on the bus trips. The discovery of the bus was still months and miles away.

El Latigo and his *policía* first spotted Mathieson, Gillon and Hannah Martin on April Fool's Day 1997. Three days later, the two men checked out of the Scirocco and moved to another hotel a quarter of a mile off, while Hannah disappeared. She would later play a significant role in the unfolding of the story. Further watches showed the Glaswegians were joined by another man, Liverpudlian Keith Barry, and on 7 April the trio were followed as they drove two hired cars to a remote villa outside Fuengirola. Had the police in Spain or Glasgow had any inkling then that Mathieson, Gillon and Barry were a relatively small part of a major drug conspiracy, the order would have been given to watch the three round the clock and note anyone with whom they had contact. Maybe a decision to hold off for the time being would have produced a very different end result. But, as far as the Spanish police were concerned, they were watching three isolated drug-dealers and the order was given to move in. Decisions are always easier with the wisdom of hindsight. What happened next was probably the reason for the ultimate failure of Operation Lightswitch.

Minutes after Mathieson, Gillon and Barry had been spotted at the villa, all hell broke loose as police cars and even a helicopter swooped to find their suspects unloading 470 kilos of hash with a street value of more than £1 million. Robert Gillon had a logical explanation. 'We had been in Spain just a week,' he would later say. 'We met an English guy in a bar and he offered us the chance of work painting this villa. We went to have a look and had been there about two hours when the police arrived. The Englishman ran off and got away.'

After their arrest, they would spend 11 months in jail before being sentenced to three years each in March 1998. As for the hashish, Chief Inspector Bulanyos was in no doubt that it had been destined for Britain – probably Scotland While he was chalking up one more victory, yet another party, this time of 14 singing, cheering, happy holidaymakers from Glasgow, were on their way to Torremolinos. They arrived on 7 April, blissfully unaware that only hours earlier two of their fellow citizens had been hauled off in handcuffs. Twelve days after setting off, the bus was safely back in its Scotland Street garage, hash worth £1,600,000 nestling in clingfilm under the floor.

By the time it returned, Tam McGraw was also back from his break in Tenerife. As the Mercedes bus had been about to set off from Spain, he was on his way to Dumfries to collect his old friend Manny McDonnell, who had called to announce he was catching the ferry to Stranraer and could he scrounge a lift to Glasgow? He had a meeting to attend. Tam said he would be delighted to help out, unaware that, as he and his son William collected the man from Belfast, their every move was being watched by the Central Surveillance Unit.

In Glasgow, at the Marriott Hotel, The Man and The Irishman sat down in the comfortable armchairs that litter the main lounge and shared a pot of tea. The Irishman needed to get things off his chest. He was not getting on well with Big Ted, who, having run a trouble-free operation for so long with considerable success, did not appreciate the relative newcomer's evident paranoia over the lack of and need for security. The over-exuberance, often bordering on nastiness, of Craig, Trevor and Billy was attracting unnecessary attention. More crews had moved into the area and the arrests of Gillon, Mathieson and Barry had excited the attention of *El Latigo*. 'Too many people seem to be being brought into what we're doing,' he said in his Belfast accent. 'This is such a brilliant scheme it would be a tragedy if it all went pear-shaped simply because of a few wrong words. Maybe we need a rethink about the way the whole thing is being run.'

The Man had been expecting this. He knew a change of plan was on the cards, but for a different reason. During a lengthy telephone call from Benalmadena, Big Ted had dropped a bombshell. He had decided to quit. End it. Go home. 'It's all changed so much,' he said. 'Craig's gone and I don't gel with some of the others who have been coming over. I know you'll think I'm mad, but the life is killing me. It sounds crazy, but I'm sick of looking at so much money. I could stay on and be a multimillionaire, no bother, but there are so many other crews moving in. They just don't give a fuck for the locals and something is sure to go wrong. The Scourge is down here now and the arrest of the three guys in Fuengirola may be the writing on the wall. I've had a brilliant time. You've been brand new. It's such a good scam I'd hate it to go off the rails, but I think it's time to move on for you also.'

Never one to be accused of being emotional, The Man knew he would miss Big Ted. The two had seen fortunes made and spent, they had been friends, drinking buddies, totally reliant upon one another.

'I'm sorry, but I understand,' he said. 'You got much stashed away?'

'Not a sodding peseta,' was the reply, astonishing for a man who had made millions. 'I'm skint. I've lived like Frank Sinatra for the past few years, but now it's time to get out. It's becoming too regimented and too many Brits are giving the wrong impression. The cops have had an idea something has been going on, but while it wasn't flaunted in their faces, they turned a blind eye and took a few backhanders. Now, it's obvious there are heavy teams around.

'I was at Cheers Bar last week having a quiet drink and couldn't believe the number of flash vehicles parked outside. There were Rollers, Bentleys, Porsches, Ferraris, and the guys climbing out of them looked what they were, hard cases up to no good. It was obvious the motors were ringers that had been nicked in the UK and driven over. The police turned up and were asking who owned this deep blue Bentley. It was clear they had found out it was stolen, but nobody admitted it belonged to them. The cops were no mugs. They realised what was going on, so started pointing out all the big cars and asking the owner of each one to come forward. Nobody said a word or moved. So the police called in a fleet of lorries and towed the lot away. It was no big sweat for the drivers. They were boasting about how quickly they'd be on the phone home to order a nicked replacement.

'That's not the way it used to be. Discretion's gone out of the window and before the busies call on me I'm going. I'll miss the fun and the people, the way they used to be. You've been a helluva good friend but I'd hate to see you in bother because of something some other prick says or does.'

So Big Ted loaded up one of his jeeps and took the long road home to happiness. His words did not fall on deaf ears. The Man knew it was time for change, but first there was another bus to load and fill, another party on whom Colin O'Sullivan wished to spread his largesse. Another million to share.

Time was running out on The Costa del Crime. So many high-profile villains were there that their presence had become an embarrassment to the Spanish government. Their authorities had regularly promised to ship the worst of the bunch back to Britain, in particular, but in reality had done little. Now, politicians were bemoaning the reputation the Costa was getting as a result of hosting these men of guns and evil. Their complaints were being reported and The Man was an avid follower of current affairs. He read about the stirrings of discontent and added to these the words of Big Ted. The outcome was that, by June 1997, he had satisfied himself, and the others, the time had come to move the operation to Benidorm, where he himself had stayed. Because of its distance from the known centres of drug-smuggling in the south of the country, it attracted less suspicion of being used by those running the trade. More than four million visitors flocked to its hotels and beaches every year. Just one more coach among thousands of others would hardly cause crime-fighters to sit up and begin asking awkward questions. Many bus parties had already stayed in the Costa Blanca resort, almost always for the second half of a two-week trip, loading hash into the bus at the beginning of the holiday and simply leaving it there until everyone was back in Glasgow. Yes, he mused, there were many advantages of a move, not the least being the fact that the overall journey would be shortened by around 650 miles. The only question mark was whether the hash could be delivered to the bus at Benidorm instead of in the Malaga area.

After the departure of Big Ted, the group had opted for dealing directly with Mohammed. Desperate not to lose his valued Scots customers, who paid with the funny money, he was effusive in his assurances that such a thing was possible – for a fee, of course. The hash would be delivered by van. The Man had no reason to distrust Mohammed, but, without Big Ted around, he was taking no chances. His team would arrange their own driver. What if a vanload of hash worth £1.6 million were to disappear between Benalmadena and Benidorm? He ordered The Irishman to check around Benidorm for suitable villas to rent and announced he would fly over for a look around himself.

It is said that no matter where in the world you are from, if you stand under the statue of Eros in London's Piccadilly Circus you will eventually meet someone you know. When The Man flew to Benidorm in late June 1997, he remembered that old adage. There was someone he wanted to meet, but it was essential that no one else knew of it. He had a particular reason for feeling comfortable about the decision to move north; it was home to the old friend, whom we are calling Frenchie, a sidekick of a man who was a legend in the world of drug-smuggling. Frenchie knew everything and everyone. A fluent Spanish speaker, nothing moved in the area without someone telling him. No police operation began without his knowing. If new players moved in, he got to know. He had his finger on the pulse of Benidorm and it beat to his timing. He was delighted to have taken the telephone call telling him The Man was about to pay a visit. It would be good to see him once more.

Frenchie had reason not to want it known where he had based himself. Police in Glasgow would have given their right arms to find him. They had been searching for him for years and wanted to ask if there was any truth in their suspicions that he was a major player in the smuggling racket. And there were others, high-ups in the Customs investigation branches in particular, who would have welcomed a chat about his old sidekick, a man who featured prominently in their files. Determined their meeting would be a total secret, he and The Man arranged a rendezvous in a tiny village near Callosa d'en Sarria, in the hills overlooking Benidorm. Arriving separately, the two old friends embraced, then sat in a corner behind a pillar drinking beer. Outside, birds sang and they heard the shouts of villagers making their way home for their afternoon siesta. All was at peace. Until, that is, they heard the unwelcome sound of what was almost certainly the engine of a coach. It was followed by the murmur of voices as passengers alighted, a slight gasp and a voice asking The Man, 'Is that really you? How did you get here? You're not with us, are you?' The face was that of a near neighbour from the East End of Glasgow. It was time to make an excuse and move elsewhere. But, by the time the two men separated later in the day, The Man had had his thoughts confirmed. The future lay in Benidorm.

Just over two weeks later, on Thursday, 17 July 1997, the Mercedes, with 14 passengers made up of mums and their children, left Glasgow and headed down the M74 for Dover in search of fun and sun at Benidorm. They were guaranteed not to be the only Scots at the resort that weekend. Drug-squad chief Bob Lauder and Customs investigator Brian Ferguson were headed in the same direction, flying to Alicante, where Spanish police met the pair as their jet touched down. The Scots explained what had been happening, how they were convinced an Irishman named Manny McDonnell was running a major smuggling ring and how they had been listening in to his telephone conversations. Manny, they believed, was already in Benidorm and they wanted to know who he met and what his movements were.

Around teatime on Saturday, 19 July, as hundreds of weary, burning and hungry sun worshippers slowly heaved themselves towards hotel rooms, the police began their watch in appropriate style, sitting in Rocky's Pub, one of the favourite drinking holes for Brits. The disappearance of the sun did little to cool the air; instead it brought on the appearance of swarms of evil, blood-hungry insects which hovered, swooped and bit, forcing the police to roll down the sleeves of their yellow Berghaus-style jackets. They were sure Manny would appear. Tapping into his telephone conversations, they had heard him arrange to meet a fellow Irishman at this same bar at two in the morning, telling the unknown man he would be booking into the Hotel Presidente. And they were not disappointed. Sure enough, they watched him strolling through the bar with a companion. Neither would stop for a drink and later the police would comment on how Manny seemed upset.

No wonder. As he walked out of Rocky's Pub, he had already sussed the nature of the two tall, neatly trimmed strangers. 'They're cops,' he told his companion.

'Cops? You're fucking kidding. How do you know?'

'Who else but cops are going to sit in boiling heat with yellow Berghaus coats zipped up to their chins and down to their wrists? They look like fucking bananas. It's like something out of an Inspector Clouseau film.'

In the street outside, Manny heard a Scots accent, a voice in the darkness, telling someone, 'The Glasgow polis are in Rocky's. They're wearing fancy dress.'

This was worrying. Manny had already checked into the Hotel Presidente. If they knew he would be arriving at Rocky's, then they were sure, too, to know about the hotel booking. And his luggage had been left in his bedroom. He shrugged in a gesture that said it was too late go back. He was convinced that already his bags would have been opened and searched. He knew there was nothing incriminating inside them, but had heard stories about drugs and guns turning up where they had not been earlier. Manny and his friends were there to holiday, but maybe it was time to find out if they really were the targets.

For the police, the sight of Manny, suspected of being a major drug-smuggler, brought a tingle of pleasure. It meant their long vigils listening to thousands of telephone calls had been worth it. They had been spot-on with the rendezvous and bang-on with the hotel where he would be staying. Now it was a case of following him to see who he met.

Leaving Rocky's, Manny and his companion were joined by a third man, who started off towards the Hotel Presidente but then began nipping in and out of side streets. The police recognised this as an anti-surveillance technique but did not realise it was being carried out specifically because they had been spotted, their cover broken. As far as they were concerned, the men had no idea there were police in town. The trio were watched as they returned to the Presidente at 3 a.m., and again the next day when they left in a taxi from a rank outside the hotel which returned, empty, a few minutes later. Brian Ferguson, who had lived in South America at one stage and spoke perfect Spanish, strolled over to the driver and asked where he had just been. 'Hotel Don Pancho,' the cabbie said – three words that were to spell devastation.

In the meantime, it was Sunday, the very holiest of days for the staunch Roman Catholic Spaniards, a day for attending mass, lying on the beach and basically doing little else. Spanish police had agreed, with some reluctance, to maintain a watch on the Presidente, but it was Tuesday before they had anything of significance to report. The three checked out, hopped into a taxi and left, moving into an apartment owned by a friend in a different area of town, to continue their holiday.

For the police, the trail seemed to have died out. Manny and his associates may have acted like men with something to hide, but they had done nothing wrong, broken no laws. There was no sign of drugs or smuggling. Maybe it was time to move on – but where? There seemed only one answer: the Hotel Don Pancho, where, according to the taxi driver, they had been dropped off on the Sunday. It was the only lead the police had. And it was there, on Thursday, 24 July 1997, that Bob Lauder, later to be tagged 'Benidorm Bob' because of the frequency of his visits to the resort, spotted a white Mercedes bus parked in an adjoining street. The lettering on the side read 'BMH Travel, 191 Scotland Street, Glasgow'.

At that stage, the police had simply seen a bus that had evidently come from Glasgow. There was nothing obviously significant about its presence in Benidorm. Or was there? Tour coaches from Scotland in general, and Glasgow in particular, travelled to Continental resorts every day of the summer weeks. Was it a mere coincidence that a man they suspected of being a drug-smuggler had been to the same hotel where it now stood? Or was there more to the story than that? Lauder was a highly rated, intelligent detective, convinced that, in following an ultimately cold trail, he had stumbled on another growing warmer by the minute. He ordered a round-the-clock watch on the Mercedes. A spy camera was fitted above a chemist's shop opposite the hotel. Yards of tape would run but produce nothing.

On the streets of Benidorm, knowing locals chatted about the presence of the Scottish police. It was inevitable that, sooner rather than later, The Irishman would have his suspicions of police surveillance confirmed. He was not surprised to find cops watching but was disturbed. He contacted The Man on his mobile phone to discreetly put him in the picture. 'Some people are showing a lot of interest in our T-shirts. What do you want us to do?' he asked.

The reply was simple, terse but commanding: 'Dry run.'

On Sunday evening, police watched The Driver climb in and move off. He drove around a couple of blocks to see if he was being followed, after being warned by The Irishman that police were on the scene. Seeing nothing to cause alarm, he returned to his parking spot. Where, police wondered, had he gone? On Tuesday, they saw two men leave the hotel carrying suitcases, open the bus and stow their gear in the boot. They were followed by a file of adults and children and minutes later the Mercedes drove off, arriving at Calais the following morning for the lunchtime ferry to Dover.

The law, and common sense, dictates that on ferry crossings no drivers or passengers are allowed to remain on vehicle decks. Vehicles are locked up and no one allowed near until the ferry is on the point of berthing. That, at least, is the theory. It was, therefore, not surprising that when the mums prepared to take their seats as the ramp to the Dover quayside dropped, all hell broke out. Their seats and the floor were coated in sticky dog saliva; someone had rummaged through hold-alls and bags, not even bothering in some cases to zip them back up. On the quayside, as Customs officers were about to begin the more formal searches and inspections, one of the mums let rip.

'Somebody has been in the bus while we were on the ferry,' she stormed. 'What right has anybody to poke around in our personal property?'

Customs officers are used to the occasional ear-bashing, but this incident could well lead to serious trouble. Sending dogs to sniff about kids' bags was a definite no-no and the sort of crass carelessness that ended up in the press. To make matters worse, here were the so-called forces of law and order blatantly guilty of breaking into a locked bus. Unless this was sorted quickly, it could lead to any Tom, Dick or Harry writing to his Member of Parliament alleging his car or van had been burgled during a ferry crossing and his property stolen. One of the inspectors decided to play for time until someone else arrived to take up the gauntlet.

'Impossible,' he said. 'Nobody is allowed near.'

'Look,' he was told. 'It doesn't take a genius to see a dog has slavered where we're supposed to be sitting.'

'It must have been the police. They've probably let the dog have a sniff through. There's nothing to worry about, it's routine.'

It was a dismal defence. 'Don't be so fucking stupid. I'm a dog owner myself and there's no way a fucking dog can unlock bus doors and unzip hold-alls.'

The Driver remained silent throughout the confrontation. He knew the bus had been searched. Before leaving the car deck, he had closed the door then carefully lowered an aspirin on the end of a piece of thread through the almost-closed window until it rested on the inside door handle, then released the thread. When he came to enter the bus, the pill and thread lay on the floor. Back at the Scotland Street hideout later that day, he told The Man and some of the others what had happened. The general view was that the motion of the ferry had caused the aspirin to drop. 'No way,' said The Driver. 'For that to happen, somebody had to unlock the bus door and turn the handle. They're on to us.'

He knew, too, there was no way the search could have turned up anything. The space between seats and floor had remained empty. The journey had cost the syndicate, but The Man felt it was money well spent. Now, perhaps, the heat would cool.

chapter twenty

LICKED

THROUGHOUT AUGUST, THE BUS REMAINED GARAGED, THE
team attempting to let every last suspicion die down after the police had
searched it and found nothing. By September, they felt they had waited long
enough and decided to try again. The break would be a short one to Benidorm,
starting on 21 September and returning seven days later. On the day of
departure, families of the passengers waved them off. There were goodbyes,
too, for Tam and Margaret McGraw that same day, as they and three family
members flew to Tenerife. Others, less emotionally attached to the travellers,
were also watching the departures – members of the Central Surveillance Unit.

The arrival of the bus in Spain was being awaited with interest. After it had
disappeared down the M74 motorway, an unmarked police car had discreetly
followed, maintaining a distance throughout the drive. Police were certain it
would head for the Dover docks and the ferry terminal to Calais. Just in case the
pursuers were given the slip, or lost the scent, officers from Glasgow were
already hanging around the departure area, having previously checked that a
berth had been booked for the bus. The Driver had been under surveillance
since the sighting of the vehicle in July and had been spotted in the offices of a
Glasgow travel agent. When detectives called in later to ask what had been the
nature of his business, they were told he was completing payment of a booking

on behalf of Colin O'Sullivan for a group of young people and some adults. The party would be staying at the Hotel Los Pelicanos in Benidorm.

Two days after the bus left Scotland Street, Benidorm Bob was returning to the resort to watch for it and arrange a meeting with Spanish police at which their next moves would be plotted. The Irishman too was already in the resort. He and his three-man squad had flown from Scotland and Belfast on 19 September to organise a delivery of hash from Mohammed. They were on the steps of the Los Pelicanos as the bus pulled in.

'Any sign of the police?' The Driver queried, after checking in and seeing his passengers safely to their rooms.

'Nothing obvious, but there's no point in taking chances. Why not have another dry run this time and let them see we're carrying nothing?'

'No point,' The Driver told him. 'We could go on doing that for ever. We'll be OK. Let's just go ahead as if nothing has happened. But it might be worthwhile having a look around to see if there are any familiar faces.'

Next day, The Irishman and one of his sidekicks hired a motorcycle and drove about Benidorm. They saw no one. The Driver, however, was not satisfied. 'You'll never see anybody whizzing about on a motorbike,' he told them when they stopped outside the bar where he and his friend, who had helped with the long drive, were relaxing over coffee. 'Walk about, but don't make it obvious you're looking. Just blend in with the crowds.' What happened next would become part of Glasgow's East End folklore. Dressed in a white T-shirt, dark shorts and sandals, The Irishman began mingling with tourists, peering in shop windows, gazing across the street, occasionally stopping to ask for directions. The heat was searing, sweat soaked his shirt and poured down his face and neck, but there would be no relief, no chance to wipe away the perspiration. He had forgotten to remove his crash helmet. Looking akin to a Star Wars extra, he marched along the seafront to the astonishment and amusement of thousands of sun worshippers. 'If the police didn't know he was here before this, they do now,' said The Driver, undecided whether to laugh or scream in rage.

The police from Glasgow, meanwhile, sharing that same searing sun, could not be certain if something untoward was going on, or whether the bus was in any way involved. It had been checked over at Dover on its previous run, not too carefully or professionally thought a few of the Glasgow detectives, and nothing was found. Some police officers argued that the searchers may have been careless and incompetent enough to miss the obvious. On the other hand, the search had been such a direct warning signal it might have scared off a repeat performance from anyone up to no good. Lauder was convinced that if something untoward was happening, the key to the answer was the bus. Arriving in Benidorm, he headed for the giant 794-bedroom Los Pelicanos and discovered the Mercedes parked in Calle Gerona, a few yards from the hotel entrance. A 24-hour watch was ordered, but the observers noticed nothing out of the ordinary. The passengers lazed about the hotel, romping in the pool and playing football on the beach. It would later be claimed that the Spanish police, coping with their busiest time of the year, with visitor numbers at their height and trying to counter a spate of thefts from hotel rooms, were not as vigilant as they might have been. It was even rumoured that they had agreed to help their Scots colleagues, but in doing so had pointed out that the afternoon siesta, when most people in Spain went to bed to escape the best or worst of the heat, also applied to policemen. This meant that, for two hours after lunch, the bus would be free from surveillance.

Notwithstanding his peculiar and inexplicable gaffe, The Irishman and his team had been using every trick acquired on the streets of Belfast to ascertain whether the police, who had dogged them so obviously at the end of July, were back on their trail. But they saw no sign of being followed. The reason was simple: the police had concentrated on the bus, certain it was involved in some way. At some stage, something was sure to happen to explain why it was there, because even allowing for the natural cynicism of police officers, they were positive in their hunch that O'Sullivan, or whoever was behind the trips, was not paying for the party of holidaymakers out of pure benevolence. They were there as a cover, but for what? So the police continued to lie low, watching the bus from above a row of nearby shops.

To his credit, despite their apparent absence, The Irishman was convinced there were police about. And he would soon be confirming his suspicions. On the day before the coach was due to return to Scotland, he needed to talk with The Driver to arrange the loading of hash into the bus. The two arranged to meet at The Driver's hotel room, but on the way there The Irishman had a feeling he was being followed. He was. Police had broken cover when they saw him on the move and wanted to know his destination. When he vanished through the doors of Los Pelicanos, they played a hunch and sent an officer to The Driver's room. As the two suspects chatted, there was a bang on the door.

Opening it, the smugglers found, to their amazement, a tall man wearing a dark suit eyeing them both, even though The Irishman tried shielding his face. The man requested that they kept down the sound of their music. It was an odd situation. No one wore a suit in the Benidorm heat, and there had been no music. With the door closed again, The Irishman turned and said, 'I told you. I knew there were fucking police about. They've followed me here so they'd know who I was meeting and gambled it would be you. They're on to us.'

The Driver took a calmer view. 'Even if they've connected us, it means nothing. They searched the bus last time and found nothing, and for all we know they've searched it in the past. We've been stopped at least a dozen times on home runs and nobody has found a thing. We should carry on as if nothing has happened.' In the end, they agreed to make contact with other members of the gang in Scotland. There were a series of telephone discussions about the chances of a second thorough search. Those at the Scottish end of the lines were convinced the police had showed their hand and lost. They believed the hash was so well hidden and camouflaged it would not be found even in another search and the bus team was persuaded by this argument to load up as normal.

That night, after darkness fell, a shadowy figure furtively slipped from a back door of the Los Pelicanos and headed for a van parked close by. He opened the rear doors and heaved out a box, carrying it to the bus. The operation was repeated in total silence for under an hour before the man vanished back into the hotel. Spanish police had been briefed never to take their eyes from the bus, but would later claim they had seen nothing, despite a continuous watch. As dawn shepherded in blue skies and warmth, they had every reason to believe nothing untoward had transpired, even if they had taken a few moments during darkness for a bottle and a laugh to relieve the monotony. The bus was still in its original parking spot, clearly not having moved a centimetre. Had it, however, stood on a weighbridge, the scale would have shown it to be 89 kilos heavier.

While loading was going on in secret, The Irishman had been contacted. Frenchie was at Penelope's Club and needed to see him urgently. When The Irishman arrived, he found Frenchie breathless and clearly worried. He had bad news.

'You've been rumbled,' were his opening words to The Irishman. 'There are cops everywhere, the place is swarming with them, and there's even a bigwig detective from Alicante evidently on the way here. He loves to get his picture in the newspapers when there's a kill to be made. He only turns up when a lift is a certainty. My advice is to get out now.'

That, of course, was impossible. To have aborted the holiday without a clear and self-explanatory reason when most of the passengers were just in their beds would have been to invite even greater suspicion and create ill-will back in Glasgow, perhaps even making it impossible to fill seats on any future runs. There were only hours to go before starting back. The Irishman knew there was only one thing to do. And that was nothing. 'We can't leave now. The cops would know straight away that something was up. I've always hung around for a few days after seeing the buses off, and if I suddenly disappeared after the cops had seen me, they would realise there was definitely something going on. I was planning to hang on and chill out for a couple of days before going. We've got to wait until the morning, at least.'

'OK,' Frenchie told him. 'But you have to go in the morning. You must get away from here. Have you any money?'

As The Irishman hesitated, Frenchie told him and one of his associates to be in a bar near the seafront at eleven the following morning, once the bus had moved off. 'Go out the back door and two guys on motorcycles will be there. They'll take you to Valencia airport and from there you're on your own.'

Next morning, a friend of Tam McGraw's was having breakfast at a Benidorm beachfront café, tucking into the traditional Scottish breakfast of bacon, eggs and sausages, when he noticed a white Mercedes bus drive slowly towards him. He thought nothing more of it until, as it neared, he heard a serious of raucous voices screeching at all and sundry, 'See you, ya pricks,' and, 'Go on, ya fannies,' and, looking up in amazement, saw a number of young men wearing the familiar green-hooped shirts of Glasgow Celtic leaning from the bus windows. The holidaymaker, once a leading member of the notorious Barlanark Team, found it impossible not to burst into laughter, much to the astonishment of the early day strollers. He was the sort of man who had the confidence and ear of most of the leading gangland figures back home. Yet to him this was just another coach-load of rowdy youngsters heading back to Glasgow. The bus racket had been running for years, yet not a whisper of it had reached him.

As the Mercedes disappeared, two men were climbing onto the backs of motorcycles. When the coach neared the turn-off to Denia, where cars were waiting to board the ferry to Ibiza, the powerful machines sped past it. The pillion passengers each had £1,000 worth of pesetas in their pockets, a gift from Frenchie. 'The guy is sheer class, a class operator, a gem,' thought The Irishman as the kilometres ripped by. 'I hope he's OK.' He was. And still is.

The bus plodded on through Spain and France to Calais. It was not stopped or searched, and that could have proved a major blunder by police. The Man, being told that police were apparently on to the operation, had advised that the crew should get rid of the 358 bars of hash hidden in the gap beneath the floor and put the loss of a potential £204,000 down to experience. 'What's that compared to what we've all made?' he said. 'Better to limp away and live to fight another day. Tell them to stop somewhere in the French countryside, saying there's something wrong with the engine. Send the passengers for a walk and dump the stuff into the fields. They'll be far gone before anybody finds it and there's nothing to link it to the bus.' His suggestion was passed to another member of the gang who was occasionally contacted by the bus team. If it ever reached the two-man crew, it was not acted upon, and the answer to whether the message reached its destination was lost in the chaos of the events that followed. The coach crossed the English Channel and headed north.

chapter twenty-one

CLUELESS

JUST AFTER SIX O'CLOCK ON THE EVENING OF SUNDAY, 28 September 1997, the Mercedes coach passed Abingdon services area, carved into the rolling hills of Lanarkshire. It had been a long, tiring run and the driver – broad, jovial Michael 'Benji' Bennett – was looking forward to reaching the garage at Scotland Street, Glasgow, and the chance to put his feet up. On the way, as the passengers gradually wilted, the banter and singing that had marked the start of the journey had slowly died down. But heading north on the M6 motorway through England, the jollity had perked up as the result of a stop at Southwaite Services in Cumbria, where one of the youngsters bought a newspaper, to learn that Celtic had beaten Dundee United by two goals to one the previous day while Rangers could only hold Motherwell to a two–all draw. At the same time, they read that a number of celebrities and academics, including some from Glasgow, were advocating that the time had come to decriminalise cannabis.

The bus party were not the only callers at Southwaite. A detective from the Central Surveillance Unit and her colleague followed, in an unmarked car, as the coach pulled to a brief halt. They had watched it leave the ferry in Dover's Eastern Docks just before ten that morning and had been in constant radio contact with their colleagues in Glasgow throughout the day. Now, their long haul was coming to an end.

At 6.32 p.m., as the bus approached Hamilton Services, with Glasgow in sight, it was suddenly surrounded by police cars, blue lights flashing and sirens blaring, and forced to pull off the road. Officers in plain clothes stepped from unmarked vehicles They had reason to believe, they told an astonished Benji, that his coach was carrying drugs.

He protested his innocence: 'I don't understand. What are you talking about?' Police took the names and addresses of the startled passengers and arranged for them to be taken home. They would be visited, they were told, by officers who would want statements from them. But the youngsters on that trip and those who had been on earlier holidays would all tell the same story: they had never seen any of the adults who drove them abroad speaking to strangers, doing deals, boasting of having plenty of money, looking flash or throwing cash around; they had never witnessed odd packages being loaded on board, heard of or seen drugs. In fact, there had never been anything at all out of the ordinary.

Benji was taken off, along with the equally protesting John Wood, who had been the other adult on this journey. The bus was hauled away and forensic experts brought in to examine it. Measurements showed an unusual amount of space between the floor and the ground. There had to be something hidden, reasoned the specialists. But when, eventually, they found the hash, there was massive disappointment at the relatively tiny amount. In terms of drug seizures, it was comparatively nondescript.

Just a few hours after the bus had been stopped, the early editions of the *Daily Record* told of the arrests of a number of men in connection with alleged hash smuggling. That came as a surprise to some of the so-called detainees. The 'news' that they were in Strathclyde police custody had not yet been broken to them, and it would be some hours before they were actually seized. There were also others who would be surprised, among them Hannah Martin, who heard a television newsflash about the bus and quickly worked out it was part of the operation her one-time lover Graeme 'Del Boy' Mason had boasted of running. She recalled the mysterious telephone call telling 'Mr Balmer' about the bus service and presumed he would now be in handcuffs. He was.

Big Ted was in a pub with friends when a group of associates came in to tell him they had heard of the seizure of the bus and the arrest of the Glasgow crew, among them Gordon, Trevor and Billy. He had wondered how the operation had fared after he'd left and was not wholly surprised to learn the secret of the bus had been discovered. Hadn't he warned that too many people were being involved and the behaviour of some was attracting attention? Still, he was saddened by the news that his friends were in trouble. He hoped The Man, in particular, would be safe.

In the days and weeks that followed, police would spread their net wider, arresting more than 30 suspects. Among them were John Healy, Manny McDonnell, Billy McPhee, Trevor Lawson, Gordon Ross and John Burgon, who had helped to run the Highbury Boys' Club. Many of them were friends of Tam McGraw, who had returned from his Tenerife holiday just over a week after the bus had been stopped. News of the arrests caused panic in some parts of Glasgow. Souvenirs suddenly vanished from mantelpieces; reminders of visits to Euro Disneyland were given away to startled friends and relatives. Suddenly, at car-boot sales could be found, going cheaply, a spate of mementoes of Spain and the Disney park, including a cowboy Stetson along with boots, a silver gun and a knife.

When police stripped out the bus, they made two discoveries. One was a fingerprint on the cellophane wrapping. It would lead to the arrest of Liverpudlian Paul Flynn. The other was a name written on the timbers used to build the fake floor. One of the engineers at the coachworks did what many other self-respecting workers did: he left his name, details and the date of his efforts. As a result, he received a very unexpected knock on his door from Strathclyde's finest, who had a series of very awkward questions for him. He was, of course, able to satisfy them about his innocence and ignorance of anything untoward.

As the investigation continued, Tam and Margaret McGraw took themselves off to Tenerife once again on 21 October. As always, they enjoyed the warmth and relaxation the island offered, returning to Glasgow on 5 November: bonfire night. It was an omen. The heat on Tam was increasing. Two weeks later, he and a friend flew off to holiday in Malaga. When they touched down back at Glasgow airport the following week, Tam was arrested.

There were many who felt the police action in stopping the Mercedes had been premature. There seemed little hard evidence. It was not unknown for the law, suspecting a gang had been breaking it, to arrest all the members and then to sit back and wait for one of them, terrified at the prospect of spending the next decade behind bars, to spill the beans on his fellow conspirators. It may have been that they hoped for something similar in the case of the bus smugglers. If so, they were to be disappointed. No one was talking. Maybe it was time to step up the pressure. Tam McGraw was placed in segregation, the theory being that the others would conclude he had talked to save his own skin and decide in their own interests to do likewise. It didn't work, merely giving him more time to read the thousands of pages of statements taken by police and highlight the weak points of their case.

Paul Flynn, facing a long sentence because of the condemning fingerprint, was offered a deal by prosecution lawyers. If he pleaded guilty and talked, he would get no more than two years. With the time he would have spent in custody before the trial taken into account, he would only have a few weeks left to serve. And even then, it might be possible to reach an agreement. They reckoned without the courage and loyalty of the little man. Unselfishly, he announced he was pleading not guilty, certain that the case against him would deflect some of the pressure from the others. If his guilt seemed obvious to a jury, they might, he thought, tend to concentrate more on him than on his friends.

In 1998, with a trial date looming, police were still desperate for clues. They called on car dealer Thomas Wallace, whose business in Glasgow had been expanding at a rate of knots. He had done a roaring trade with some of those arrested, but having to question him caused considerable embarrassment to some of the police involved in the inquiry; they too had been among his most regular customers. He had sold at least four vehicles to Tam McGraw. Trevor Lawson was also a very regular client. In two years, he had averaged a change of car once a month. Initially, men like him and Gordon Ross were fans of the high-speed VW Golf, but having discovered the thrills of fast driving they would then constantly seek upgrades. And once Gordon had sat at the wheel of his first BMW, he was hooked on the classy German built motors.

Sometimes, Wallace told police, the group would simply return a car they had bought from him earlier, walking out with the cash without buying a replacement. Wallace was not arrested but invited to accompany officers to Aikenhead Road police station, near Hampden Park soccer stadium. Deciding discretion was wiser than being stubborn and refusing to go, he was there for six hours taking part in taped interviews, although at one stage of the discussion the recording device was switched off. He would later complain to close friends of being given a 'hard time' by the police, who took from him computer records and a considerable volume of sales invoices connected to vehicles used by the arrested men. But he would not be charged with any offence.

The Crown had decided that the initial 11, known jokingly among some members of Operation Lightswitch as the first team because of their number, would be the subject of the first of at least three trials. As the months wore on, it became increasingly evident that, despite the length of the surveillance and the huge resources devoted to it, evidence was scant, to say the least. None of the 11 had given anything away, making the point to anyone who would listen that they had nothing to tell because they knew nothing. If, as was being alleged, a gang had been running a lucrative scam sending tonnes of hashish into Scotland using concealed compartments in buses, then it was not them. In prison, they were careful not to discuss the case unless absolutely certain their conversations were not being bugged or that no other inmates or prison staff were about. There were frequent conferences with teams of lawyers and barristers who would be defending the accused men, but here, also, discretion was the byword.

Police had decided to pivot their case around Tam McGraw, seeking to portray him as the leader, the brains, the mastermind, the plotter-in-chief, the commander of the hash army. They sought to link him to the others through their monitoring of phone calls, calls made by him and Margaret from their landline and mobiles. The problem here was that a call from Tam to John Healy, for example, could hardly be interpreted as being of any special significance. It is, after all, not unusual for brothers-in-law to talk. Then the police began wondering if calls between mobile phones were actually being made by the holders of the numbers. What, for instance, if John Healy and Gordon Ross had met up and swapped phones? A transcript of conversations from their numbers, provided by the expert listeners mainly made up of Special Branch officers, would have been worthless.

There were those who felt the police tactics and those of the Crown went beyond the normal limits of what was acceptable. Rumours abounded in lawyers' offices throughout Glasgow of dirty tricks. The prosecution would hinge much of its case on records of telephone conversations alleged to have been made between the accused men. The police had spent months drawing up charts based on manual assessments of the calls, and these suggested that traffic surged when one of the buses left for Spain and when it arrived. The defence was given legal aid to have this task done by computer. The painstaking work was carried out by a highly respected company in the city, which had previously used computers on similar assignments for the American Federal Bureau of Investigation. Its findings ripped to shreds the manually derived conclusions. Police got wind that they were being outflanked and searched the firm's offices, seizing some of the computer charts, but it was too late. The issue of the telephone calls, which the prosecution had hoped would crucially swing the outcome of the case in its favour, would, when it came to trial, fade into nothing.

The police had spoken with Hannah Martin, who was still bitter over what she saw as the web of lies spun for her by Graeme Mason. Using details she provided of the dates when she and her lover had smuggled money into Malaga airport, detectives went off to Spain to search around hotel registers, looking for evidence of who had been on the parties at those times and, most importantly, who were the adults in charge. Their questioning of the young footballers and the other families who had gone on trips had been, almost without exception, fruitless. The police knew of around 16 holidays, some officers suspecting the number to have been in the high 20s, whereas, in reality, there had been at least 40. They realised, also, that no matter how much detail they were able to glean about a specific trip, it meant nothing if no one had seen any evidence of drugs being involved. Frankly, they were struggling.

Seeking to bolster his case, in January 1998 Bob Lauder was back in Torremolinos and Benalmadena, where Spanish officers joined him to encourage hotel managers to go ever further back in their records for details of holidays booked by any of the accused group. The little entourage called at the Sol Principe, Barracuda, Griego Mar, Sol Elite Aloha Puerto, Don Pedro Riviera, Bali, Las Palomas and Scirocco. In some, he hit lucky, turning up documents proving Michael Dennett and John Burgon had booked in groups and evidence showing Graeme Mason and Hannah Martin had stayed in the area. But would it be of any value if there was nothing to link the visits with any wrongdoing? Travel agencies in Glasgow would swear blind they knew Colin O'Sullivan existed, because they had heard him answering when Benji Bennett had asked for his number to be dialled. And the conversations were not about drugs but between two men discussing how to ensure young people made the most of free holidays overseas.

The policeman decided that, while he was in the area, it would be a sound idea to visit Malaga jail, where Robert Gillon, Donald Mathieson and Keith

Barry were awaiting their fate before a Spanish judge. He pointed out to the trio, and the two Scots in particular, the potential advantages to them in coming clean as to who had put up the money for the hash they had been handling when caught, who was behind the operation and to whom the drugs would go. It was a wasted exercise. None wanted to see him or speak with him. Spanish lawyers had already explained they were only weeks from their date with a judge who would set them sentences that ensured they would spend the summer months in Malaga jail but be back home in Scotland in time for autumn. They had nothing to gain, they said, and in any case nothing useful to pass on.

In February, Benidorm Bob was back in the resort that had earned him his nickname, trying to track the movements of Manny McDonnell and the bus crews. It was here that the police would have their best chance of securing convictions, having had the chance to watch the bus throughout its stay. Despite a full-time watch, no one had seen hash being loaded, yet hash was certainly there, admittedly in a limited quantity, when it was stopped near Glasgow. How did it get there? Who was the smuggler? That was the sixty-four-thousand dollar question, and no one had an answer.

The trial was scheduled to begin at the High Court in Edinburgh on 17 April 1998 and, as kick-off time neared, there were rumblings within the drug squad that things were not looking promising. Drastic action was needed. It would later be alleged that a basic human right had been flagrantly breached. Lawyers for some of the accused wrote to the then Scottish Secretary Donald Dewar – himself a solicitor – to claim that telephones in their legal offices had been bugged. Someone had stuck up two fingers at client confidentiality, that cornerstone of the judicial system. The lawyers reckoned they had noticed a suspicious change in the sound of dialling tones and had brought in experts, who carried out a sweep and confirmed bugs had been planted.

chapter twenty-two

COLD SPAM

THE FIRST OF THE TRIALS OF THE MEN ALLEGED TO HAVE been raking in hash cash by the bus-load opened on a Friday. It was scheduled to last 12 weeks, during which time 177 prosecution witnesses would give evidence.

Eleven defendants had been listed. Their fate would decide the future of two other proposed trials. Tam McGraw, along with others among the accused, would spend 55 days in the dock, and the show would set taxpayers back a cool £2 million. There would be those who would later remark that just one more bus run would have settled the bill.

By coincidence, 400 miles away in London, another Glaswegian, Paul Ferris, was waiting to face a judge, charged with gun-running. His trial ended a week after Tam's, but the fates of the two were vastly different. While one went home in a black Mercedes, the other was escorted into a prison van to start a sentence initially set at fifteen years but which was later reduced by judicial blunders and appeals to seven.

Justice is all about being fair. Defendants must be seen to be innocent until the evidence proves otherwise. That ancient cornerstone upon which the law sits was booted into touch even before the first team made it onto the field of play. Armed police escorted them from prison to the rear of the court. Someone had made the decision that it had to be made obvious to all and sundry that clearly these were dangerous men and care was taken to ensure that the jury, entering the same building, would be left in no doubt about that. One juror was even heard to complain that police had pushed him aside as he attempted to make his way in, warning him to stay well away from the 'criminals'. At least one daily newspaper found itself in trouble with the court for publishing a photograph showing the security circus.

Saturday's headlines would report that on trial were John Wood, 38; Emmanuel McDonnell, 40; Gordon Ross, 32; Michael Bennett, 37; Graeme Mason, 51; John Burgon, 41; Thomas McGraw, 46; John Healy, 40; William McPhee, 33; Paul Flynn, 36; and Trevor Lawson, 29. They were accused of being involved in smuggling cannabis into the country between 1 January 1994 and 28 September 1997 at a number of addresses in Glasgow; at the Allied Irish Bank, Donegal; at Dover, Gatwick and Manchester airports and in various hotels in Torremolinos, Benalmadena, Salou, Benidorm and Malaga, Spain.

The trial opened with acting police sergeant Ronald Arnott telling how he switched on the flashing blue light of his marked car to stop the white Mercedes driven by Michael Bennett. In the days that followed, Hannah Martin, guaranteed protection by the police if she gave evidence, told of her relationship with Graeme Mason and how the two had carried money abroad, effectively sealing his fate. But there seemed little to implicate most of the others in the dock. Hundreds of pages of telephone records were produced, which, it was claimed, showed that the accused men knew each other and, it was alleged, often called one another at times when the bus was abroad. The Crown had hoped these records would prove the ace card, but this evidence would soon crumble. The defence had been well prepared, and Tam McGraw would show his long days in solitary confinement had not been wasted.

Tam had burned the midnight oil poring over the records and discovered some of the calls had indeed been remarkable. According to the Crown experts, the men had even been telephoning themselves, ringing the very number from which they were calling and then spending some time speaking as the engaged tone bleeped on. On other records, additional numbers appeared to have been added, and a specialist would confirm major discrepancies in the dates when some of these numbers appeared to have been added. For instance, when two numbers had been shown to be in communication with each other, the information relaying this would have been expected to have been collated on the same day. But an analysis of the telephone records provided by the Crown would suggest that one of these numbers had been added at a later date.

Such apparent tinkering left a sour taste in the mouths of the alleged smugglers, who knew that, if convicted, they could be facing very long sentences. Tam McGraw's legal team had warned him to expect 24 years. As the trial wore on, they had a feeling that some of the tactics being used against them were under the belt, to say the least. It was a sensation which took on sinister overtones with the testimony of the two women detectives as to what had transpired when they sat next to Tam McGraw, John Healy and Manny McDonnell in the Chinatown restaurant in March 1997. During the meal, Manny had chatted about the fate of his niece at the hands of Customs officers when they discovered her to be over the limit with her tobacco allowance at Glasgow airport, and about how airports all over Europe were the scene of smuggling.

The version of this given by the two women was that the discussion centred on Nice airport and how it was a top-rate escape route to virtually anywhere in Europe. Tam's story of neighbours held up at Benidorm for four hours in the heat only to be further delayed by a Glasgow Customs check had been interpreted as him warning how Customs monitored passengers, while Benidorm was four hours from an unspecified point by car but longer by bus. They had also noted as important the seemingly innocuous query by John Healy about the McGraws' recent visit to Tenerife.

It was claimed that, throughout the meal, one of the detectives had been jotting down notes about the conversation on a paper napkin, to jog her memory when they later came to write a full report. After the meal, when the three men left, the women went back to their office. Normally, police take extreme pains to preserve any piece of evidence, no matter how apparently insignificant, which will corroborate statements they make and actions they take. The napkin was, then, clearly highly important. The women would merely need to hold it up in court and point to the various words marked on it as evidence of what they had been hearing during the meal. They did not and could not. The blame was put on the clumsiness of a waiter who spilled water over it. That would have been a logical explanation if only the manager of the restaurant had not confirmed that he used napkins made of cloth, not paper. Sitting in the crowded dock, the defendants listened to evidence that one of them considered had been 'refreshed', while others were more blunt. 'Cooked' was their view.

Each day, most of the defendants would turn up in clothes that the jury might have found familiar, having seen the same outfits on them the previous day and the day before that. It was a deliberate ploy aimed at giving the lie to claims that these men were members of a ring that had made fortunes on the back of selling misery in the form of wicked drugs. Appearing unkempt and unable to afford decent garb was bound to cast doubt over such suggestions and, while the reasons for juries arriving at their verdicts are never divulged, it could well be argued that, for many, the dodge worked.

The defendants had no control over the quality or otherwise of the food they had to eat, however. Tam McGraw led a bitter protest on behalf of them all about being forced to exist on Spam sandwiches for the duration of the trial. When their protest threatened to take the form of refusing to move from their cells, new arrangements were hastily made and they were assured of hot meals. Some felt the Spam onslaught was a deliberate manoeuvre on the part of the prosecution, aimed at demoralisation.

There was one more dirty trick still in store. Kari Paajolahti was a 38-year-old Finn with qualifications in accountancy but an even greater skill in the art of being a confidence trickster with the Casanova touch. Jailed for fraud in his own country, he decided not to see out his sentence and took to his heels during a short home leave. He worked briefly in Spain, then Italy, before heading to Scotland, where he was arrested after failing to pay his bill at a Highlands hotel. A routine check with the Finnish authorities revealed Paajolahti was on the run and, in the normal run of things, would have been shipped home on the next available flight. But Customs officers saw in him great potential for a spot of dastardly work. He spoke first-rate English and they wondered how effective it would be to set a thief to catch other thieves. At a meeting with two Customs officers in Edinburgh, one of them Brian Ferguson, the Spanish speaker whose conversation with a taxi driver in Benidorm had been of such significance, the Finn was offered a new career: infiltrating the accused hash-smugglers and reporting back not just on what they discussed but on any plans they had for life on the other side of their trial. His return to Helsinki would be delayed by 'documentary problems', allowing him to spend time in Saughton jail waiting for these to be resolved – time he could use to garner information.

He would be encouraged to gain the confidence of the Glaswegians and to keep in contact with them once he had returned to Finland to finish his sentence. And Customs investigators would see no problems were put in his way about him returning to the United Kingdom in the future. They had a very interesting bonus awaiting if he managed to gain the confidence of the gang. Paajolahti was sent to Saughton's remand wing, where he immediately set about his task of discovering what his targets were all about. His instructions were to mingle with them, not to appear over-curious and to find out whether their guards might be lowered to a foreigner trapped in a strange country. Getting near the men he was briefed to deceive would not be difficult; they were all held in adjoining cells.

The Scots had no idea that their new companion was other than what he told them: a man who spoke four languages – his own, English, Spanish and Dutch – who had run out of money after being ripped off in a deal to buy a forged passport and who was desperate to consider anything that would give him enough to make a decent start once he had served out his jail spell in Finland. They found him affable and friendly. During a visit by his friends in Customs and Excise, he told them he was sure he was making headway. In reality, the group, at first cautious, had become suspicious and felt that for a man facing a potentially unhappy time in his own country, he was too interested in their own predicaments and plans. In three weeks, he discovered nothing of significance, apart from a contact number for one of the accused, but was glib enough on the day he left to convince his Customs handlers it was worth their while helping him to stay in contact with the Scots. By the time he completed the outstanding three months of his sentence in Finland, the trial of the smugglers was over, but a second attempt would then be made to take the mickey out of the gang through the Finn.

chapter twenty-three

MINCE AND TATTIES
ON THE CARDS

DURING THE HEIGHT OF THE ULSTER TROUBLES, THE savagery of many of the paramilitary groups shocked because it knew no bounds. The age, sex and innocence of victims failed to discriminate in their favour when bombs were planted, shots fired. That savagery occurred not only between paramilitaries on opposing sides, or those in competition with one another, but also within a particular group's own ranks. Those merely suspected of stepping from the party line could expect not mercy but bullets in the back of the knees, if they were lucky, and elsewhere, if they were not. Each group had an obsession with its own security that bordered on paranoia. Each set about sniffing out touts with the vigour of witch-finders from centuries past.

Manny McDonnell had spent time in prison because of his dedication to the Republican cause. Support for, and membership of, the paramilitaries had earned him his own Special Branch file. Frequent trips between Belfast and Glasgow and then to Spain had made him the prime police suspect in their search for a Mr Big of the drug-smuggling rackets. He was a known friend and associate of Tam McGraw. Why, wondered Provisional Irish Republican Army commanders in Belfast, had he not conformed to the rules and offered them a piece of the action? As the trial opened, sympathisers in the west of Scotland were ordered to ascertain the extent of the smugglers' operation and, more importantly, how much money they had pocketed. Their reports, if true, of fortunes being made, signalled bad news for Manny. It was permissible to freelance, provided the cause got its cut. But he had and it had not. The men in dark glasses and black berets wanted to know why.

A close relative of Manny's, living in Glasgow, was approached and questioned, but it was immediately apparent the family had not grown rich on the spoils of hash. Indeed, their sole concern lay in getting him home. PIRA, too, now shared that ambition. It could not allow a man who had made such sacrifices to wither away in a British jail, and it wanted to know the complete extent of what had been going on. After all, if the police allegations were true and the scam had been so successful, could it be revived from Ireland? Manny's protestations of ignorance fell on deaf ears; as his relative was told by the two PIRA representatives who called, he was still in the dock, wasn't he?

At a meeting in Belfast, it was decided their comrade needed help. A number of alternatives were proposed and these were passed to Manny during visiting time in Saughton. He was horrified by what he heard. Plan one involved a gun being smuggled to him with which he would be expected to shoot his way to freedom. Under plan two, the van taking Manny and the others back to prison each evening from court would be ambushed at traffic lights, the escorting police disabled and he and his friends sprung. If these failed or were considered unworkable, plan three would be adopted. It seemed the least crazy. After each day's sitting, the courtroom was locked up, with the evidence left inside. Volunteers would simply use incendiary bombs to burn it down, thus destroying any case against him. It was an audacious scheme, which had been attempted unsuccessfully in the past in the Glasgow trial of the notorious XYY armed-robbery gang. If it failed this time, the implications for all the accused would be horrendous, the finger of suspicion over the would-be arsonists inevitably pointing in their direction and almost surely guaranteeing convictions. In the event, the matter was taken out of the hands of Manny and PIRA by the trial judge, Lord Bonomy. On the 45th day, he ruled Manny, Gordon Ross and John Wood had no case to answer and sent them home.

That decision spelled the end of terrorist interest. If Manny had not been involved, then he had nothing to tell. For the others, there were 13 more days to endure. The Crown case, led by Advocate Depute Philip Brodie, was that Tam McGraw was the linchpin of the entire plot, providing the money and the brains. 'The picture seems to be of a resolute person well able to make advantageous arrangements on his behalf,' Philip Brodie told the jury, reminding them that Tam did not pay income tax yet had coughed up £135,000 to buy the Paradise Bar in Donegal and that the money John Healy had been caught with during a Gatwick Airport Customs check in 1994 was his also. Tam's favour to his brother-in-law had come back to haunt him.

Tam McGraw's lawyer was Donald Findlay QC, the best known and most skilled defender in Scottish law courts. He had savaged the police case and, in particular, the versions given by the two women detectives of the Chinatown conversation. He pointed out during a dramatic and enthralling closing speech that one of the female detectives who had given evidence was, at the time of the trial, suspended, having being accused of lying during another case. He would add that Tam was 'really an Arthur Daley figure, ducking and diving in the black economy, doing a bit of this and a bit of that and not paying income tax or VAT. Coupled with his legitimate business activities, his objection to paying income tax explains why he is in possession of huge sums of money. His cash has come from a cash-and-carry business, ice-cream vans and the Caravel public house. There is not a single scrap of evidence in this whole case which, in any way, connects Thomas McGraw with the bus, with holidays in Spain or anything else. There is not a single scrap of evidence that one penny piece of his money reached Spain and was given to somebody to supply drugs.'

It was a superbly crafted address and one which convinced enough of the jury members. They spent two and a half days deliberating and when they returned announced the cases against Tam and Benji Bennett were not proven by a majority verdict. In the public gallery, there were muted cheers and whispers of 'yes'. Billy McPhee and Trevor Lawson went free as a result of unanimously not proven decisions. The jury unanimously found John Burgon not guilty. That meant eight of the original eleven accused had been cleared and could go home. The news for the remaining three men was not so good. Hannah Martin's ex-lover Graeme Mason and tiny Paul Flynn were each found unanimously guilty and given eight and six years respectively. John Healy was convicted on a majority decision and jailed for ten years. There were many who felt John made a fatal mistake by deciding to go into the witness box and give evidence on his own behalf. He had given details of his private life which clearly did not impress women jurors. Had this discriminated against him? No one would ever know. Lord Bonomy had clearly been unimpressed with the presentation of the Crown case. He praised the jury for the way they had gone about looking at 'the welter of evidence which emerged in a fairly disjointed fashion as the trial proceeded'.

Tam McGraw had never doubted that he would be freed. He would never forget the advocacy of Donald Findlay, but at the same time knew an immense amount of preparation to enable every individual piece of Crown evidence to be attacked had been made by his defence team of Liam O'Donnell, Billy Lavelle and Brian Geraghty, the case being put together by Liam O'Donnell.

But there was another reason why he was so certain he would be sitting down that night to watch a rerun of a favourite *Star War*s episode. Margaret had told him so. She had talked over the case with a close friend and the two women had read the outcome in the tarot cards, which they were so adept at interpreting. Outside the court building, Tam, thin and pale after months on prison food, headed for a black BMW in which a friend would drive him to Glasgow. 'You for a beer, Tam?' asked one of the passengers. 'Naw,' was the reply. 'Home. Margaret will be expecting me. She knows I'm coming. She's making my favourite meal – mince and tatties.'

For the police, the outcome was devastating. Years of hard, expensive work with virtually nothing to show for it. Tam's defence had been funded by legal aid, and when the costs were added up it would total £218,000, slightly less than that for John Healy. The total legal-aid bill for the trial exceeded £1.5 million. There would, inevitably, be recriminations. Five days after the trial ended, Lothian and Borders police force, which had shouldered the everyday task of providing armed escorts for the accused men to and from the court, pointed out this had cost them £500,000 when, in fact, the case was nothing to do with them. Strictly speaking, the case involved Glasgow, but because the defendants were well known, it had been decided, in the interests of impartiality, to hold the trial 50 miles away in the capital city. Just for whose benefit that was, no one ever said.

On Friday, 10 July 1998, the men and women involved in Operation Lightswitch drove back to their Pitt Street, Glasgow, headquarters and in a lecture room were thanked by Bob Lauder for their efforts. But he failed to hide his disappointment. The virtual collapse of the case, certainly its failure in terms of convictions, left the Crown little alternative but to scrap other proposed trials of suspects thought to have been involved on the fringes of the smuggling gang.

Someone else would have been disappointed at the end result: the stranger who had sent unsigned cards to those of the accused held in prison on remand over the Christmas of 1997. Inside had been a simple message: 'Wishing you a Happy Christmas – in prison for the next 20 years.'

As for The Man, there were many, including police, who would say he was Tam McGraw. One story that circulated in Glasgow was that he had been spotted sitting in Verde's, the swish Tenerife restaurant, watching buses pull up outside and noting that kids were not seated high enough to see out of the windows. Was he the genius who had dreamed up and controlled the entire enterprise? But then, it couldn't be Tam, could it? The jury cleared him.

The trial would, once and for all, dispel any suggestion that he was hand-in-glove with the police. The same force with which he had been accused of collaborating had striven with all its might to get him convicted. Moreover, when the going got rough, this force tried dirty tricks. No avenue with a door leading to Tam's possible imprisonment had been left unexplored. Teflon Tam, they could call him. But if accusations failed to stick, then that was hardly his fault.

The Irishman, said the gossips, bore all the characteristics of Manny McDonnell and The Driver's role was identical to that played by Benji Bennett. But that couldn't be right, either, could it? The jury cleared them too.

As for Big Ted, he was never caught. He went home never regretting the lifestyle he gave up, with a woman he loved and loves, to dig in his garden, watch trains whistle by on the other side of his hedge and prune his fruit trees.

How much did the bus runs net the smugglers? Only one man knows and he is not telling. The police suggested there had been around 20 journeys. The figure is probably nearer double that, with the gang sharing in the region of £35 million.

Some saved, some spent. But while it lasted, it was some party.

chapter twenty-four

DUMPED

BUT FOR FATE, TAM MCGRAW MIGHT NEVER HAVE SEEN Glasgow, let alone become one of its best-known citizens. His ancestors had spent decades battling the elements in the Hebrides, eventually deciding enough was enough and moving to the mainland. They settled in Dunbar on the south-east coast of Scotland, a town best known nowadays to golfers playing the many superb courses that litter the coastline. One of his distant relatives became prominent in local politics, but lack of opportunity saw them heading into Glasgow and settling in the Calton, a close-knit scheme on the fringes of the Glasgow Gorbals.

It would be a misnomer to describe the Calton as a working-class area. The majority of those living there had no jobs, meaning they had little money. Despite their poverty, they had old-fashioned standards, pride and an innate honesty. Among the families there was a kinship, a common suspicion of strangers and the police and, at least among themselves, honesty. Folks could lie in their beds at night without worrying over whether they had remembered to lock the back door. And, while gangs of razor-carrying youths might roam the streets, their targets and victims lay outside the scheme.

More and more television sets were appearing, but housewives would have to make do with finding the goods shown in TV advertisements in their corner shops. The nearest most came to a supermarket was looking at photographs of the phenomenon in glossy magazines. Not even black-and-white television programmes or the cinema could change the habits of the Calton menfolk. For them, entertainment was meeting friends in the bars that seemed everywhere, with the only woman on show being the barmaid or landlady. Restaurants were the domain of the wealthy – Glasgow's working classes revelled in a take-out from the nearest fish-and-chip shop.

A certain family from Dunbar realised that those living in the Calton had many hungers to satisfy and, accordingly, one branch of the family invested in a chippy, public house and corner shop selling everything from newspapers to tins of treacle from early in the morning until the door was finally closed at ten each night.

Janet McGrow was heavily pregnant when she decided to holiday at Lennoxtown in February 1952. In those days, the beaches of Spain were the preserve of school geography classes; holidays tended to be taken in the chillier surroundings of the Ayrshire seafronts. Many would travel over the Border for the annual and frequently notorious 'Glasgow fortnight', exploring the fairground attractions of the White City at Whitley Bay, near Newcastle upon Tyne. Yet others would spend the vacation in sparse bed-and-breakfasts or caravan parks a bus ride from home. Hardly was Janet's break under way when she went into labour, giving birth to Thomas in hospital at Lennoxtown. When the family arrived back in the Calton with the new addition, Tam became an instant favourite of an aunt who ran the businesses.

How the name-change came about, nobody would know. But when he was first formally registered for school at St James's primary in Calton's Green Street, Tam was listed as 'McGraw'. Maybe it was a slip of a master's pen, maybe his 'o' looked like an 'a', but the new identity stayed and has followed him throughout the remainder of his life. From St James's, he graduated through St John's at Glasgow Green. When his grandparents asked if he would like to stay with them at their home in Barlanark, nine-year-old Tam leapt at the chance. His own home, with his folks, two brothers and a sister, could become crowded. It was the beginning of a love affair with the East End that is strong to this day. Tam stayed there during the week, usually returning to the Calton at weekends. He was enrolled at Pendeen School, where, on virtually the first day, he became firm friends with a younger boy, Drew Drummond. In turn, Drew brought another pupil, John 'Snads' Adams, into the company (the nickname had come years earlier from a school game of juggling with the letters of his surname and replacing the 'm' with an 'n'). That first meeting of the three signalled the birth of the Barlanark Team, an event that might not have had huge significance at the time but which would spell trouble for police forces throughout Scotland as the years rolled on.

Tam spent more and more time at Barlanark, especially after the death of his father from cancer when he was aged 12, but still frequently returned to his mum's home for weekends. He revelled in the rough and tumble at Pendeen School, but, being from the Calton, was looked on as an outsider by many of the other pupils. Two in particular picked on the younger boy, knowing there was no possibility of an angry father knocking on their door after school hours demanding retribution for the blood and bruises they left on his face. He had no option but to suffer their bullying. Some years later, though, the pair would have cause to sorely regret their roles. Tam was seated on the top deck of a bus, heading for home in Barlanark after an evening out with pals in Glasgow, when, as it pulled away from one of the many stops, two heads with loud voices emerged from the top of the stairwell. The recognition was both mutual and immediate. As the sources of such misery from the past began pushing their way up the aisle towards the rear, they were surprised to see their one-time victim stand to block their way. Before a word could be exchanged, Tam launched into his erstwhile tormentors, punching and booting them further and further towards the back seat. His friends, realising their assistance in the dispensing of justice was not required, sat watching the fun and then came up with a suggestion. The vehicle was of the type that had an emergency exit, for anyone on the top deck unable to get out via the stairs. This involved pulling up two handles to open the back window and pushing it outwards on its hinges. While Tam's companions gave an impromptu demonstration of how this worked, he heaved his battered, bleeding and subdued opponents through as the bus came to a halt at one of its routine stops, their cries fading amid insults, catcalls and the laughter of fellow passengers.

By the age of 16, Tam was virtually out of control and constantly at odds with the law. Other teenagers played football or wandered aimlessly about the streets of Barlanark, but he, Drew and Snads felt time was too valuable to be wasted on such irrelevances. They set about thieving with a skill and fervour that more than matched that of the keenest young footballer. Their attitude was that, if something was not bolted in place, it could be carried away and sold.

Their careers in crime began with stealing car hub caps, graduating to car wheels and inevitably progressing to the removal of motors from outside the homes or from the parking places of their owners. Contemporaries stayed away from the trio, warned off either by their own instincts or the sanctions of parents. Mostly the threesome achieved their aims but there were occasions when flight, regardless of consequence, was needed. It was during one of these escapes that Tam badly gashed his hand and arm and was taken home by Snads to have the wound repaired.

The patient was 17 and his nurse was Snads's sister, Margaret. The young couple had seen one another about the streets many times before, but, if this could be classed as such, it was their first formal meeting. Tam went to the house wounded and in pain. He left on cloud nine. He was in love. A year later, when he was 18 and his bride 19, they were married, settling into a flat in Burnet Road, Barlanark. Margaret worked in a Queenslie knitwear factory and her husband was a bus conductor by day and a thief by night.

Not long after the marriage, Tam was persuaded to join a relative of Margaret's who ran a building company, on a site at Spateston, near Johnstone, Renfrewshire. Off he would go each morning with his favourite piece – an astonishing sandwich concoction of brown bread, jam and Cadbury's milk flake. He was given the task of driving a dumper truck, weaving his way through the site each day carrying bricks, rubble, oil drums and, worst of all, sticky wet concrete. His fellow workmen had dug deep pits into which would be sunk massive foundations, and Tam's job was to carry and tip load after load of the mixed concrete into the holes. For a young man with ambition and imagination, the job was monotonous, and he found it increasingly boring. Even worse was the fact that there was no protection from the rain that seemed to fall unceasingly. There came a day when he decided the rain also had its uses. Tam was constantly reminded that it was his job to make sure no concrete remained in the tub of the dumper, so, at the end of each day, he would be left behind with a hosepipe and brush to scrub it clean. It was a messy chore, and frequently he would arrive home with his clothing soaked and spattered with cement. When the rain fell, it effectively did the job for him, washing away the remnants, but blue skies and sunshine meant the residue dried and settled on the metal tub. At the end of one shift, Tam forgot his cleaning duties, with the result that the next day, his colleagues had to drill the rock hard mixture from the tub. The lapse cost the young man a ticking off from the foreman. But he promised there would be no repeat. Like many others in years to come, the gaffer was to discover that Tam was a man of his word. A couple of days later, when it came time to pack up, Tam was reminded his truck had still to be cleaned. 'Leave it to me,' he said. 'I'll take care of it. You'll be able to eat your breakfast off it in the morning.'

His solution to the problem of the mucky truck was simple. Waiting until the others had left and he was alone on the site, he steered it towards the edge of the pit, switched off the ignition, removed the keys, jumped off, gave it a helpful push and watched as it continued on its suicidal run into the mass of still-setting concrete.

'Glug, glug, glug,' was its parting, accusing shot at its driver as it disappeared below the surface. Next morning, Tam was as baffled as his workmates by the case of the missing dumper. He swore it had been spick and span and safely parked when he left and even produced the ignition keys. His innocence was unquestioned, but Tam decided the future had to be brighter. At the age of 20, in 1972, he and his young wife headed for the bright lights of London. They had no jobs, only their savings.

They stepped onto the soil of the capital at Victoria Station but were appalled by the price and filthy state of most of the hotels and guest houses in the area. While they were not entirely penniless, Tam and Margaret were determined to conserve their meagre savings as far as possible. The young couple discovered that by cuddling together during the night the scores of halogen lamps lighting the station gave off enough heat to keep them warm. By day, in between searching for work, they lived off burger bars and in greasy spoon cafés.

They soon discovered they were not alone. Other young Glaswegians had followed the trail to the streets paved with gold – including Snads and Drew. Helpful down-and-outs tried persuading Tam and Margaret that they would be welcomed in Salvation Army hostels, but a quick look, and an even quicker sniff, persuaded them the platforms at Victoria were considerably cleaner. They met scores of others in the same penniless, homeless predicament and a camaraderie developed among the young people. Friends from the East End who had moved to London years earlier offered the couple rooms in their homes, but Tam's pride was evident even then. He felt that to accept would have been to take charity, however kindly meant. The young people believed in one another and were never in doubt that a different sort of salvation lay just around the corner. And their confidence was rewarded.

In Victoria Station, they spotted London Transport advertisements offering work on the buses. Tam's previous experience in Glasgow put them in good stead and both were accepted at their initial interview. A day later, Tam and Margaret went to work as bus conductor and conductress respectively. They moved into a flat in Wimbledon and were confident their move south was about to pay off. It was, but not as they expected. No Glaswegian with an eye for the main chance was going to pass up the opportunity to make money that Tam saw had been thrust his way. He noticed how the majority of passengers paid him little heed as he handed back tickets in exchange for the preferred fare, instead keeping their heads down in books or newspapers or gazing through the windows at a vague panorama of housing estates and shops. Many, as they were leaving, would throw the ticket on the floor, or leave it on a seat. Tam collected the discarded tickets and resold them as new. No one noticed and the scam doubled his wages.

After a year, they decided it was time for a change. Tam was offered work in an electroplating factory at North Cheam run by Changewear, and, if the couple thought their luck had truly turned, it had indeed, because Margaret found a job almost literally across the road, with a company at Morden manufacturing parts for Concorde, which had first taken to the skies four years earlier. Tam's fellow workers were a motley gang, many of them long-haired bikers whose faces showed the scars of many battles. The work was easy, the money not bad and some enjoyed the chance to laze about and smoke a hash pipe or sample blow. Their new Glaswegian colleague wasted no time in picking up the series of stages involved in the electroplating process. Soon he was promoted nightshift foreman.

At the beginning of each shift, the night team would be confronted with a huge vat filled to the brim with hundreds of items to be plated. When they clocked off, the vat would normally still be half-full, the remainder being plated by the dayshift and a newly filled vat being rolled in for the nightshift to start the process all over again. At the beginning of one shift, Tam called his team together and made an offer they could not refuse. If they emptied their vat, plating every item in it, instead of working until six in the morning he would let them go home at four, and he would stay behind until six to stamp their time cards at the official leaving hour. The gang might have had difficulty in understanding every word of his Glaswegian accent, but words like 'increased bonus' and 'early bed' had a stimulating effect. They worked so effectively that, after completing their day's allocation of work, there was time to ride their bikes into the factory, chromium plate every visible part and still be able to leave early. Every item had been plated, and plated perfectly. With the bonuses, the young Scots shift foreman was picking up £600 a week – a fortune then. Within a week, the dayshift found itself arriving with the vat empty and nothing to do until a new batch of unplated material had been delivered.

Tam and Margaret moved to another rented flat, this time in Worple Road, Wimbledon, where they discovered one of their neighbours was the one-time pop singer turned successful actor Tommy Steele. Most mornings, the Cockney would exchange a greeting as Tam passed on his way to bed after yet another nightshift.

Everything seemed to be rosy, yet there were snags to the arrangement. Drew and Snads, homesick for the East End of Glasgow, had returned to Scotland. And as the weeks and months rolled by, Margaret increasingly missed her family. Most weekends she would catch a bus back to Glasgow, leaving Tam working. She longed for the familiar closes, the chatter of her young friends, the comfort of seeing the familiar and loving faces of her own family. Tam sensed Margaret's homesickness. The money was good, he revelled in the responsibility but he too missed the buzz of a Friday night in Barlanark, that familiar Saturday trip to the city centre and the thrill of danger he and the others felt when the Barlanark team was on a raid. In whichever direction they steered their futures, there would be regrets, but then the decision was made for them.

In 1974, Tam was lucky to survive a horrific accident at his works. Attempting to free a section of machinery that had jammed and was causing a blockage in the electro-plating process, he slipped and fell into a vat filled with boiling-hot chemicals, including caustic soda. Fortunately, he plunged in feet first and hauled himself out within seconds. But the pain was excruciating. On some parts of his legs, the skin had literally been burned through to the bone. An ambulance rushed him to hospital. On the way, he lost all feeling in his legs. Burns specialists wrapped them in gauze soaked in soothing oils, but it was weeks before feeling returned. Three months later, he was well enough to be discharged, with the advice of doctors that he should not return to the works ringing in his ears. He visited a lawyer, who promised to win him substantial compensation – and who kept his word. It was time to go home.

chapter twenty-five

ICY CLOUDS

TAM AND MARGARET ARRIVED BACK ON THE STREETS OF the East End in 1974 with their savings and the kernel of an idea. Around every housing scheme in Glasgow, the familiar chimes and catchy jingles of ice-cream vans rang out, no matter what the weather or time of year. To any child, their arrival was the equivalent of return visits from Father Christmas. They sold not just ice cream in many colours and varieties, but cigarettes, sweets, crisps, cans of soft drinks, chocolate, some even offering themselves as unlicensed mobile shops. Each van had its own allocated round, which had been won over the years, often not without challenge from others. For a van to stray over the boundary of a competitor, whether by accident or in a deliberate act of confrontation, was to invite trouble. Owners usually met to sort out disputes peaceably. After all, no one wanted the sight of vans warring for business with the bulk of the custom coming from children and their mothers. When a van was sold or rented, the round came with it, the price reflecting the wealth the round could be expected to produce. Having a van meant long hours on your feet but a guaranteed income of around £300 a week: good money then.

Renting a van often meant having also to agree to buy stock only from the vehicle's owner. This is a common enough condition in any business, but it means being at the mercy of an owner who might decide to increase prices whether or not a hike in cost could be justified. The answer was to buy a van outright, but this solution was not as simple as it sounded. A potential buyer first had to find enough cash. With ownership came freedom of choice, but many of the families who owned the vans were reluctant to part with them. Everyone in the schemes knew the security that having an ice-cream van could provide, but few had the means to come up with enough money for deposits, advances and the cost of stocking up.

Margaret had started working at the W.D. and H.O. Wills cigarette factory to keep the money coming in. She was made redundant, however, when the factory, a familiar city-centre landmark, became caught up in a UK-wide production cutback. It turned out that this was a blessing in disguise. Combined with their savings from London, Margaret's redundancy payment meant that they now had enough money to buy into the ice-cream market.

The Marchetti Brothers, based in Bishopbriggs and run by the Mitchell family, was a long-established name in the ices business. Dozens of Marchetti vans plied throughout the city, and the fleet manager, Jimmy Mitchell, confirmed he would be glad to rent a van to Margaret and Tam, but on the usual condition of tying themselves to Marchetti stock. The McGraws had no alternative. If they wanted to get on the carousel, they had to pay the price, and Marchetti Brothers charged more than most. It was an awkward arrangement because the van had to be garaged nightly and stocked up at the Marchetti depot, which meant Margaret having to travel between her Barlanark home and Bishopbriggs. This was made even more frustrating by the fact that a rival supplier, Fifti Ices, was already based in the East End. Being able to deal with Fifti Ices would have considerably eased the work burden.

Tam would help out and sometimes two friends worked the van for them, but, more often than not, Margaret was left in command and would return late at night to an empty home. Other business needed the attention of her husband, and sometimes that business could take him away. The insatiable appetite of youngsters for Margaret's ice cream saw the McGraw van build up a healthy profit. Of course, others were making considerably more. While he was doing a stint in the van one day, Tam was stopped for a routine police check. Satisfied all was in order and licking his free cornet, the policeman became affable. 'You should be using this to sell drugs. Word is everybody else around the East End is doing it,' he suggested. Tam told him, 'Not a chance. I've never done drugs in my life, and I'm not starting now.'

Eventually the profit from their hired van brought in enough to raise the necessary £12,000 for the McGraws to become owners. The van purchase meant the end of their commitment to Marchetti Brothers, because now they could deal with Fifti Ices, almost on their own doorstep. For a time, things went well, until they began experiencing mechanical problems with the vehicle. Tam bought a replacement on a three-year-contract lease, at the end of which it would be his. He saw how a couple of competitors on similar arrangements were having cash problems, stepped in and took over their contract leases. Having more rounds meant bigger turnover and profits, which Tam and Margaret used to buy more vans. As the mid-1980s approached, they owned around ten and the annual profit was into six figures.

It was good, clean money that meant they could afford holidays abroad and discover Tenerife, where they would invest in an apartment. It also enabled them to give up their flat in Barlanark and move three-quarters of a mile to a detached house in Mount Vernon and invest in the El Paso pub. But holding on to ice-cream rounds came at a cost. There was the constant threat from pirates bent on forcing rivals, sometimes literally, off the road and out of business. The authorities who granted health-and-safety licences allowing vans to trade were continually hearing complaints about cutting in and cutting up but preferred to take the standard pen-pusher's view that these were the affairs of others.

And for those who bought the ice creams and Mars bars, other, more pressing, matters were dominating the headlines. A mineworkers' strike was looming that would see unheralded scenes of savagery. In February 1984, thanks to the help of his pal, Arthur 'The Godfather' Thompson, safebreaker Paddy Meehan had been awarded £50,000 compensation as a result of being wrongly convicted and jailed for the murder of Mrs Rachel Ross at Ayr in 1969 – what, people wondered, would he do with the money? Scots daily read their newspapers dreading to come across stories that yet more of their countrymen had been blown up or gunned down by terrorist madmen in Ulster, where atrocities were commonplace. The time was approaching, though, when the seemingly harmless business of ice-cream selling would bring a tragedy to their own doorstep.

chapter twenty-six

SHOPPED

THERE HAD BEEN ANOTHER MOTIVE FOR TAM WANTING TO
be back in Glasgow. He was keen to link up once more with his old pals Drew
and Snads. So, while the scoops and dollops of ice cream flowed with increasing
profitability, the Barlanark team was reformed.

The gang that had once been guilty of snowdropping, the street term for
stealing washing from lines as it hung out to dry, now found itself the subject of
police reports littered with offences such as 'housebreaking', 'obstruction',
'hindering an emergency worker' and the strangely entitled 'opening lockfast
places'. In other words, they had been leading the forces of law and order a
merry dance. The team would provide the music and call the moves for almost
a decade and a half, although Tam would occasionally be required to adjourn to
a rest room in the shape of one of Her Majesty's prisons, courtesy of the
Scottish legal system. He knew the value of doing his homework, hearing from
their own lips the tales of woe from other villains who had successfully thought
of a way in on a score, but not a way out. Organisation, Tam knew, was the key
to staying one step ahead of the boys in blue, and the antics of the Barlanark
team would not only become legendary but would also inspire others to follow
in their wake, adding to the headaches and confusion facing the hunters.

Every potential target would be carefully cased and every detail noted: the frequency of police patrols, the positioning of telephone wires to surrounding houses and properties, the siting of electricity cables, the types of padlocks used. Did there appear to be young people living nearby, because they would be most likely to stay up late? Did curtains twitch as they walked past, indicating an overly nosy neighbour? Were there dogs in the vicinity? Where were the least noticeable spots to park up and, most importantly, where were the routes leading to and from them? It was essential to know from which direction police might come and which were the easiest ways to main roads. Were there, the team would wonder, unmarked cars coming from police stations and, if so, what were their registration numbers and colours? Crafty busies had been known to give their vehicles quick respray jobs or switch plates around, but these changes were carefully monitored too. Having spent time looking over all the possibilities, the team might not return to the target scene for days or even weeks, reasoning that if they had been spotted looking things over, then the police might have been alerted and could be lying in wait.

Tam and his crew kept a fully equipped robbers' kit containing shortwave walkie-talkie sets, a huge variety of bolt and wire cutters, spare screws, screwdrivers, files, hacksaws, jemmies, including some specially made by a friendly blacksmith for opening safes, dozens of spare car keys, oil cans and ladders. And always a variety of padlocks. They would rarely carry out single jobs. Having done one, they would move on to other pre-arranged jobs in that same night, burgling, breaking and stealing until dawn and the onset of the morning rush allowed them to blend in with traffic as they made for home, having already shared out the loot. Time was money and the raiders might be out at work three nights in a week.

Tam, Drew and Snads would recruit others as the years rolled by, but they would always form the core of the Barlanark Team. And those who found themselves lucky enough to be asked to join were chosen because they had a particular skill, perhaps a knowledge of electricity, plumbing, working at a height or being a driver. A team might be the three main players or perhaps six, the number normally depending on the network of roads to be watched. Each of those selected would know they had to be sure they were not followed, that they had a cover story guaranteeing that no worried wife would contact police to report a missing loved one. Apart from the core trio, no one knew the extent of the night's planned programme or the identities of his fellows. It meant if one man was taken, he would genuinely be unable to spill all the beans to his interrogators. The night's crew would be telephoned, or met earlier in the day, and given simply a rendezvous and a time. Once at the scene, a man would be handed a walkie-talkie and sent to a particular location – perhaps watching a police station, a bar with a reputation for staying open or, more usually, a roundabout or main road – with orders to whisper a warning should danger appear to be heading in the target's direction.

This was before the advent of the mobile, so an essential first ingredient of any break-in was to snip the telephone wires of the target building and those of nearby houses, where someone sufficiently keen of hearing and filled with public spirit might decide that the slightest noise warranted a call to the nearest police station. That meant the only way of alerting bobbies that something was afoot would be on Shanks's pony or by clambering into a car and driving for help. And who would fancy being a Good Samaritan and coming face to face with thieves on the way? Potential have-a-go heroes were not to know that the worst they might encounter would be an anxious robber eager to give reassurance that nothing was amiss. The rule, instilled into everyone ever taking part in a Barlanark Team raid, was that no violence would be tolerated. While Tam attempted to allow for every eventuality, the members of the team were expected to use their own initiative should they find themselves facing the unexpected, but thuggery or violence of any degree brought vicious retribution from police and courts. If a passer-by intervened, they would not be molested or threatened. This peace-at-all-costs policy caused jobs to be aborted, but at least it kept them on a relatively low profile in the eyes of the police.

There would be one exception to the no-rammy rule. One of the team members, T.C. Campbell, would tell how he was on guard duty beneath a motorway underpass when he was forced to take cover to avoid being spotted by a courting couple. They could run through the *Kama Sutra* undisturbed, as far as he was concerned, provided they stayed well away from the action that really mattered. But it soon became evident that the girl was not game for a night's thrashing around in the undergrowth, a fact that only propelled her partner to even greater efforts to persuade her to cooperate. Determined to have his wicked way, he was in the process of ripping off her clothes when T.C., a big man by any standards, whacked the amorous adventurer over the head with his jemmy and then watched as the rest of the team laid the attacker out cold. The young woman, all tatters and tears, was patted on the back and helped on her way by her knights in dark clothing who had appeared from nowhere. It meant aborting the raid and leaving a bulging safe behind, for it to be discovered by baffled police the next morning.

When the jobs were successful, the night's takings would be shared out before everyone made their way home. This meant that no one could nurse any thoughts of having been ripped off. While there was an emphasis on the security of the team, Tam and the others realised that the more men a job required, the less reward there would be for each. A safe might produce £20,000, but with a seven-man team that meant under £3,000 each. Admittedly, this was enough in the late 1970s or early 1980s to provide half the cost of a new home or a bar, but it was still not a fortune.

When it came to deciding the fate of the money, the team had none of the problems facing the modern-day crook, who is expected to provide his, or her, bank manager with evidence of the source of the proffered few thousand pounds. Money laundering was an accepted, though despised, activity, but it was not then fought with the enthusiasm and ingenuity now shown by the authorities of law and order. The robbers simply carried their loot to the nearest bank, where no nasty manager would demand to be told how it had been obtained. As a result, the wisest of the team saved and invested. Many of the others blew the swag as if the stream of sterling would never run dry, but, in Margaret, Tam had a financial adviser to rival that of any corporation.

Some of Tam's reunions after returning to Glasgow came sooner than he had hoped. The early activities of the team led to his being arrested in late 1974 and, in March the following year, awarded a three-month stretch in Barlinnie from a Glasgow sheriff for attempted housebreaking and obstruction. In 1976, he was again arrested and held in Perth prison to await trial and there he met up with a close pal from his Barlanark days. Colin Campbell had become a brilliant engineer after leaving school, but his reading of history and his family name had also taken him into the world of the Irish nightmare and the Ulster Defence Association. Colin became a dedicated and, most dangerously, an active UDA supporter. Like most of the terror groups, the UDA was dedicated to raising cash wherever it could to be used in the fight against Republicans. In Glasgow, it became aware of the success of the then burgeoning Barlanark Team and decided to try its own experienced hand at robbing a sub post office at Mount Vernon. The raid was a badly planned disaster. Staff were threatened with a sword and the sub postmaster attacked. The haul was just £995, and the robbers left so many clues that the police had a comparatively simple job in tracking them down.

Detectives were helped by an anonymous tip-off that the group was part of a UDA unit, and a search of a house in Calton unearthed sticks of explosives and detonators. Special Branch became involved, and at the High Court in Glasgow in June 1974 Colin, then 21, and four other sympathisers were jailed. Malcolm Nicol, described as a top-ranking UDA officer, was given ten years. George Collingwood, Alexander Scott and Samuel Tyrie were each jailed for seven years, with Colin, who admitted stealing a car and taking part in the sub post office raid, being sent away for six. It was the first of several prison terms that would destroy him, including a spell in grim Peterhead, overlooking the fishing port on the north-east coastline of Aberdeenshire, at that time reserved for Scotland's hard cases, men who refused to buckle, who defied discipline and authority and were suspected of plotting escapes. In Perth prison after the post-office debacle, he met up with Tam, who was horrified to find that his friend had given in to the one escape from the boredom and hopelessness of jail life, the cataclysm of drugs. He was not alone; most of the other inmates were hooked. Tam, a fervent non-user, was an exception. He tried persuading Colin to abandon their use but could make no headway.

Despite his personal problems, Colin never lost his bizarre sense of humour. Someone (Tam suspected it was him) slipped heroin or a heroin substitute into Tam's prison tea one evening. The next day, Tam was still hallucinating, seeing three teacups, two spoons. It was a nightmare experience, but he had a perverse sort of revenge. Colin's circle of users wrapped their illicit haul, smuggled in with the help of prison staff, in cellophane and taped it to a filing cabinet in the office of one of the governors. They kept the stash a secret but were suddenly transferred to Glasgow's Barlinnie jail shortly before their release and, on the outside, would bemoan having had to abandon it. By that time, Tam was already free, being let off with a £350 fine at Perth Sheriff's Court in August 1976 for a series of offences of store break-ins and opening lockfast places. The court decided that his stay in prison on remand had been sufficient punishment.

Despite many brave attempts, Colin would never succeed in overcoming the slow death that was his addiction to an increasingly potent array of drugs. He became cunning, signing on with three different GPs in Glasgow and managing to be prescribed by each prolific quantities of painkillers. These were meant to be taken in twos or threes, but he would polish off an entire box at one sitting. Such was his dependency on heroin that he would shoot up as he crossed the city in cars or buses. Each week, he would visit his friends in Barlanark – Snads, Tam and others from the past – who tried, but failed, to hide their despondency at his decline. Eventually, his body could take no more and he perished, angry over the prison system that had set him on the path to self-destruction, and bitter that his offers of becoming a human guinea pig by touring schools to demonstrate to children the effects of drugs had been rejected.

Back in mainstream Glasgow, a chance conversation was to alter the course of the Barlanark team. During a casual meeting at a bar, Tam discovered he was talking to an engineer with the Royal Mail's telephone service, which some time later became British Telecom. By accident, the conversation moved around to new technology and security. The engineer began talking about post offices and sub post offices: how poorly guarded they were, the lack of sophistication of their security and alarm systems. The engineer was not a man who discussed his business with just anyone. He knew that his job required discretion of the highest order. He fancied himself as a professional down to the last terminal and screwdriver. But something clearly bugged him, and he confided his concerns to his listener. Most sub post offices had no alarms. They relied, for keeping their cash safe, on time locks that were so basic they could be disabled quite easily, and on the fact that, if something did go wrong, the safes were too well made to open and too heavy to cart away. At least, that is what the men responsible for postal-service security seemed to think.

His listener could hardly believe his ears. Here were hundreds of thousands of pounds, probably even millions, evenly distributed throughout Scotland, waiting to be deposited in other safes: those used by the banks at which members of the Barlanark team did business. Tam realised his engineer acquaintance had not been telling tall stories. The man genuinely believed the set-up was too lax, too inviting. Well, there was only one way to discover just how right he had been. Within weeks, his words had been put to the test. The three musketeers targeted a sub post office in a sleepy suburb to the north-east of Glasgow. Entering through the front door at night-time by cutting the padlock, they opened up the rear, replaced the damaged padlock with a new one, then switched on a torch and could hardly believe their luck. Between £9,000 and £10,000 was lying in bundles on the floor, postal orders stared at them from open racks and sheets of stamps for buying electricity and authorising television-licence cards, as well as postage stamps for letters and parcels, lay in stacks. It was an incredible haul, but the real target was the safe.

It was dragged outside, heaved into a stolen motor and taken to a deserted quarry outside Glasgow's East End, where the trio set about it with sledgehammers.

At first, the confidence of post-office bigwigs that their safes could never be opened without a key appeared to be justified, and the gang thought they were licked. Then, as dawn introduced more light, they realised that, rather than being a single moulded unit, the safe had simply been made in sections and was riveted together. Within seconds, two crowbars were at work on the rear and rivets were popping like bubbles in a champagne glass. With the back removed, a flimsy block of fire-resistant material was ripped away by hand and minutes later the gang was looking at £50,000 in cash. The total haul for the night topped £60,000, equivalent nowadays to about £165,000.

The success of this post-office break-in led to a whole string of raids, although not all of them went smoothly. On one occasion, so strenuous were Tam's efforts to move a safe by lying on his back and using his feet to push against it, his body needed stitches for his self-inflicted gaping wounds. Another venture ended when the safe toppled on top of one of the gang. A sally into Glasgow's Mosspark ended in a bizarre comedy of errors. Tam was putting so much effort into heaving a heavy safe outside, where it could be loaded into the getaway vehicle, that the strain caused one of his teeth to pop out. It was pitch darkness, the only light coming in bursts during infrequent appearances by the moon from behind the clouds.

'Leave it,' the others urged as Tam fingered the offending hole. 'Get the dentist to stick another one in tomorrow.'

'I'm not leaving it.'

'What's the problem? It's only a tooth.'

'It might be only a tooth to you, but it's my tooth, and if the cops find it, they'll be looking at all the usual suspects to see if they have one missing. They could call on me and try matching it. There's no way I'm leaving it behind.'

'Look, there could be £50,000 in this safe. We'll have to get out of here before somebody hears the din.'

'I don't care if there's £50 million. We stay here till we find it.'

The trio crawled around feeling for the offending tooth. Half an hour later, it was found. And there was still time for a getaway with both safe and tooth.

As the raids continued, the wealth of the Barlanark Team grew. The hired help were advised not to show signs of sudden riches that could attract unwelcome curiosity and jealousy. The sudden appearance of a new car at the front door, or even a new suit or coat for a man's wife, could result in awkward questions from the neighbours as to how it had been afforded.

Yet this was a time when individual enterprise was being enthusiastically encouraged like never before, if not the sort of capitalism practised by the Barlanark Team. The Labour government of James Callaghan was running out of steam and Margaret Thatcher was waiting in the wings to unleash a new reign of Toryism in which adventurism and money-making were to be the order of the day. Like the team, she was all in favour of getting rich quick. And anyone working with Tam McGraw made money – nothing was wasted. It would be said that the team took away enough perforated sheets to ensure that for 20 years they did not need to buy a stamp, pay an electricity bill or cough up for a television licence.

Of course, there was no way the police would take all of this lying down. An investigation by a detective inspector into one break-in saw Tam the victim of an attempted fit-up so amateur it would have been laughable had the consequences not been so serious. It centred on a black Mini, seized along with Tam after the raid. The inspector called in a minion and ordered him to search the vehicle. When the constable reported the car was clean, his furious boss ordered him to search again, even instructing him where he was to 'find' incriminating clues. It was obvious the constable realised he was being cajoled into a glaring fit-up and, to his credit, the man refused to play along. The senior detective was forced to bring in another, more pliant, rookie. 'Try the hub caps; try the glove compartment,' he was ordered, and, sure enough, the charge sheet would reveal detectives had 'discovered' three sets of keys that could be used to steal cars, hidden in a hub cap, while in the glove compartment lay a map of Scotland conveniently marked with crosses on the locations where post offices had been robbed. How remarkable that a skilled team of professional and highly organised robbers should carry with them a map recording their every crime. Arrested and carted off to a police station for a grilling, Tam discovered things had worsened and decided there was no advantage in arguing. He decided to go with the flow, reasoning that the police would report not what he wanted to say but what they felt he ought to have confessed to.

In court, he was asked by the procurator-fiscal about incriminating statements he was alleged to have made to police in an interview room. 'I would have admitted sinking the *Titanic* just to get out of there,' he said, adding, to peals of laughter from the jury, who were clearly dubious about the credibility of much of the police evidence: 'The detective inspector wants to be chief constable, and the more convictions he gets, the better his chances.'

There was to be a bizarre sting in the tail. Tam's usual lawyer had been unable to represent him during the early stages of his arrest so, naturally, he was apprehensive about the understudy who was being called as a crucial defence witness. The lawyer said one of the police officers had admitted to being 'slapped about' by his inspector and warned he would be in trouble if he did not help in fitting up Tam. It was highly questionable evidence and the Sheriff, later to become a High Court judge, intervened to ask about the lawyer's background.

'I spent nine years in the police force before training for the bar, my Lord,' he said.

'And what about that training?' he was asked.

'Two years under you, sir,' was the reply.

The verdict was not guilty.

'I am sorry you've been put through this,' was the Sheriff's apology to the jurors.

Such an outcome was not always the case for Tam. Tracked down after raiding a sub post office at Bathgate in late 1976, Tam ended up at Linlithgow Sheriff Court before a jury who were unsympathetic to his pleas of innocence. The result was 12 months' imprisonment.

Police would, from time to time, visit members of the team to apply heat, more as a reminder they were around than to confront their adversaries with hard evidence. Pressure from the authorities was a fact of life that all criminals strove to accept, but a 'visit' by the team to a bowling club in Glasgow in 1978 brought down heat in a form they could never have expected. The only way in was through the roof, and to ensure the gang could work in the relative security of darkness, alarm wires were cut immediately upon arrival. Unfortunately, a back-up system was in operation which automatically turned on spotlights illuminating the entire front of the building. The solution, suggested by the gang's electrical expert, was to lie them face down on the roof, with the inevitable effect that within minutes it was blazing merrily. Everyone scattered but Tam, who, still blinded by the fire, drove into a policeman manning a road block, throwing him onto the bonnet and breaking the man's legs. It was a pure accident, but he was arrested and charged with the attempted murder of a police officer. However, after a trial the charge was found not proven.

Fate was against the team when it descended on the village of Logan, near Cumnock in Ayrshire, in the early 1980s, to target the local sub post office. The job began with a near disaster. Heading to the scene of the intended robbery in a nippy Mini Cooper car, the vehicle overturned near Strathaven, the car leaving the road on a tight bend. Amazingly unhurt, the gang of four clambered out, righted the car, cut it free of fence wire, pushed it back on the road and continued on their way. Reaching Logan, the Scots were in a merry mood as they forced their way in through the front door, singing and even doing a mock dance to celebrate the unscheduled opening up of the shop. Plundering the premises of everything in sight, they were halted in their tracks by two youths who wandered up, having seemingly appeared from nowhere.

'Any chance of a cig, mister?' one asked.

Tam was feeling generous. 'Help yourselves, lads. Take what you want.'

The two wandered in. Apparently, the sight of the post office being wide open at two in the morning, with strangers carrying out the safe, was not unusual in Logan. They re-emerged clutching cartons of cigarettes, even asking one of the burglars for a light before leaving. On their way out, they turned to murmur a gruff thanks. Their gratitude, it would later emerge, had been short-lived. For now, though, the team paid them no heed; they only wanted to be on their way back home with their haul. Naturally, the money would come in useful, but so would the cigarettes, chocolates and soft drinks removed from the shelves. They would sell well in Tam's ice-cream vans. However, if the outward journey had been difficult, it was nothing compared to what awaited them on the return. Just out of Logan, a flock of errant sheep decided the roadside grass was infinitely preferable to that in their field. It took ten minutes to persuade them to move aside. Further on, the road was blocked again, this time by the police, who had, it emerged, been tipped off by the two young smokers. The four, by now wholly disillusioned, robbers were given a lift in a police van to Ayr, where they were held for four days before being released for lack of sufficient evidence. As they gathered their belongings and prepared to complete the trip back to Glasgow, they were visited by a senior detective. 'Don't come back to Ayr. Keep off my patch or I'll have you,' was his cheerful message.

'But I'm coming to Butlins with the wife and kids,' he was told. 'Does that count?'

The inspector's screams of rage followed them out of the police station.

Ayrshire was not the happiest of hunting grounds for the Barlanark Team. Two of its members visited Dalry late one night to examine possible targets. They had been spotted leaving Glasgow and a general alert was issued for police to be on the watch for them. At Dalry, as Tam and a close friend, Eddie McCreadie, trooped around the village, Eddie announced he was in desperate need to answer a call of nature. He was compelled to disappear from sight and drop his trousers before, much relieved, he could rejoin Tam. Months later, a detective, listening to his protestations that he had never been to Dalry and had only read about the antics of the Barlanark Team in newspapers, interrupted to assure him he knew he had been there. There could be no doubt about it, said the officer. Eddie disputed the claims until the man described, in detail, every action of that night, telling him, 'You squatted beside a bush, and I should know, I was hiding in it. You missed me by inches. We'd been warned to keep an eye out for you, but I never expected to get so close.'

Another time at Kilmarnock, Tam, Snads and Eddie were in the process of carrying off a post-office safe when the brothers-in-law began arguing over the best way to lift it.

'Whoa, hold it there.'

'I'll need to put it down.'

'No. Hang on till I shift my grip.'

'I'm telling you it's breaking my arms.'

'Just hang on till I move around.'

'No. I'll move around; you hang on.'

'No. It's easier for me. Stay where you are; keep it up.'

'Look, ya prick. I'm putting it down.'

'Who you calling a prick?'

'You, ya bam.'

'Listen, ya prick, don't put it down till I get a better grip.'

'No, you listen, ya bam. Don't call me a prick.'

'I'll call you a prick because you are a prick.'

And so it continued, insults flying over the safe as Eddie, at first bemused, then astonished and finally horrified, waited in vain. The gang had been tipped off that the safe could contain as much as £40,000, but no degree of arbitration could settle the dispute and, thanks to the noise they had made and the time they'd already wasted, the sealed treasure was eventually abandoned to the pavement.

There were other setbacks. During a raid on a coal depot at Baillieston, Glasgow, the gang hauled themselves up three flights in a rickety wooden building. The safe was cemented into a concrete base and there were some who doubted whether the effort of moving it would be worthwhile. With the aid of crowbars, it was eventually forced out, only to vanish through the wooden floor. A member of the gang on the floor below was surprised to hear a rumble and cracking from the ceiling, followed by the sight of the safe appearing, dropping and vanishing from a spot near his feet. He looked up to see the surprised faces of his accomplices and down to a cloud of dust. The team rushed downstairs and found the safe on the ground floor. Deciding it had at least saved them the problem of heaving it down three staircases, they jemmied it open to find only a few pounds inside.

During a foray to Livingston, two of the gang were busily attacking a safe freshly hauled from a sub post office when a police car unexpectedly arrived. To attack a cop was out of the question, so, still clutching crowbars, the pair took to their heels, leaping fences but ultimately realising the fitness of the young officer chasing them was winning the day. There was nothing for it but to stop, turn and face their pursuer. 'Right, give yourselves up,' he ordered, unable to hide his nervousness while his confidence visibly drained away. What little authority he had vanished as he turned to discover he was alone.

'Clear off or we'll stick these crowbars up your backside,' his adversaries promised, and the policeman took to his heels, back in the direction of the safety of his car, howling for help.

'He'll go far,' said one of the crooks. 'Probably end up a chief superintendent. What a shitebag.'

Over the years, around 14 men would be involved in Tam's Barlanark Team. Its activities were indeed prolific, but even he began wondering at the scale of the raids attributed to the gang. There seemed to be one a night, sometimes two a night, in different parts of Scotland. The reason was, of course, simple. Others from Barlanark had formed their own gangs and had a similar modus operandi to that of Tam and his men. There were at least two other teams, and it was one of these that would bring Tam as close to major grief as he would ever come.

Sub post offices were such soft targets, it was difficult to resist them. Tam's advice was that nothing traceable should be taken away, such as postal orders, because, while often adding up to many thousands of pounds in face value, each carried its own individual serial number and had to bear the name of its authorising post office. The team soon received an indirect lesson in the importance of this precaution. During an attempted raid at Condorrat, Tam and other members of the gang were arrested on suspicion of planning a break-in. They were taken to Cumbernauld police station and, to their surprise, held amid conditions of unusually strict security. The reason would soon become apparent.

Two men entered the interview room where Tam was being questioned and waved out the detective constable, who had been attempting to persuade him to make a statement. They introduced themselves as Special Branch officers.

'We heard you're the post office specialist,' said one.

'Don't know what you're talking about,' said Tam.

'Of course not, but somebody has been doing sub post offices.'

'Not me.'

'Naturally, but whoever has been doing them has been very naughty. They've been taking away very high values of postal orders.'

'I wouldn't know a postal order if you put one in front of me.'

'And sending them over to Northern Ireland.'

'I don't know anyone there.'

'Certainly you don't, but the point is these are being sold and the money distributed to paramilitaries.'

'What are paramilitaries?'

'Well, the UDA, IRA. We suspect these are being given to the UDA. Their people cash them in and use the money to buy guns and explosives that kill innocent people and even our own soldiers. We know from the serial numbers that the postal orders are from Scotland. We can even identify which sub post offices they've come from and these are always places where there have been break ins. Do you know anything about this?'

'Absolutely, honestly, no.'

'Have you any political leanings? Do you support any of the terrorist factions in Northern Ireland?'

'Definitely not. I'm just not interested in politics. I'm for Queen and country, right behind our soldiers. I even know the families of some of the boys out there, so I'd hardly be likely to do anything that would help the bastards trying to kill them.'

'OK, Tam, we believe you. We didn't think this was your style but we had to ask. We're not asking you to tell tales, but any idea who's behind this?'

'Sorry, no.'

'Right, well, you're clearly a public-spirited sort of man who would want others not so upright as yourself to know that if this continues, the heat is going to come down on everyone from a very great height and at a very strong temperature.'

'I understand, but I just can't think who would do this.'

'All right, but a word of free advice. Never touch banks; that's how you get the big boys coming after you. Banks get you into trouble.'

'The only time I'm near a bank is to put my wife's money in.'

'OK, off you go. Your pals are free to go as well.'

Tam was furious. He realised that one of the other teams was behind the traffic to Ulster. It was sheer stupidity, because the presence of the Special Branch had shown just how seriously the authorities would regard help for terrorists. Back in Glasgow, he put the word about the streets of the city that it had to stop. If it did not, then the perpetrators would need to answer to him. It ceased. But the team realised this was an awkward development. Until the matter was shown to have been sorted and had gone away completely, sub post offices would be monitored all the more carefully. Maybe, they wondered, it was time to diversify. And for a time they did.

Little went on in the East End of Glasgow that was not widely known. It was impossible to keep a total secret of who was doing what and, sometimes, who was doing what with, and to, whom. This knowledge hardly ever left the schemes, though, which were worlds to themselves. Barlanark was effectively a big village where strangers were looked upon with suspicion and the police regarded as outsiders. What went on there was the business of Barlanark folk and no one else. Many knew who made up the Barlanark Team and the identities of those in its replica groups, but that was the business of the boys involved and nobody else. And the boys paid for that discretion with little kindnesses, especially around Christmas time and Hogmanay.

A store somewhere might be robbed of its safe and discover the entire contents of its deep freeze had also gone in the night. Maybe it was purely coincidence, but East End families might be eating well on roasts and turkeys for a few days afterwards. The Barlanark Team itself was known to take on jobs because a member needed to pay for a special occasion. One robbery was planned specifically because money was needed to fund a family christening, another to pay for a particularly precious first communion. These were important occasions in the lives of the children of team members and had to be celebrated in a style that would make them long remembered.

Then the team was constantly being sounded out, with massive discretion, of course, by parents wondering if a certain type of stock, say, household furnishings or electrical items, might be available at some time. This was not stealing to order, but it did raise awareness of the fact that if a certain item appeared, there was a ready market for it. Hard-nosed corporation men would say this was simply the law of supply and demand, which was what business was all about. In Barlanark, few knew about Mammon. For most, life was a perpetual struggle against increasing costs and diminishing income. Yet hard-up families with little money and few prospects were still proud of being able to invite neighbours and visitors to a clean, comfortable home. Admittedly, the furniture might be scuffed and fitted carpets a rarity, but every now and then an opportunity would come along for some home improvements.

So it was that, during a snowy evening, an articulated-lorry driver made the mistake of parking his vehicle in the East End of Glasgow. The man regularly brought his lorry up from England to a major store in the city centre. Usually, he would arrive by day, unload, book into a bed and breakfast and return south the following morning, well fed and rested. This time, he had a motive for changing his routine. During his unloading, he had become friendly with one of the store assistants, a married woman whose husband happened also to be a lorry driver, specialising in runs to the Continent that could take him away for a week or ten days at a time. The driver had invited her for a drink, and, much to his delight, the invitation had been accepted. As in these matters, one thing led to another and it had been suggested that the driver might wish to make an alteration to his programme. When her husband was next away and he was due to deliver to Glasgow, what if he arrived in the evening and unloaded the next morning, then headed for home? And, instead of checking into a bed and breakfast, why not stay with her? The driver had gone along with the suggestion and, following her directions, had driven his articulated lorry along Edinburgh Road and into Barlanark, where he had parked up for the night and headed off for the promised frolic beneath the blankets.

The woman greeted him wearing a particularly revealing baby-doll nightdress. The man appeared to be in a trance, besotted, and knew paradise awaited. But then, she had a particular reason for wanting to make sure his stay would be a long one. As the lovers snuggled up, their antics steaming up the bedroom windows, outside in the cold other East Enders were also busily engaged in frantic activity. The woman had happened to pass word to a member of the Barlanark Team that a visitor from the south would be coming up bearing gifts and where these might be found. A unit of the gang had been primed to be ready and, minutes after the driver locked up and abandoned his vehicle, it was as though piranha fish had arrived in the area.

In the reflection of the moonlight on snow-covered roads, a passer-by would have seen the rear doors of the wagon jemmied open and bundles of carpets hauled out, the gang heaving them along the ice to a quiet spot where locals queued up with their flooring measurements as sections were snipped to order. Tables and chairs disappeared, and even a sideboard, but it was fair to say that not everything was stolen. The next morning, the driver, discovering the theft, would have the good sense to take his motor to the city centre before calling police, angrily cursing the fact that his load had not even been safe in a well-lit street. There was fresh snow on the ground when he next called on the wife. This time, he was taking no chances, leaving the lorry within sight of Strathclyde Police headquarters in Pitt Street and taking a taxi to Barlanark, where he failed to notice the new carpet as he padded across the bedroom floor.

It was not the Team's only successful venture into the carpet trade. They were tipped off about a huge stockpile of top-grade carpets and rugs being stored in a factory warehouse in Templeton, Glasgow. During a reconnoitre, the gang leaders realised that this was more than simply a case of pulling alongside with a van, loading it up from a factory side door and making off. There were so many thick-pile carpets that lorries, not vans, would be needed for the getaway – and giant articulated lorries, at that. Three self-drive vehicles were hired. A night was chosen for the job and a team assembled. The date had been selected with care because the last thing the gang needed was a nosy policeman catching them in the act. And what would keep scores of Strathclyde's finest occupied elsewhere? An Old Firm encounter, of course.

This particular game was being staged at Parkhead, just along the road from the factory. Admittedly, having the match played at Ibrox, three miles to the west, would have been better, keeping the law even further out of the way. But the gang had been warned a major stock clearance was in the offing and delaying the robbery could leave them with a comparatively tiny haul. So, muffled by the sound of cheering and screaming crowds – a noise level that would have drowned out the loudest rock band – a giant heavy metal roller guarding the main delivery point eased its way upwards and articulated vehicle number one backed in. Willing hands loaded it up and it was on its way. In moved the second lorry, but there were so many carpets the job of loading up was taking longer than had been bargained for.

Still, the referee at Parkhead might have been checking his stopwatch, but not the players further along the road. This was quality stuff, worth a fortune and there for the taking, and if extra-time was needed then so be it. In went lorry number three, but as the last shag-pile was thrown in, the whistle sounded, bringing the game to an end, and within seconds hordes of police officers appeared as if from nowhere, on foot, in cars and vans, riding motorcycles and even on horseback. Cursing, and muttering that they should have cleared out while the going was good, even if it meant leaving some carpets behind, the remaining team members were convinced the game was up and began mentally concocting coincidences for being in the area. Next minute, a policeman was standing at the front of the remaining lorry, blocking its departure.

There was absolutely no chance of a getaway. Thousands of fans were streaming past – a human river totally blocking the way to the safety of the main road – while a solid phalanx of cars was creeping along London Road, the route by which they had planned to leave. Police were swarming around the junction that the previous lorries had used as their escape route. The gigantic vehicles were now miles away, heading to a fence over in the east of the country. Then, as if by a miracle, the boys in blue were stopping traffic, football fans, anything or anyone who moved, all for them: giving them an opening to freedom. There was even a friendly wave for the driver as he heaved the steering wheel in the direction of safety and speechless with astonishment and nerves, stalled the engine before driving off. It was a narrow squeak, but then there were many.

During a raid near Stirling, the gang were surprised by police and took to their heels in varied directions. One of their number had obviously drawn the short straw and was chased by a police officer. The bobby was accompanied by a particularly evil-looking Alsatian that gave the impression it had not been fed for some time and was looking forward to sinking its teeth into him. The villain crashed through a hedge, clean into, and out of, a greenhouse, destroying much of an amateur enthusiast's tomato crop and, his body entwined in creepers, came to the edge of the admittedly fledgling River Forth. Urged on by the sound of the dog, he did not hesitate for one second, plunging in and making for the opposite bank while the mutt did likewise. The swimmer was momentarily halted by the pleadings of the policeman.

'Come back, you daft bastard.'

'Who, me? Not likely,' shouted the crook as he ploughed on.

'Not you. My bloody dog. It can't swim.'

Happily, both man and dog made it to their respective banks.

Tam would not show the same daring when water impeded his escape after a raid at Drongan in Ayrshire went wrong. Just a week before a bonfire night, they discovered the shop they had targeted was packed with fireworks. Shelves were crammed with boxes of rockets, Catherine Wheels, sparklers, whizzers and bangers, which were loaded, as an afterthought, into a stolen transit van. Unfortunately, neighbours had heard noises in the night and called the police. A dramatic chase followed, with the van careering along narrow country roads until it failed to negotiate a bend near Galston, finally coming to a halt halfway through a garden fence at a dead end. Emerging from the battered van, Tam saw a bewildered couple peering from their bedroom window. The occupants of the transit took to their heels, splitting up in the darkness. It seemed to Tam that he ran for miles before coming to a river. There was no way, he decided, he was risking death by drowning, but his luck was in and he was able to escape by shinning across a water pipe. When the thieves were reunited the next day, he told them what had happened.

'Jammy sod,' one told him. 'I fell in.'

The unexpected was always expected – like the night outside Cumbernauld when the team was in the process of trying to open a safe and the sound of a woman's voice came from the darkness.

'What's going on?'

'Mending a puncture, missus,' one of them answered.

'Aye, that'll be right. You keep your spare tyre in that safe? I'm off to phone the police.'

'Aye, away ye gaan, hen,' he said, directing her to the nearest telephone kiosk, knowing every wire in the vicinity had been cut an hour earlier.

Men invited to go on a raid were carefully vetted beforehand and, if they could take orders, be discreet and get the job done, they would be asked back. Jonah Mackenzie, one of the Barlanark old boys, joined the gang, but when Tam discovered he was also working with a rival team, he was told his services would never again be needed. It was a sensible precaution, but Jonah felt bitter at being dropped.

Glasgow Road, Denny, in Stirlingshire, is a pleasant street sloping downwards to join Denny Road, taking traffic from Dunipace and Denny towards the M80 and M876. On one side, a hedge hides fields from passing cars, buses and lorries. These occasionally stop at a store midway down the gentle incline. That store was the scene of an astonishing drama involving the Barlanark Team.

The gang had carefully cased the place and identified the most likely sources of trouble. One man, carrying a walkie-talkie, was stationed at the foot of the hill, another near the summit and, as darkness fell, the team leader was in touch with each, making sure the communications were working and they were alert. During their daylight reconnaissance, the team would already have gazed upwards and followed the paths of wires leading into estates and houses in the vicinity. In Glasgow Road, they knew precisely which wires needed to be cut. Never an easy job, this was usually left to the team leader. There was always a risk element, because the actual snipping involved receiving a 12-volt current of electricity, normally safely absorbed by the double rubber gloves that held the long-handled wire cutters.

Nobody knows quite what went wrong on this particular night, but an almighty flash and bang was followed by the sight of the man being blown completely over the road, through the hedge and into the field opposite the store. Tam lay there, looking at the stars and wondering if he was dead or seriously injured. Realising that neither was the case, his brain immediately began working. 'Get to fuck, get to fuck,' he repeated to himself.

The rest of the gang, having seen his unchartered flight, preceded by an impressive display of sparks and bangs, were by now already thinking along similar lines. As a blackened, scorched apparition emerged through the hedge, hair standing on end, his face masked in bewilderment, to the accompaniment of a flood of bedroom lights switching on, they gathered what equipment they could find and took to their heels towards their getaway car park, sited in a nearby housing estate. From there, they watched a squad of police arrive, uncertain as to whether the cable had been severed by accident or design. Policemen wandered to and fro, chatting to nearby residents, then sat in their cars waiting for post-office engineers to turn up. For the Barlanark Team, the fact that the police were where they could be watched and the telephone system was out was too good an opportunity to be missed. Having lost out on one target, they simply burgled a nearby off-sales while waiting for the fuss to die down.

In addition to what was stolen during these raids, the damage done to Royal Mail and Post Office Limited was, in terms of cost, horrendous. Teams of engineers would effectively follow the burglars around central Scotland repairing the damage. Officials of the telephone and postal service set up a special squad to try trapping the gang, by being on-hand to identify, in double-quick time, sudden and unexplained cable faults. Someone even costed that it would be cheaper for the Post Office to offer the gang compensation to give up their exploits.

To the gang, the whole affair was a game, but their sense of humour was not shared by the Scottish Crime Squad, which took the job of trapping them seriously. The robbers were convinced that the hunters would go to any lengths to put them behind bars, even to the extent of manipulating evidence – a threat that inspired them to take even greater care and precautions. Yet, despite this, a club in Gartocher Road in the East End of Glasgow was robbed three times. The KSC social club in Moodiesburn had its takings removed. The El Paso pub in Barlanark, which would be bought by Margaret McGraw, was burgled. And, again in Moodiesburn, the sub post office was to suffer a similar fate, inspired by the need of one of the gang to pay for a family party.

The post office's security consisted of a time lock, and the team reckoned that inside the safe was at least £100,000. The pod holding the time-lock unit was disabled in seconds with the aid of a giant crowbar. The gang, experienced in such matters, had already prepared a padlock identical to that on the post office. It took just a minute to cut through the original, get entry, open a door to allow others inside then replace it with a spare. Inside, they discovered an Aladdin's cave. There was so much money around that the safe would not hold it. Cash was strewn everywhere, thousands of pounds in silver coins having been left in bags on the floor. The safe was hauled out and one of the watchers given the bags of silver to look after. He laid them on a wall outside the home of a nearby resident. But the safe was so heavy the robbers realised their own car would not be big enough to carry it. Two of the gang then set off to steal an estate car.

When they returned an hour later, they discovered, to their horror, no sign of the others, whose confidence had waned with the passing of the minutes.

Thinking the expedition party had been caught, those left waiting had made their getaway in the car, forgetting the bags of silver, which were never subsequently found. Meanwhile, the car thieves hunted high and low but eventually, finding no trace of the car they had arrived in, decided there was nothing for it but to abandon the search and head home. Heaving the safe into the stolen estate car, they drove off along back roads towards the Easterhouse suburb of Glasgow. On the way, they stopped at a bridge, dragging out the safe and opening it with a series of movements with jemmies, not unlike the unpicking of stitching, before setting merrily off over fields singing and carrying the swag in sacks. They had got away with it yet again, but at the back of his mind Tam had an uncomfortable feeling that all was not well. He wondered whether their luck was running out, or was there a more sinister element seeking to bring the gang down?

When the Barlanark Team next decided to score at a sub post office in Cultenhove Road, St Ninian's, Stirling, they took along a car and a van. Tam had mentioned their target was in Stirling, being no more specific than that – and he had made a mental note of exactly who knew even this small piece of information.

They broke into the rear of the building after taking out telephone lines and replacing the padlock. The safe was hauled out but, unknown to them, two police officers were on duty nearby and were leaving a house where they'd been having fun with the wife of a man with a criminal record. Their unmarked car had been parked a few yards from the sub post office, with the team spotting it but not knowing who it belonged to. The van and car containing the robbers sped off, but police, already tipped off about a raid somewhere in the town, set up road blocks and stopped both car and van. The occupants of the car were asked where they were going.

'Heading for Aberdeen. We came into Stirling to try to find something to eat.'

It was three in the morning but fortunately the police believed the tale and told them, 'On your way,' even directing them to the all-night Stirling Services a couple of miles away.

The drivers of the van were not so lucky. When the police opened up the back of it, there stood the safe. Billy McPhee, the driver, ended up in front of a High Court judge, who, astonishingly, gave him community service. It was a punishment that amazed everyone, except Billy, who told his bemused associates, 'I knew I'd get away with it. Somebody in there likes me. We use the same swimming baths.'

The outcome might have been a lucky one, as far as the gang was concerned, but it had left a nasty taste. Tam was convinced a fly had landed in the ointment, that someone was grassing. His natural suspicion pointed towards Jonah, who was bitter, irked, at being left out in the cold. But he would never learn the truth.

And so, as the curtain began inching down over the 1980s, the era of the Barlanark Team came to an end. The decision to put the operation into cold storage was Tam's. Margaret had become increasingly worried over the years by police attempts to trap her husband. She knew of cases where police had been accused of framing suspects to guarantee a guilty finding, and she did not want that to happen to Tam. An appearance at Glasgow Sheriff Court in February 1983 brought Tam a six-month stretch for theft, break-ins and opening a lockfast place. He loathed prison, missing freedom and especially Margaret's home cooking, and it would be seven years before he was again in a courtroom, fined £50 for theft at Glasgow District Court in January 1990.

The couple's son, William, was coming into his adolescence and Margaret dreaded the prospect of the boy's father being hauled off for a long prison stretch. In any case, the scam had run its course. Sophisticated security systems were being installed even in minor businesses, chief constables were equipping their men with high-tech communications systems which by-passed telephone landlines and neighbourhood-watch groups were recruiting honest citizens as amateur lookouts. It was time to move on.

One East End Glaswegian was never to know he had played a leading role in the gang's success. For almost two years, he parked his Rover car outside his home each night, locked it and climbed into bed. Regularly, in the early hours, the team opened it with a set of replica keys, climbed in and drove off on raids, piling cigarettes and spirits, cash and the other contents of post offices into the boot. After sharing the loot, the car would be filled with petrol, wiped down and returned to the exact same spot. As one of the team said: 'The owner ran around in the car for two years and never once needed to buy petrol. Either he knew what was going on, or he must have imagined he had a fairy godmother. He climbed in each morning to find his petrol tank full but never ever complained to the police.'

No one counted the number of scores they took down, and to this day no one is saying how many, but it probably runs into hundreds. That they were able to survive was due to professionalism and no small degree of luck. Some police officers grudgingly admired the meticulous planning, even down to the gang occasionally stripping naked before reaching home after bursting open a safe to avoid tell-tale dust being carried onto carpets and floors.

chapter twenty-seven

JURY SERVICE

IN THE EARLY HOURS OF MONDAY, 16 APRIL 1984, NINE members of the Doyle family were asleep in their top-floor flat four storeys up at Bankend Street, Ruchazie, when flames were spotted coming from their only exit door. Firemen were on the scene quickly but their gallant efforts and those of paramedics, doctors and nurses, both at the scene and in the next few days, were unable to prevent mass death. Six of the family perished: Christine Doyle Halleron, aged 25; her baby son, Mark, 18 months; James Doyle, Snr., 53; and his sons James, Jr., aged 23; ice-cream-van driver Andrew, 18; and Anthony, 14.

As public outrage shrouded the aftermath of the tragedy, stories began emerging of bitter rivalry between those running the ice-cream vans. There was talk of vehicles trying to run one another off the roads and even of shots being fired and windows shattered, and that the ice-cream business had been taken over by gangsters. Glasgow's housing schemes, declared the media, were the battleground for 'Ice-Cream Wars'.

Rather than diminishing, as the days rolled by, public hysteria and frenzy increased, finally reaching the team of detectives, led by Chief Superintendent Charlie Craig, set up to investigate the six murders. Craig, big and overweight and with a liking for pulling the straps of his braces while confronting cowed suspects, was under extreme pressure to produce a result. The longer cells remained empty, the greater became that pressure and the shorter Craig's temper and that of his deputy, Detective Superintendent Norman Walker.

The consequences are well documented. Thomas 'T.C.' Campbell, Joe Steele, William 'Tamby the Bear' Gray and Gary Moore were arrested on the word of a liar, William Love, who said he overheard them in the Netherfield Bar in Glasgow plotting the fire. In Glasgow's Barlinnie Jail's 'C' hall, they met up with Tam McGraw. He had been strolling along Edinburgh Road, Barlanark, when three police cars had blocked his progress. Without being told why, he was put in handcuffs, taken to a police station, shackled to a radiator and told by a red-faced and angry Craig that he was suspected of killing the six Doyles and also of attempting to murder Andrew Doyle six weeks before the fatal fire.

The police based their allegation on two claims. One came from a woman who declared she had seen him carrying petrol into the home of T.C. Campbell. The other was that he had been seen in a Ford Escort in Bankend Street around the time the fire began. As did the other accused men, Tam angrily protested his innocence from the outset. All were warned by friends that they would become victims of a police fit-up. The word was that high-ups had unofficially given Craig and his troops virtual carte blanche for six weeks to run riot through Glasgow, at the end of which if there was no result, well, Craig could find himself back in uniform.

It would later transpire that the accuser of Tam and T.C. had a wayward son facing serious criminal charges, which mysteriously and coincidentally evaporated around the time she told the police of her petrol and car sighting.

The circumstances of the story of the Ford Escort were even more sinister. Tam had decided to buy Margaret a new black Ford Escort XR3i and the sale was to be completed on 13 April. He went to the suppliers in Rutherglen on that day but discovered that a door panel on the new motor had been damaged. Assured it would be repaired, he insisted on a totally new vehicle and, to make sure he was not given the original with the damage made good, he carried off its registration plates. He took delivery of a brand new replacement on 19 April, which meant he could not have had a Ford Escort on the night the Doyles were burned alive. Through his lawyer, Tam gave this information to the police, who visited the car suppliers. Margaret would later be warned that detectives had attempted to pressure the salesman into making a statement to the effect that the McGraws had the car on the 13th, and not six days later, thus enabling them to put Tam at the murder scene. To his great credit and courage, the man refused, and Margaret was told, 'The police are fitting your man up.'

Craig tried bluffing to Tam that he had evidence of involvement. But he was forced to release him. Tormented by the need to appease his superiors, Craig would have hung on to Tam had he the slightest fragment of evidence against him. He did not. Gary Moore would be cleared of the murder but had to suffer the ordeal of a trial. Tamby Gray was also acquitted of murder but convicted of blasting a shotgun at the ice-cream van driven by Andrew Doyle and given 14 years. For T.C. Campbell and Joe Steele, the wait for justice lasted almost 20 years before judges decided they were victims of a miscarriage.

Charles Craig would die from an apparent heart attack in 1991, aged 57, his career blighted by allegations that he was a notorious liar and fit-up merchant. Norman 'Norrie' Walker drove out of Glasgow one day four years after T.C. and Joe were sentenced to life imprisonment, attached a hosepipe to the exhaust and went to sleep forever as he breathed in death to the sound of the running engine. The careers of both policemen were left stained by ignominy.

The tragedy of the Doyles impacted on many others: those who were wrongly jailed; those such as Tam, who suffered then and still suffer the stigma of having been accused; and those decent police officers working on the case whose only ambition was the honest prosecution of the genuinely guilty.

Not long before the trial of the men accused of the Doyle murders at the High Court in Glasgow, Tam and Margaret McGraw received official letters. They contained routine instructions to report for jury service. After a telephone call, they were assured they would not be required.

chapter twenty-eight

CLOCKING OUT AND IN

TAM DESPISED 'THE LICENSEE' TAG BECAUSE IT HAD BEEN used to allege he had an agreement, a licence, with Strathclyde police to get away with crimes in exchange for passing information.

There would also be those who would unkindly suggest that the Caravel, under Tam's and Margaret's management, became a meeting place for villains. Others would criticise it as being a den of thieves, a nest of gangsters. Certainly, the bar attracted its share of men with money-making ideas that were outside the law. The respective members of the various Barlanark Teams would meet from time to time, but purely to socialise and not to discuss business. That took place in the open air or the privacy of a car, where there was no possibility of being overheard.

Gordon Ross and, later, Chick Glackin would become regular callers. Gordon had people to meet. He was part of a busy service driving hashish from Spain into France, where vans and later buses would smuggle the contraband into Scotland. But he was aware of Tam's aversion to drugs and would only speak in hushed tones, out of his hearing. John Healy would often pop in for a chat with his brother-in-law. John would earn a reputation in the Thornliebank district, where he had his own pub, for not tolerating trouble or drug-dealing. It was said that, after he was imprisoned for his role in the hash-smuggling enterprise, heroin dealers took advantage of his absence to move in, causing mayhem.

Trevor Lawson was another frequently seen at the bar or sometimes at the pool table, where he fancied himself as a man to be reckoned with. One night, the smugglers, after a gathering at the Marriott Hotel in the city centre, adjourned to the Caravel. It was a night for fun and laughs and drink flowed. Trevor was soon at the pool table taking on all-comers. It always added to the excitement to have a small flutter on a game, and the stakes were £10 a match – too much for the ordinary Barlanark regulars but a drop in the ocean to the smugglers, for whom money was not so much a necessity as a toy. Some of the games were tense, and the stakes became higher. Sometimes the matches were between individuals; on other occasions, the players would split into teams. One team match was played for £500 a side. It was clear that Trevor and John were the pick of the players, and John proposed a £1,000 bet on a single frame of pool between them.

'No,' Trevor said. 'Let's play for £10,000. You put up the cash and if I lose I give you my Rolex watch. It's worth a lot more than that.'

The room went silent. It was clear the other smugglers were worried about this development. Twenty thousand pounds might not have been a fortune in their terms, but it was still an awful lot of money. The winner might go home happy, but would the loser feel bitter and angry? Might the loss lead to resentment? Disharmony among the gang, no matter what the motive, could not be allowed. It was at this point that Tam intervened and refused to allow the gamble. The relief at his decision seemed to extend to the players. There were times, the others decided, when they relied on the authority of The Licensee.

Tam's moniker had a further possible interpretation. Running the Caravel was effectively the equivalent of being presented with a licence to print money. Most pubs were relatively quiet mid-week, but the Caravel, with its bar, lounge and off-licence, could run £4,000 through the till in a single day. At weekends, it was generally heaving. Takings of £14,000 were not unusual, and Tam showed how acute was his head for business by charging punters who wanted to drink late an extra £2 a head to stay, telling them he had to meet additional overheads. Despite attracting most of the local hard cases, and some from further afield, there was rarely trouble. Joe Hanlon's presence was clearly a factor in this, and occasional doorman Snads Adams had a name as a man who was to be trusted. Anyone intent on bother would usually find himself talked out of it by Snads.

With the profits from the ice-cream business as well, Tam and Margaret were able to afford regular holidays overseas. At the beginning of the 1980s, they had been introduced to the delights of Tenerife by friends. They fell for the island on their first visit and made the most of every subsequent chance to fly over. Their early stays were mainly in the north, in the temperate area around Santa Cruz, but the livelier and decidedly more cloudless south impressed them even more. In the Torviscas zone of Playa de las Americas, they bought a villa, though when demands on their time back home meant fewer chances to stay, they swapped it for an apartment.

Arthur Thompson had considered offering to buy the El Paso from Tennent's when word leaked that the brewers were selling. It was a Barlanark pub, though, and Arthur's base was Provanmill. The idea was never on.

It was while Tam was in the Caravel one day in 1985 that he first received an emissary acting for Arthur Thompson. That would lead to the first of only three meetings between the men. Dubbed 'The Godfather' by the media, Arthur was a one-time club bouncer, fruit merchant, scrap-metal dealer, joiner and demolition contractor who became wealthy as a result of many nefarious rackets. One was money-lending. Another was drug-dealing. Another, it was said, was carrying out duties as a heavy for the infamous London Kray Twins, who hired him to help put the squeeze on anyone brave, or simply stupid, enough to refuse to pay for the protection they so kindly offered on what they considered to be ultra-generous terms.

As the years had rolled by, Arthur – stocky, barrel-chested – had felt less and less comfortable about leaving the security of his lavish one-time council house in Provanmill Road, dubbed 'Southfork' and 'The Ponderosa' after a series of extensions and enlargements. He had enemies who made it their business to try to permanently destroy him. In 1966, he had been found not guilty of fatally shunting two long-time rivals, Arthur Welsh and James Goldie, off the road and into a tree. That same year, a bomb exploded under his car as he drove his mother-in-law. She perished while Arthur almost lost a leg. Three members of the Welsh family were charged but found not guilty.

The call to the Caravel resulted from an attempt by Tam to do a good turn. Bar gossip had it that Jonah Mackenzie was selling drugs in Barlanark, a common enough practice but one that should have been done carefully. In Jonah's case, it was not, and one night, as Tam drove his son William to the cinema, he realised he was being followed. Working out his pursuers were policemen, and knowing the streets of Barlanark inside out, in no time he had turned the tables. Later, discreet enquiries revealed that these were drug-squad officers who suspected Tam might be part of a team involved in dealing heroin. He knew he was innocent, but he telephoned a friend to suggest that Jonah be advised the police were aware of a smack-selling operation in the area. The warning went unheeded and, as a consequence, the team of suppliers, including Jonah and Arty Thompson, was arrested. Young Thompson was in serious trouble. He had been supplying heroin, and the drug was regarded with just as much distaste by the authorities back then as it is now. Arty was looking at a long prison sentence.

The message brought to the Caravel was a polite summons. Would Tam meet Arthur Thompson in a bar at Cambuslang? Arthur had business he wished to discuss. Tam had never met The Godfather and took along Drew Drummond and Bobby Glover. When they arrived, they were met by Arthur Thompson and two associates, including Tam Bagan. Tam McGraw was checked over for hidden weapons. As it was, he had gone along to the meeting unarmed. After all, his path and that of Thompson had, as far as he knew, never crossed. He was, all the same, curious to know what the subject up for discussion was.

Arthur came straight to the point. 'I want to give you £20,000.'

'£20,000? What for?'

'So I can impeach you.'

'Why would I want to be impeached?'

'Arty is in trouble. They are tying him to heroin. I don't want Arty to go down. I want you to say the stuff wasn't his.'

'No chance.'

'Why not? £20,000 is a lot of money.'

'I don't want the money and I'd advise you not to try this. In fact, you can stick it up your backside. Your boy's problems belong to your family and not to anyone else. I'm not involved and this is not my responsibility. He got himself into this; it's up to him to get himself out. Frankly, your boy is an idiot.'

'Whether or not you take the money, I can have you called to give evidence.'

'That's up to you, but I wouldn't advise it.'

It was a suggestion that Arthur ignored. Tam was forced to turn up at the High Court in Glasgow and the defence called him into the witness box. He made it plain he was there under duress, telling all and sundry, 'If I'm asked any questions, then I'll say exactly what I want to say and I will not be blamed for the consequences. I'd advise you to ask nothing so I say nothing.'

Arty had hoped to show that ice-cream van owners such as Tam were aware that heroin was being sold from the vans, rather than by people like Arty. It was an allegation that would have had horrendous repercussions for the trade, and Tam was angry and adamant. 'I don't do heroin. I don't do drugs. I don't even know what heroin looks like. I can't have my name linked to drugs. This is rubbish.'

Tam knew that Jonah Mackenzie and Arty were indeed dealing in heroin. Arty's case was that it was Jonah, and not himself, who sold smack and it was done through ice-cream vans. Tam knew this was not true. Ice-cream vans did not sell drugs. Had he been forced to go into further detail, then telling the truth would have destroyed Arty's claims, and he did not want to do that. It was obvious to Tam that, as far as the defence was concerned, the less he said, the better. And nothing more was asked. Arty had shot himself in the foot. After a trial lasting a month, he went down for 11 years and would never again experience the same freedom he had once enjoyed. Jonah was sentenced to seven years. All he could see regarding Tam's role in the matter was that he had not wanted to speak for the defence.

While Arty and Jonah settled down to cold, bleak years in prison, someone else was turning up the heat at the Caravel – by setting fire to the roof. Damage was not severe, but this could not be allowed to pass. There were those who hinted that the culprit was The Godfather's youngest son, Billy, encouraged from jail by Arty and Jonah, but no one would ever be certain. Whichever way it was looked at, though, the incident, coming so soon after the failed impeachment ploy, seemed to point to the hand of the Thompsons, and Tam set off to Provanmill Road. It would be the second time The Godfather and The Licensee stood face to face. The door was answered by Rita Thompson – small, feisty and intensely loyal. She called for her husband.

'My pub is damaged and it's down to you. I don't give a fuck who you are, you don't frighten me, and I want something done about it,' said The Licensee.

'Don't worry, I'll sort it,' he was told.

That day, Tam had his third and last meeting with Arthur, when Arthur turned up to inspect the damage for himself.

'It's not bad. Look, come down to my yard in London Road and you can have your pick of timber for mending the roof.'

Was it a genuine offer? Or an invitation to turn up and be confronted by a gunman? Only Arthur would know, but Tam was taking no chances. 'No way. I'll get it done and you pay,' was his answer.

A car was passing as the two men left the Caravel. It stopped and out stepped Tam Bagan, a one-time debt collector for Thompson whose gradual distrust of The Godfather had brought the relationship to a bitter end. With him was a relative. It was clear the loathing was mutual and, as Bagan approached, from his jacket pocket Thompson pulled a handgun, a .45, and put it to Bagan's head, pulling the trigger. Nothing happened. He tried again and heard nothing. The trigger had evidently jammed, so Thompson cracked the gun against Bagan's skull, knocking him to the ground. At this point, Thompson was grabbed by Bagan's cousin and, as the pair fought, Bagan climbed to his feet and joined in the attack. Thompson was knocked to the pavement, where he was kicked and punched unconscious. Bagan seized the gun, clearly set on shooting the older man, but Tam realised the heat such a murder would bring. One of the inevitable repercussions would be the closure of the Caravel. 'Leave it,' he told Bagan. 'Nobody wants this.' Bagan walked off, used the weapon to smash the lights of Thompson's car and drove away. Tam helped Thompson to his feet and reminded him he was not involved in the war with Bagan.

'You're here to sort the roof,' he said. 'I don't want second-hand wood. I'll have it mended and you can pay.'

Wiping away blood and dust, Arthur protested, but in the end handed over £5,000, all in £10 notes. The actual bill was £600. No one would say how much the insurers settled for, but rumour put the figure in the £20,000 range.

After that attempt on the Caravel, Tam was warned by his closest friends that there might be another. For a week, three men hid in a school across the road from the pub, keeping watch. One of the trio had been a loyal member of the Barlanark Team, with a reputation that would have been envied by a commando. Watching and waiting for signs of danger during robberies had taught him to lie on a roof or in a hedge without moving. Each night, he and the others hid on the school roof, gazing over at the Caravel. Their wait was rewarded when they saw a man, holding what appeared to be a petrol can, attempting to climb onto the pub roof. They hauled him down and he was dragged into nearby wasteland, where his interrogators kicked and slashed, demanding to know who had paid him to set fire to the building. Utter terror showed through the blood on his face and he passed out. Convinced he was dead, the attackers set off to get shovels. They would bury him in the wasteground and no one would be the wiser. On the way, though, they heard the sound of sirens and saw the lights of police cars. A neighbour had heard the commotion when the would-be arsonist was taken and had called for help. There was nothing for it but to leave the body where it lay. Next morning, and in the days that followed, they scoured newspapers and listened to radio bulletins for news of the discovery of a body and the start of a murder hunt. But there was nothing. No one asked questions at the Caravel. When Tam heard what had happened, he assumed the victim had recovered and made his way to safety. And the fire-raiser, realising that to complain could lay him open to a charge that carried a potential life sentence, said nothing.

Three years after the roof blaze, in 1988, the Thompson faction was again blamed for an example of crass stupidity that might well have cost innocent lives. Tam was at the bar of the Caravel when what appeared to be a potato was lobbed in through the front door. No one took any particular notice. It was not unknown for youngsters to play pranks against elders having a few beers. It rolled around the floor. A group of drunks began kicking it about in a mock football match, until someone, tiring of their antics, picked it up and threw it back outside. Next day, a passing police patrol noticed the potato and stopped to investigate. What they saw prompted a major emergency and the appearance of an Army bomb squad. The soldiers were horrified to discover that what had been turfed around the crowded bar was a Second World War hand grenade. It could not have gone off, because the firing pin was broken, but there were those who wondered if it had been a serious attempt to blow up Tam.

For the Thompsons one tragedy was to follow another. Not long before the grenade incident, a gunman had walked into Arthur's yard and shot him in the groin. The assassin would always remain too scared to admit to the shooting, fearing retribution from Thompson family friends in London. Arthur drove himself to Ross Hall private hospital on the outskirts of Glasgow, where he told doctors he had been working with a drill when the bit snapped and shot into his leg. His story would never be disputed because surgeons decided it was safer to leave the fragment of metal where it was, rather than risk extracting it and perhaps leaving Arthur with a permanent limp, or worse.

The following year, his daughter, Margaret, died tragically young of natural causes at just 28, and in 1990 Thompson survived a murder bid when two men deliberately drove over him as he walked home from the Provanmill Inn. The assassins fired at the prone figure, but missed, then left the gun beside him to make it appear he had been the gunman. Despite suffering a broken leg, he recovered. That was not the end of the Thompson family's troubles, though. In August 1991, allowed a weekend off from prison as he neared the end of his sentence, Arthur Thompson, Jr. was fatally shot three times outside the family home. On the day of Arty's funeral in September 1991, the bodies of Joe Hanlon and Bobby Glover were discovered in a car dumped outside the Cottage Bar in Darleith Street, Shettleston. They had both been shot with two handguns: a Smith and Wesson .44 Magnum and a .38 revolver. One had been used for the head shots, the other for the chest injuries. The Cottage Bar had been a favourite drinking hole of many East End gangsters. Tam McGraw would often call in, and it was Bobby Glover's local. But that was not why he and his friend Joe were left outside, to be discovered in the early morning by publican Allan Cross. The significance of their resting place was that it formed part of the route Arty's funeral cortège would take. The murders of Arty, Bobby and Joe have never been solved, with some characters seeking to take credit by denial. One fallacy is that, after being killed, the bodies of Joe and Bobby were taken to a back room of the Caravel, laid out in Tam's presence and offered for inspection by The Godfather, who declined to pay his last respects. In fact, the dead men were carted to a warehouse in the east of Glasgow city centre, where they were left before being delivered to Shettleston. The warehouse was owned by a businessman friend of Arthur Thompson, who, to this day, considers himself an unofficial protector of the family reputation. Arthur too would die unexpectedly, but in his bed from a heart attack in 1993.

To have attempted to haul two dead bodies into the Caravel would have been folly. Even after closing time, the pub would be surrounded by customers laughing, chatting, arguing, reluctant to go home. Sometimes, up to 200 people congregated, waking up neighbours and, much to the annoyance of the McGraws, dumping rubbish in the grounds of the school opposite. Local busybodies would sometimes complain about the racket, so Tam came up with a solution that would later be seen as a stroke of genius. He set up a taxi company. The idea was solely to serve the Caravel, but his Glasgow Radio Cars was such a success he realised that there was a fortune to be made in the private-hire business. Customers wanting a car rang a central number, where controllers would find them a taxi through a radio service announcing details of the client's request. Drivers were constantly listening to the service, having paid around £60 a week to tune in. Tam paid associates to run the service and would eventually have 800 Glasgow private-hire cabs paying for the system.

By the beginning of the 1990s, Margaret was finding it increasingly difficult to continue running the Caravel. Suited men carrying clipboards and bundles of regulations were increasingly calling to pass on complaints that the pub attracted undesirables. Each year, she had to scrap to have her licence renewed and sometimes the legal bill would run to £20,000. She wondered, finally, if it was worth it.

Tam, meanwhile, during another of the family holidays in Tenerife in 1996, had met up with two friends from Glasgow, who pointed out to him that the ever-growing demand for inner-city land on which to build housing would send values soaring. He owned land around the Caravel, which would have been ideal but for the siting of the pub. After all, who would buy a new house just yards from a busy, raucous pub? When he returned home, Tam discussed the problem with Trevor, who had invested some of his hash return in a demolition business. 'Leave it to me,' he told Tam. The next morning, the Caravel was flattened. It was as if one moment it was there, the next it was gone, carted off to be dumped on wasteland near Glasgow Forge. Some would claim the destruction was in order to hide possible evidence linking the bar to the murders of Bobby and Joe five years earlier. That was fantasy. The truth was that, by clearing away the Caravel, a site had been created big enough on which to build 22 houses. A company, Carrick Developments, was set up to do just that. It was simple economics, not forensics. Carrick Developments would later be sold and become CRI Properties.

So the Caravel, the 'Paso', became history its memories floating off like ghosts in the wind. Regulars had to find another watering hole in which to gossip and scheme. Some would wander off and be forgotten. Others would find a very different resting place.

chapter twenty-nine

ABSENT FRIENDS

GORDON ROSS HAD LOOKS THAT MANY A MOVIE STAR might envy. But the only cameras Gordon would face were those of policemen taking mugshots. His chosen career was crime.

Tam did his best to steer Gordon away from trouble, and the two would become close friends, with Gordon a regular visitor to the McGraw home. However, Gordon's good looks caused problems no godfather figure could resolve. Dark-haired, broad-shouldered, he smiled with green eyes, showing even white teeth, and the picture opened the doors of a thousand bedrooms. His early ventures into lawbreaking involved driving cars filled with hash out of Spain to Disneyland and Scotland. He was an original member of the hash-smuggling crew, but after his jailing in 1989 he sought advice from Tam at the Caravel. The Licensee told him: 'Invest. Spend some money, sure, but remember good times never last. There are too many envious people who will want to bring you down. Think of the future. Always remember the day may come out of the blue when it will all come to an end.'

Gordon knew this made sound sense. He had known hard times and troubles, especially after the break-up of his marriage to wife Elizabeth. Setting up home with the beautiful blonde who would put her own freedom on the line for him in France, they scoured newspaper columns for fiver bargains with which to furnish their modest flat, but even then Gordon paid unsuspecting vendors with forged banknotes. When they had first met, at a party at the home of a friend, she had been lured by his looks but found him courteous, gentlemanly, quiet. 'He's terribly shy,' she would tell a friend. 'He's incredibly handsome and all the women go for him but when we go to a dance or a party he seems to prefer sitting on his own in a corner clutching a drink. He needs to open out.' As time passed and his fortunes changed for the better, Gordon did just that.

The early drugs money was modest by comparison with what was to come later. He would not be described as flash, but splashed out on a BMW nevertheless. Sometimes, on impulse, as they watched television together, he would whisk the girl off into his car and they'd drive from their home in Rutherglen to Ayr, simply to eat fish and chips while gazing at the setting sun. His confidence increased in line with his bank balance and one day he took her Citroën runaround to the garage for minor repairs and swapped it for a brand new Ford Escort convertible.

In Chick Glackin, he found a soulmate. Chick was the more showy of the two, although both were fun-loving, always on the lookout for a laugh and ready with a joke. Gordon heeded Tam's advice and bought an ice-cream van, using it on a round in East Kilbride. His second van came not long after and was based in Cranhill, in Glasgow's East End. Eventually, he and Chick would buy vans but always Tam kept an eye on the younger man, sometimes turning up at a party to order him home, reminding him he had an ice-cream business to run and giving him a tongue lashing if he suspected he had been dabbling with drugs. 'That's one for the noted,' Gordon would say, his favourite response to someone making a telling point.

On holiday with his girlfriend, he would be tucked up in bed by nine at night with a book about crime, or sitting quietly listening to REM singing 'Everybody Hurts' or, his special favourite, Elvis Presley's, and later UB40's, 'Can't Help Falling in Love'. As the buses began plying between Glasgow and Spain with their million-pound loads, Gordon used his share to buy a holiday chalet at Trevor's farm. He became obsessive about his fitness, playing football regularly and sometimes climbing onto a bicycle and going off on a two-hour ride with a black plastic bin liner wrapped around him in an attempt to lose weight.

Unfortunately, though, when money changed Gordon, it was mainly for the worse. The girl noticed he was becoming less tolerant, more demanding, less

219

patient. She knew he was unfaithful, but more times than not it was the woman who threw herself at Gordon, rather than the reverse. She could only guess at what he got up to during his frequent trips to the Costa del Sol or Benidorm and became increasingly disheartened over his friendship with Billy McPhee, who would telephone their home asking for a meeting to discuss business. 'I don't want to go out, but Billy needs to see me,' Gordon would say, then disappear for a fortnight. When they had first met, his favourite drink was Bacardi, but later he felt it was more macho to guzzle beer with the rest of the boys. The relationship deteriorated, despite the birth of a son, and they split up. The girl's love for Gordon, though, would outlast Gordon himself. To this day, she says she still speaks with him, although, if he listens, she can never hear his responses.

After the break-up, Gordon became a devotee of the opposite sex: a one-night-stand specialist, loving and leaving and building a reputation as being totally ruthless in matters of the heart. His conquest of the Manchester footballer's girlfriend left the player a laughing stock. But Gordon made no distinction between friend or stranger. During a foray into Glasgow one night, Billy was surprised to have his suggestion that a dark-haired girl accompany him home at the end of the evening accepted. Married Billy took her to Gordon's flat, where the two men chatted to her and shared more drinks. It was clear that the girl's inducement in following Billy was that Gordon, too, would be going along. So it was no surprise when Billy fell asleep and awoke to find the girl, absolutely naked, straddling Gordon on the settee right beside him. The only shock was Billy's reaction. He roared with laughter.

During a break in Tenerife, Gordon shared a hotel room with a friend of Tam's, who decided to take a mid-afternoon shower. He soaped himself, unaware that Gordon, reading a newspaper poolside, had been picked up by a stunning Swedish girl, naked except for a thong. Within minutes, they were in Gordon's room on his bed making love. So loud were her shrieks of joy, the roommate emerged from the shower to investigate and was forced to wait behind the shower curtain until nature had taken its course. A visit to the Irish Rover bar at Playa de las Americas saw Gordon seduced by an older woman, who took him to her holiday home, where her husband acted very reasonably by insisting upon watching the two sport in the marital bed.

Another trip to Tenerife saw Gordon meet up with two well-known Manchester footballing celebrities. All three were drinking in the H_2O club when the Scot became exceedingly drunk after a long session on Martini and lemonade. He knew there was always the possibility of a boozy session leaving him incapable of looking after himself, so would hide the bulk of his cash in his socks. That night, he was seated on a wall outside his hotel, trying to focus on a spinning moon, when a taxi drew up and out stepped a very attractive black girl. She was wearing a halter top and miniskirt and her appearance sobered Gordon. With barely a word, the girl went down on her knees, unzipped his trousers and proceeded to perform fellatio on him. Then she left and disappeared into the hotel. The act encouraged Gordon to have another drink but, back at H_2O, he discovered his secret hoard was missing. 'Cow,' he screamed to his companions after telling them of his remarkable experience. 'She blew my money while she was blowing me.'

Tam and Margaret watched their friend's lifestyle spiral out of control. Gordon survived the 1998 hashish trial, but he alternated between euphoria and depression, frequently brought on by the troubles that seemed to follow the sons he'd had with Elizabeth: Gordon, Jr., born in 1982, and Stephen, born five years later. At the end of the trial, Tam took his friend to Tenerife to cheer him up, and the holiday appeared to do the trick. But time was running out. On 24 September 2002, Gordon left the home he shared with a girlfriend in Coatbridge, Lanarkshire, to meet up with a pal in a pub at Shettleston, Glasgow. They had planned to watch a televised football match, but the barmaid was unable to switch to the channel they wanted because the key giving access to the equipment was held by her absent boss. They decided to move on. It was a fatal mistake, and had they waited ten more minutes the keyholder would have arrived. In the Sheiling Bar, insults were exchanged with the relative of a long-time rival, whom they ordered to leave. This man made a telephone call and, some minutes later, Gordon was advised that someone was outside the pub with a message for him. As he went through the door, he was confronted by a gang, his arms pinioned by one while another fatally stabbed him. It was a cowardly murder and one in which the identity of the killers is known. The news was immediately telephoned to Tam McGraw, who set off to search for the murderers, but they had fled, and are still running.

The McGraws were devastated. Gordon was only 36 when he died, yet he had packed a score of lifetimes into those years. He left behind an estate worth over £1 million and a memory for each pound.

His death came only five months after tragedy had ended the life of Trevor.

Trevor had used his hash-smuggling cash to buy Broomhill Farm at Dunipace, Stirlingshire. The spot was only a few feet from the M80 and Trevor would frequently take a short cut across the motorway to drink at pubs in nearby Denny. In April 2002, he had been with friends at The Pines when a fight erupted. Trevor had confided he felt he was being watched, suggesting enemies might be interested in the whereabouts of some of his fortune. A careful man, he was thought to have hidden tens of thousands of pounds in paint tins, which he had buried. Not wishing to become involved in the brawl, he took to his heels in the direction of home, but, crossing the M80, was hit by a car and killed. He was 32. Tam McGraw, who had once saved his life outside the Caravel, was devastated, but there was more to come.

At the funeral of Gordon Ross, in February 2003, Tam and Margaret were among the mourners. So was Billy McPhee. His grim looks could have been accounted for by the fact he had been shot in the face five months before, but this was not the real reason behind them. At that gathering in honour of life and death, Billy had been told his own days were surely numbered. Billy was a hard man who had grown up in Barlanark under the wing of Tam and Margaret, who were neighbours of his parents. He had an adoring wife and two delightful children. His problem was that he believed his reputed invincibility was a licence to go where he wanted and do as he wished. Billy took advantage of the daughter of another Glasgow gangster. The girl was a willing enough participant in the sex orgy which followed, but she was vulnerable and easily used, a fact Billy knew and which should have been enough to persuade him to stop. But he had not and now, he was being told, a price would be exacted. The same gangster had meted out rough justice to two leading Glasgow footballers who had been less than gentlemanly in their treatment of the same girl, and both had hastily left the city.

The warning persuaded Billy to begin wearing a bullet-proof vest. He took it with him when he went to the Springcroft Tavern, a bar–restaurant not far from his Baillieston home on Saturday, 8 March 2003. He was looking forward to watching a televised rugby match and drinking with friends. Inside, it was crowded and someone suggested to Billy he should remove the vest, which he did. Almost immediately, a telephone call was made, a car drew up and a man emerged. He knew precisely where Billy was seated, walked straight through crowds of parents and children enjoying an early dinner, confronted his target and without speaking plunged a knife into Billy's neck, immediately disabling him. The knife was driven into his head and body a further 18 times before the killer vanished. His identity is known. He has never been caught.

Billy McPhee was the fourth to die of the eleven men who had appeared in the dock at Edinburgh. The first had been Paul Flynn, whose task It had been to drive a transit van packed with hashish from Benalmadena to meet up with the Mercedes coach at Benidorm. A solitary fingerprint had condemned him to prison. An Arthur Askey lookalike, the short, wholly reliable Scouser was known in his native Liverpool as 'Mr Glasses'. He was not to know he had a congenital heart condition and, while taking a prison shower one morning, collapsed and died. He was only 37. At Paul's funeral, Tam was taken to one side by his friends and thanked for the way the little man had been treated. 'Good turns done are good turns owed,' they promised.

Sometimes a favour could take an unexpected turn. Tam and Margaret agreed to an old comrade from the Barlanark Team having use of their Tenerife flat for an extended holiday. They were not to know that Tam's friend was on the run at the time from detectives in Glasgow, who had impounded his gleaming blue BMW car and towed it to a city police station. He had spotted it there, realised trouble was headed his way, made his way to Manchester and from there to the island. Arriving in Tenerife, he rang Tam and asked if he could stay in the empty flat. 'Of course,' said Tam, telling him the name of the concierge who held the spare key. 'Stay as long as you wish, but tidy up before you leave. Is everything OK?'

'No problems, I just need to keep my head down and have a wee break. I'll look after things.'

In Tenerife, the comrade, whom we shall call Ernie, soon became bored and sought out a friend who ran a bar in Playa de las American. 'I need a job. Got anything going?'

'Not really. Oh, hang on, I could do with a DJ to do nights. It's only introducing a few records and maybe running the karaoke. Can you sing?'

'Sing? Oh aye, no bother. Leave it to me, I'll have the place rocking.'

He was as good as his word. While police in Glasgow hunted his whereabouts, he proved such a hit on the island that he made it onto the front page of the *Tenerife Times*, together with a photograph. It had not occurred to him that thousands of Glaswegians annually took their holidays on Tenerife, including a proportion of the city's police officers. Some days after publication, Ernie was taking a break from his DJ duties, enjoying a beer at the bar, when he began chatting to an attractive young woman. Her first words told him she was a Scot.

'Where you from, hen?' asked Ernie.

'Glasgow. And you?'

'Aye, the same, more or less. You on holiday?'

'Sure, going back tomorrow. I'm due back at work tomorrow night.'

'Tomorrow night. What do you do?'

'Oh, it's not important. You stay here?'

'Aye, I'm looking after a friend's flat. It's just around the corner. You with your husband?'

'No, not married. And before you ask, there's no boyfriend either.'

'You're kidding, a lovely girl like you . . .'

'Forget the patter. Heard it all before. I was in a relationship until a few weeks ago and the holiday is to put it all behind me. You want another drink?'

'Aye, but let me. I get them cheap working here. Now, you going to be in here long?'

'Could be . . .'

And Ernie knew he had pulled.

At close of play that night, he and the woman strolled the few yards to the flat. 'I'll need to get a taxi back to the hotel. My flight's just before lunch,' she said.

'Don't worry,' he told her. 'I'll get you a cab – in the morning.'

That night, as they made love, they talked, and he pressed the woman about her work.

'All right,' she said. 'I try forgetting about it when I'm not there, but I'm in the police.'

'Police?' Ernie gulped. 'Glasgow police?'

'Yes, Strathclyde.'

'Which station?'

And she told him. The fact that beneath him was one of those who sought to deprive him of his freedom, take him from his family and steal away his beloved BMW stirred him to even more frantic efforts. It was as if, in his lovemaking, he sought to quench the loathing he felt for police in general. Yet the only result was the ever greater satisfaction that the woman's cries told him she was achieving.

In the morning, he rang for a taxi and when it arrived, showing an abundance of gallantry, he helped her in. Before waving her off, he asked, 'You still going to work tonight?' The woman assured him she was but was left ashen-faced at what followed. 'Well, when you get to work, nip round the back of the station because there's a beautiful blue BMW there. Give it a fucking wash because it's mine.' Weeks later, he would discover through his lawyer that the procurator-fiscal was not proceeding and he was free to return home. He tidied Tam's flat and flew back to Glasgow, where one of his first tasks was to collect his car. There were signs it had been washed.

Tam would also arrange favours for other friends. Donnie McMillan had once been falsely accused, in 1992, of being offered £50,000 to murder Arthur Thompson. It was a silly suggestion but left Donnie wondering if he should be reclassifying friends as enemies. He had met Tam some years earlier at the Cottage Bar when he entered for a drink with Joe Hanlon. His first impression was that Tam appeared wary of him, but for all that seemed ordinary and up-front. In 1995, Donnie was asked, by rivals of the McGraw faction, to give evidence at a robbery trial to the effect that Tam was 'a policeman without a uniform'. He refused point blank. When Tam heard about this, he telephoned and, together with Gordon and Trevor, called on him to ask exactly what had been wanted. Next day, Donnie received a telephone call summoning him to a rendezvous at Glasgow Forge. As he stood about waiting and wondering, a stranger approached, handed him £2,000 and flight tickets to Tenerife for him and his wife. Tam later did Donnie another kindness that he would not forget. Following a spell in prison in 1996 for theft, Donnie was visited by Tam, who, realising he was down in the dumps, sent him and members of his family on holiday to Spain.

If there were criminals trying to set up Tam McGraw, so too were law officers. The attempt to sucker the hash-smugglers into giving away their secrets in Saughton Jail to Finnish scoundrel Kari Paajolahti had failed but not died. Months after the end of the trial, he telephoned one of the group and travelled to Glasgow for a meeting. Before it took place, he had secretly rendezvoused with two Customs handlers, who gave him an astonishing document. In it, Paajolahti was given written permission to take part 'in a particular crime, the importation of controlled drugs, providing the part I play is a minor one when judged against the criminal proposal as a whole'. And he would agree 'not to take a major role in the planning or committing of the offences and not to act as an agent provocateur'. It was a blatant and crude attempt to use the crook to set up the freed smugglers. He could break the law and get away with it. Two of the men who had shared the Saughton remand wing with him met the Finn, who returned to his Customs controllers with a story that he was to take £48,500 to Amsterdam and return to the Molly Malone pub in Glasgow city centre with heroin hidden in a workman's haversack. The Customs officers urged him to go through with the plot, but Paajolahti decided otherwise. He fled. For Tam, and the other men the Finn had been sent to frame, it was a frightening example of the law running wild. But it was not to be the last.

chapter thirty

SEVEN IRON

Daily Record, 27 April 2002:
'Licensee fights for life after gangland hit.'
Underworld boss Tam 'The Licensee' McGraw was fighting for life last night after a murder bid.

He was stabbed six times in the stomach yesterday morning, yards from his home in Glasgow's East End.

Sunday Times, 28 April 2002:
'Gang-war fear after Glasgow stabbing.'
Police are on the alert for expected tit-for-tat killings after the daylight stabbing of a notorious Glasgow gangland boss.

Police say the attack on McGraw has not been reported to them. Detectives do not believe the victim or any other potential witnesses will cooperate with their inquiry.

The Glasgow Herald, 29 April 2002:
'McGraw: I am fit and well after attack.'
One of Glasgow's most notorious underworld figures broke his silence yesterday to say that he was fit and well and had not been stabbed repeatedly in a street attack.

Thomas McGraw, who is estimated to have amassed a personal fortune of about £10 million, dismissed reports that he was critically ill in hospital after suffering multiple stab wounds in the attack near his luxury home in Mount Vernon, in the East End of Glasgow, on Friday.

Daily Record, 29 April 2002:

'How hitmen tracked "The Licensee".'

Months of planning went into the attempted murder of underworld boss Tam 'The Licensee' McGraw.

A gangland rival launched a major intelligence operation on the 49 year old, who was stabbed on Friday.

McGraw had been living in Tenerife but the rival knew exactly when he returned to Scotland.

Daily Mail, 30 April 2002:

'Gang-war fear as police link the stabbings of city criminals.'

Police last night feared the eruption of open gang warfare across Glasgow after the stabbing of Thomas 'T.C.' Campbell, one of the men convicted of the so-called Ice-Cream-War murders.

Campbell was attacked yesterday – just three days after underworld boss Tam 'The Licensee' McGraw was stabbed outside his home in Glasgow.

Last night, police said it was likely the two incidents were linked.

Police sources believe they might have been masterminded by Glasgow gangster Paul Ferris in a deliberate attempt to provoke a turf war.

Mr Ferris, who is believed to have been present during the attack on McGraw on Friday, is thought to have organised yesterday's attempted murder on Campbell to make it look like retaliation.

Daily Record, 1 May 2002:

'The Licensee watched as rival T.C. hit.'

Underworld boss The Licensee watched as a feared enforcer ambushed a deadly rival.

Gangland and police sources said Tam McGraw looked on as henchman Billy McPhee tried to stab Thomas 'T.C.' Campbell.

SEVEN IRON

Daily Record, 2 May 2002:

'Ferris blade duel.'

Mystery surrounded the whereabouts of gangster Paul Ferris last night after he was knifed in a street fight with a sworn enemy.

Underworld sources claimed the notorious criminal was the man who left Tam 'The Licensee' fighting for his life on Friday.

It is understood that Ferris was also stabbed twice during the vicious battle.

Press Association, 3 May 2002:

'Gun-runner Ferris back behind bars.'

Gun-runner Paul Ferris was tonight behind bars after turning himself in to police.

The reformed gangster from Glasgow, who vowed to go straight when he was released on licence earlier this year, surrendered to officers in Durham on Thursday night.

He was immediately arrested for being 'unlawfully at large' after allegedly breaching his parole conditions, said a spokesman for Durham Constabulary.

Daily Record, 4 May 2002:

'Police: McGraw is next.'

Detectives last night told crimelord Tam 'The Licensee' McGraw: 'Your days are numbered.'

The warning came after his gangland rival, Paul Ferris, was thrown back in prison.

News of the World, 5 May 2002:

'When the golf club broke on my head, I was still standing!'

'I've read reports that the people who tried to kill me were McGraw and McPhee. I am not naming names but those reports are accurate.'

Thomas 'T.C.' Campbell told last night how he fought a desperate battle for his life when he was ambushed by two would-be killers.

The freed Ice-Cream Wars suspect grappled on the ground with a knifeman before he had a golf club smashed over his head.

CRIMELORD

Daily Record, 6 May 2002:
'Licensee ready to flee.'

Underworld crime boss Tam 'The Licensee' McGraw is set to return to his luxury Tenerife bolthole.

Gangland sources said McGraw was preparing to leave ahead of a new wave of violent confrontations with rivals.

Daily Record, 8 May 2002:
'Cops quiz McGraw.'

Crime boss Tam 'The Licensee' McGraw was hauled in for questioning by police over a street fight yesterday.

Detectives quizzed McGraw over the attack on convicted Ice-Cream Wars killer Thomas 'T.C.' Campbell near his home.

Daily Record, 9 May 2002:
'Inside the madhouse.'

For a man who never speaks in public, gang boss Tam 'The Licensee' McGraw was in a revealing mood yesterday.

McGraw didn't only drop the silence he has kept since being unmasked in 1988 as Glasgow's top gangster. He dropped his Y-fronts as well.

As I watched, Glasgow's most feared criminal stripped naked in his kitchen to prove he had not been stabbed.

He shouted: 'I'm here and there's f*** all wrong with me. Want to see?'

McGraw then pulled his top over his head to reveal his unmarked torso and turned through 360 degrees.

He asked loudly: 'There, do you see any f***ing stab wounds?'

News of the World, 12 May 2002:
'McGraw denies plans to flee to sunshine bolthole.'

Gangster Thomas McGraw has rubbished rumours that he's fleeing to his Tenerife hideaway.

Underworld rivals claim The Licensee is running scared after being implicated in a string of recent street fights in Glasgow.

But the 49 year old has told friends he's not quitting his plush Glasgow home for the Canaries.

He told them: 'I run several businesses and there's no reason why I shouldn't make sure they carry on being successful. I intend to stick around.'

News of the World, 26 May 2002:
'Medics: no knife wounds on Ferris.'

Former gangland enforcer Paul Ferris has had a full-scale medical behind bars – in a bid to rubbish claims he was stabbed in a street brawl.

Doctors at Durham Prison found no sign of injuries on Ferris, 38, during the two-hour check-up.

Daily Record, 14 June 2002:
'Ferris back on the street.'

Gangster Paul Ferris was back in Scotland yesterday after being freed from jail.

Ferris was locked up six weeks ago after he was linked to a spate of gangland incidents while out on licence.

SO, WHAT REALLY HAPPENED?

The 'months of planning' consisted, in reality, of a chance encounter as Tam McGraw drove his 4 x 4 along Burnmouth Road at Barlanark in Glasgow's East End on the morning of Friday, 26 April 2002. Motoring towards a traffic-calming section, he spotted a familiar face in an oncoming vehicle: Paul Ferris's. With him was Mark Clinton. The two had met for the first time that morning, after a mutual friend had asked Ferris to give Clinton work with his security company. Neither Clinton nor McGraw knew one another. Tam forced the other car to a halt and both he and Ferris immediately leapt out. According to pals of McGraw, there followed a brief scuffle, during which Ferris was thrown to the ground, where he attempted to roll into a ball for protection. McGraw then opened the rear door of his jeep and grabbed the first thing that came to hand – a golf club – and began aiming blows at his adversary. At this point, Clinton decided to intervene on behalf of his prospective employer and, despite a warning from McGraw to stay away, produced a thin-bladed knife and began hacking at the older man. At least fourteen – not six – stab wounds were inflicted on his right arm and shoulder – not his stomach. Before watching locals could summon police, the fight broke up and McGraw, realising he had been injured, drove to Glasgow's Victoria Infirmary. During the five-mile journey, there was no bleeding, but damage to his muscles meant he was unable to lift his right arm and had to lean it on the driver's door rest, his hand simply lying on the steering wheel. Curious hospital staff wanted to know what had happened, but he gave a false name and address and said the marks were the consequence of an accident while carrying out DIY work at his home. After being examined and patched up, he was unable to drive himself home and had to call for help from his son, William.

Three days later, on the afternoon of Monday, 29 April, while driving through Barlanark with McGraw, Billy McPhee was involved in a vicious fight with T.C. Campbell next to the local community centre. Campbell would later allege there were attempts to stab him and he was hit on the head with another golf club – this time a nine iron.

There was no mystery about the whereabouts of Ferris, out on licence from his gun-running sentence. As a result of police getting to hear about the fight, the licence was revoked and he was back in Durham prison. McGraw was not beating a hasty retreat to Tenerife, not having been to the island for three years. Nor was he being questioned by police. He was at home in Mount Vernon stripping naked before a *Daily Record* reporter whose interest appeared to be in the wrong part of his anatomy. He failed to see the livid puncture marks around McGraw's shoulder. Clinton would send an apology for his role, explaining that had he known the identity of the man he stabbed he would certainly not have taken part. In a well-publicised charade, McPhee was interviewed by police but said nothing. A detailed transcript of his conversation with detectives appeared in a local newspaper. Two days later, Tam and his lawyer, Liam O'Donnell, quietly and voluntarily went to Stewart Street police station in Glasgow over the T.C. Campbell incident. Tam made no comment and refused to answer questions.

Neither incident would amount to anything and both were allowed to quietly drift into oblivion, but not without a comment that left even Tam amused. In the *Daily Record* on Tuesday, 7 May 2002, the excellent journalist Simon Houston described a fantasy Ryder Cup golf match between Tam and the world's best player, America's Tiger Woods. Watched by an admiring crowd, Tiger smashes a long drive down the middle of the fairway before Tam, from the back of his 4 x 4, produces the [. . .] seven iron:

He snatches the seven out, swings it around his head and makes a mad dash for an unsuspecting Tiger.

'Yer gettin' it, ya big eejit!' screams McGraw, whose outburst brings a chorus of disapproving murmurs from the spectators.

The world no 1 – somewhat taken aback by the actions of his sinister-looking opponent – decides to run for his life and scampers down the fairway.

chapter thirty-one

BULLET-PROOF DUFFEL

WITH THE EXCEPTION OF HIMSELF AND MARGARET, NO ONE knows precisely how wealthy Tam McGraw has become over the years. It has been variously estimated at between £5 million and £30 million, but the true figure is probably around £14.5 million.

At the Edinburgh trial of 1998, much was made of the fact that he was involved in a series of businesses but did not pay income tax. That has since been resolved, but the stories about his money continue, invariably coming to conclusions well adrift of fact. The Paradise Bar in Donegal was confiscated by the Eire government's Criminal Assets Bureau in February 1998 on the grounds that it had been bought with cash made from crime and was being used to launder drug money. It cost £120,000 but was sold at auction for £215,000. The move has been embarrassing for the Irish. Unable to prove their claims about the source of the McGraw's funds for buying the bar, or the criminal use he allegedly made of it, the government has been forced to cough up the original price plus interest.

In the summer of 2004, police stopped the McGraws on the M8 and discovered they were carrying £6,000 in cash. The Crown Office's Civil Recovery Unit grabbed the money under the Proceeds of Crime Act, an incredibly sweeping piece of legislation under which any member of the public found with a hefty bundle of money in his wallet or her purse can find themselves having to explain in court where it came from. Again, there were official red faces when the haul was found to have been payment for a group holiday. It was handed back, along with £20 interest. In August 2004, Tam was declared bankrupt after failing to appear in court to challenge a sequestration order for failing to pay a tax bill of £12,794. The media had a field day. Unfortunately, the facts were far from dramatic. A letter from the Court of Session telling him of the bankruptcy hearing was sent to his home, rather than the office of his lawyer. Tam was not there and the hearing went ahead without him. The bankruptcy was later recalled. Officially, according to the Accountant in Bankruptcy, he has assets of £116 and does not even own a car. The house that is home to him and Margaret cost her £80,000 in 1991. It has been extensively modernised and extended and has probably increased tenfold in value. But it is unlikely ever to come on the market. Margaret's roots, in particular, are too deeply set in the East End.

The couple are said to spend much of their time at their Tenerife apartment. In fact, a four-day trip to the island by Tam in March 2005 was the first he had made there for three years. The fact is that he prefers sitting in his breakfast room drinking copious amounts of tea, smoking up to 30 tipped cigarettes a day – a habit that keeps him slim but which he is constantly urged to cut down – listening to Robbie Williams or Phil Collins. Giving him the microphone at a karaoke night then trying to get it back after a single number can be a risky business. He is once reputed to have laid out a DJ who pointed out he had sung half a dozen numbers and should step down to give some other hopeful a shot. Margaret prefers listening, but not necessarily to her husband. One of her favourites is 'Christian', born Chris McClure in the Ibrox area of Glasgow, who used to play in the same kids' football team as former Scotland manager Andy Roxburgh. Friends will tell you the couple's house is filled with televisions. Tam is an avid watcher of history programmes and science-fiction shows, in particular the *Star Wars* and *Stargate* series. It is also rare for a visitor not to be there. Until recently, Tam's favourite newspaper was the *Sunday Times*, but even in that hallowed organ, yet another figment of a journalist's imagination finally brought his faith in the newspaper to an end.

His speech is quick, interspersed with a series of calls on his mobile phone. One of the favourite stories with which he will entertain callers is that of a close friend who appeared before the High Court in Glasgow in 1992 charged with scams involving goods worth nearly £2 million. He was cleared, after the longest fraud trial in Scots history, which had followed a long and costly police surveillance operation, not unlike the later investigation into holiday-bus hash-smuggling. For almost two years, the man had been followed everywhere he went. He could not enter a snack bar without the details of how long he spent inside and what he ate being noted. On 16 April 1990, two of the shadowing detectives spotted him and a friend heading to Glasgow airport. The men were booked on a flight to Heathrow but, dressed in jeans and loose sweaters and carrying scuffed bags, they looked out of place among the smart suited businessmen and well-dressed holidaymakers who made up the passenger list. What, the police wondered, were they up to? A quick call to a senior officer authorised them to catch the same flight and, at Heathrow, they hopped into a taxi and ordered the driver to follow the cab carrying their targets. To the cops' astonishment, it stopped at the Dorchester Hotel, one of the swankiest and most expensive in the capital. The two looked so out of place, even their taxi driver believed something underhand was about to take place. To make sure they were genuine, he accompanied them to reception, where he was surprised to hear their booking of two rooms for the night had not only been confirmed but the bill had been paid in advance. The two police officers were forced to sit glumly in reception, not daring to take a quick drink or bite to eat in case their quarry reappeared unexpectedly. In fact, both were in their rooms, showering and changing before striding out to waiting taxis, stopping only to shake the hand of Sean Connery. Again, the officers were forced to follow, this time to Wembley Stadium, where their suspects disappeared into an office and emerged with large plastic tags around their necks bearing the words 'Access All Areas'.

Nelson Mandela was in town to attend, in person, an international tribute concert. As the Scots headed for the VIP lounge, the police tried following but were told in no uncertain terms by a no-nonsense steward to clear off, and quickly. Gobsmacked, they could only peer in through a window from the outside as the men chatted on first-name terms with politician Neil Kinnock, media mogul Robert Maxwell and the American evangelist and civil-rights campaigner the Rev Jesse Jackson. After the concert, they were off again, with their hunters in hot pursuit, this time to the Natural History Museum to mingle with the concert stars: Peter Gabriel, Lou Reed, Tracy Chapman, Neil Young and Patti LaBelle. Then it was back to the Dorchester, the police having to wait around all night to follow them back to Heathrow and Glasgow. The story of the concert brought hilarity when it was told to the High Court, as police recounted the results of their monitoring. What, one was asked, had it all proved? 'That they are better connected,' was the reply.

Another anecdote concerns a visit made by a friend to Glasgow Sheriff Court, where a minor case was in progress. As the evidence droned on, a member of the public was noticed chewing from a packet of chocolate éclairs, even offering the sweets to two fellow members of the public gallery. At this point, an officious usher intervened, ordering the man to put away the sweets. An argument ensued, developing into a commotion that forced the clearly indignant and annoyed Sheriff to halt the proceedings.

'What's going on?' he demanded to know.

'This man is eating sweets, sir,' boomed the usher. 'He's even dishing them out. I've ordered him to stop.'

Tam's friend was ordered to stand. 'You realise you are in a court of law,' asked the Sheriff.

'Yes, sir.'

'And do you take this seriously?'

'I take it very seriously.'

'Yet you are eating sweets?'

'Yes. May I ask if you have watched *Schindler's List*?'

'Yes, I have,' replied the Sheriff.

'And do you think that was a serious film?'

'Of course it was.'

'So did I, but that didn't stop me buying a hamburger and bottle of cola on the way in.'

The court erupted in laughter while the remainder of the sweets were handed around.

Visitors to the McGraws' Glasgow home will often comment on the absence of a family pet. But the McGraws still mourn the death of their Rottweiler Zoltan, who died of a heart attack in 1995. Zoltan shared their bed and love and is buried under a tree in the front garden.

Tam McGraw is a man who makes friends easily. The Paradise Bar became a favourite haunt of many television soap stars, and while in Tenerife he has been spotted chatting with singing star Daniel O'Donnell. Tam has known many friends come and go violently, but the deaths of Gordon Ross and Joe Hanlon hurt the most. Joe was given the nickname 'Bananas', a tag that stuck after he and Billy McPhee put on fancy dress for a charity event at an open prison. Joe would never be allowed to forget his banana outfit. Ironically, despite the absence of violence in the criminal forays with which Tam has been associated, sudden and cruel death has never been far away. Friends and enemies have perished. And so prolific at one stage were the threats against Tam that he was persuaded to wear protection. He refused to cast off the duffel coat which was his trademark for years, but a close inspection would have revealed a Kevlar bullet-proof vest sewn into the lining. He is constantly being reminded by his friends of the need to be vigilant, although it is difficult for him to know for certain which of his new acquaintances can and can't be trusted.

However, in early 2005 an attempt to breach his defences was exposed. Who was behind it remains a mystery. Out of the blue, a man calling himself Marvin Rummens telephoned Tam. He was, he said, aged 50, German-born, and as a youngster had moved with his parents to Arkansas, where he completed his schooling, graduating 8th in a class of 120. He studied investigation at a school in Dallas, Texas, becoming a specialist in private enquiries, security and tracking missing people. He had moved back to Germany, working as a store detective, but was potentially very useful to Tam. He had been a personal bodyguard with the Mexican Federal-Judicial Police to Florentino Ventura Gutierrez, carried out undercover assignments for José Antonio Zorillo Perez of the Directorate Federal Security in Mexico City and worked for the Panamanian Defence Forces under the personal command of ex-president Manuel Noriega. Rummens offered to work for Tam, but was evasive about where he had got the Scot's name. Simple checks of his background showed they were fictitious. Rummens, or those behind him, had not done their homework.

So who is the real Tam McGraw? Is he the ogre portrayed by adversaries as cunning, responsible for most of the gangland murders and horrors that have blighted Glasgow in the past two decades? Is he a criminal, seen by police as the brains behind the two most successful gangs to blight Scotland in the past three decades? Is he, perhaps, the Hyman Roth of the *Godfather* saga, a man who always made money for his partners? Because, guilty or innocent, Tam McGraw created riches for those around him. Some saved, some spent, some wasted, some gambled, some squandered, while he saved. Is he a man living on the edge, nervous, constantly looking over his shoulder for the past to catch up on him? Or is he the family man seen by friends as witty, generous and inventive?

There is a bizarre saying that 'In Glasgow, they'll spend 50p to stop you making £1', and certainly the city reeks of jealousy. Breaking the eighth commandment – thou shalt not steal – in Glasgow and getting away with it is more likely to induce envy – one of the seven deadly sins – than a call to the police. And that may be the key to Tam McGraw, a man painted not in his own image but by the standards of others.